WORLD ARCHAEOLOGICAL CONGRESS CUL
HERITAGE MANUAL SERIES

Series Editors:
Claire Smith – Flinders University, Adelaide, South Australia, AU
Heather Burke – Flinders University, Adelaide, South Australia, AU
F
A

THE UNIVERSITY OF
WINCHESTER

For further volumes:
http://www.spring

Some readers comments

'An entertaining and useful introduction to practices, processes and peculiarities of British archaeology'. (Peter Hinton, Institute for Archaeologists)

'Here is an interesting book – it's a Rough Guide to British field archaeology, written in an informal way but packed with information for those wishing to come to Britain to work in archaeology and also helpful for a younger generation of Brits making up their minds whether archaeology is for them. And a source of entertainment for old lags...' (Jane Grenville, University of York)

'An accessible and readable introduction to aspects of archaeology in Britain, aimed primarily at audiences outside the UK'. (Dr Mike Heyworth MBE, Council for British Archaeology)

John Schofield · John Carman · Paul Belford

Archaeological Practice in Great Britain

A Heritage Handbook

 Springer

John Schofield
Department of Archaeology
University of York
King's Manor, York, UK
john.schofield@york.ac.uk

Paul Belford
Nexus Heritage
Unit 6, Coppice House, Halesfield 7
Telford, Shropshire, TF7 5AX, UK
paul.belford@nexus-heritage.com

John Carman
Institute of Archaeology and Antiquity
University of Birmingham
Edgbaston, B15 2TT
Birmingham, UK
j.carman@bham.ac.uk

ISBN 978-0-387-09452-6 (Hardcover)   e-ISBN 978-0-387-09453-3
ISBN 978-1-4614-3035-3 (Softcover)
DOI 10.1007/978-0-387-09453-3
Springer New York Dordrecht Heidelberg London

Library of Congress Control Number: 2011928681

Springer is part of Springer Science+Business Media (www.springer.com)

Preface

This book is one of the series of cultural heritage manuals which, by providing overview and 'key-facts', is intended to help people work as archaeologists around the world. Many people associate archaeology with travel and adventure – not surprisingly given its image in popular culture – and many people come to Britain to learn about and 'do' archaeology. Wherever you are, archaeology has certain universal core principles. Archaeology is about exploring society and culture through its material traces, learning about the influence the past has had on the present, and using that knowledge to help shape the future. But despite our networked modern world, many aspects of archaeological methodology and practice are still very localised, and owe a great deal to the culture which produced them. This is the case in Britain, which is not really considered a country so much as a series of connected regions and localities by some people. We have therefore prepared this book to help newcomers to Britain learn how to get along – not just in archaeology, but in some other areas of life as well.

Before explaining what this book is and what it can do, it might be better to describe what it is not. It is not a complete guide to the archaeology of Britain – you will not pass your first-year course in British archaeology by just reading Chap. 3. Nor is it a history of archaeological practice, although you might find much which is useful and interesting in Chaps. 1 and 2. And it cannot hope to provide an intensive review of the laws relating to planning and heritage protection. Nor is it a guide to methods, ethics and standards – reading Chaps. 4–8 will not help you rise rapidly to the top.

What this book does provide, however, is an overview of all of these areas. The authors are together experienced in all of the four main sectors in which archaeological practice takes place in Britain – universities, local and national government, museums and commercial archaeology – and have drawn on that experience to produce a practical handbook for the first-timer in British archaeology. Specifically, we have tried to do four things:

- Explain how British archaeology has evolved, who is involved with it and what roles they perform.
- Provide an overview of the 'archaeology of Britain' – a snapshot of three-quarters of a million years in a little over 15,000 words!

- Describe the way in which archaeology works today – the legal framework, the profession, and how to actually get involved with survey, excavation and research.
- Provide sufficient background in all these areas to enable you to actually get on and do it!

As with any archaeological book, the information here is always subject to change. New discoveries change our understanding of the past, and who knows what discoveries will be made while the book is in press. Equally, the planning and heritage protection regimes are changing, so these too may be different when you read this book from how things were when we wrote it. Supplementing this book with online searches will reveal any significant changes in these areas. We have tried wherever possible to point you in the direction of other resources which may help, and we provide lists of reading and Web sites at the end.

With such a considerable breadth of coverage, and with the foundations of heritage practice constantly shifting (and especially so now, it would seem), there will inevitably be shortcomings and omissions in this book, shortcomings and omissions which some readers – and especially those 'in the know' – may find irritating. We have tried to reduce these to a minimum but are aware that we may have subconsciously adopted an Anglo-centric perspective on some topics, with less consideration of some aspects of Welsh and Scottish archaeology, and the text boxes (such as on health and safety, vehicle maintenance, or landscapes) also reflect personal views. It was never our intention to be definitive. Rather, what we provide here is an introduction, a way into a subject that is both complex and fluid. All of the relevant information is available, most of it online, and we provide links to many of these resources. But above all, our advice is to use this book in the way it is intended, as an entry to a complex and potentially confusing world.

Britain was really where modern archaeology began, resulting partly from contact with the New World which provoked thinking about national identity. National identities have always been constructed in relation to others, and for the first time from the sixteenth century it was possible to look at non-European 'others' and surmise how distant ancestors may have lived. From the seventeenth century, the rise of scientific empiricism during the Enlightenment encouraged a culture of quantification, and the two things came together in the eighteenth century with the discovery of landscape and the picturesque. As the nineteenth century gathered pace, fuelled by industrial enterprise and increasing scientific understanding, new approaches to 'natural philosophy' encouraged the development of individual areas of science – and of these geology, ethnography and natural history were all highly influential in transforming antiquarianism into archaeology. During the twentieth century, we have seen fluctuations in the balance of archaeological power and authority – museums and universities are no longer alone at the cutting edge of archaeological research for example; they have been joined (and some might say overtaken) by entrepreneurial private enterprise in the now well-developed system of professional commercial archaeology. The story of archaeology in Britain is, therefore, an echo of the story of modernity.

The structure of archaeology today is like many aspects of life in Britain – it is probably not the system that anyone would have been created given *carte blanche*. Parts of the laws relating to cultural heritage go back to the middle ages, and most of the legal and administrative framework can be traced back to the late nineteenth century. The present-day planning system is an amalgam of various legislative initiatives during the twentieth century – and even recent attempts to streamline this have fallen foul of the British preference for slightly muddled precedent. British archaeology contains a mixture of state institutions, private enterprise and charitable bodies – each with overlapping areas of responsibility and interest. The system is therefore a complex field – both for those familiar with the more rigid state-controlled systems in much of the European Union, and for those coming from the New World where the idea of a state-funded organisation which sends people out to survey earthworks for research purposes might seem ridiculous. For many of us working here, the flexibility and compromises inherent in the British system are one of its great strengths. It allows individual ideas to be tested, and new methodologies to develop. Discussion is open, free and fair, and there are very few 'sacred cows' which people are afraid to topple. Indeed many aspects of the culture of British archaeology actively encourage thinking 'outside the box'.

One of the disadvantages of this system to an outsider is that it may be very difficult to figure out who is responsible for which aspects of archaeology, and how to get anything done. That is where this book comes in!

John Schofield
John Carman
Paul Belford

Acknowledgements

This book has been a collaborative effort both in the sense that the lead authors have worked closely together, but also in the co-operation of additional authors who contributed text boxes. We are grateful therefore to the following for their commitment and effort: Chantel Conneller (University of Manchester), Vince Gaffney (University of Birmingham), Jon Humble, Paul Jeffrey (both English Heritage), Adrian Myers (Stanford University, USA), Cassie Newland, Josh Pollard (both University of Bristol), Guy Salkeld (National Trust), Martin Short (Ministry of Defence), and Kathryn Whittington (IfA). We are indebted also to those who commissioned this book, both at the World Archaeological Congress (Claire Smith) and at Springer (Teresa Krauss), and thank them for their professionalism, good humour and their patience.

We are particularly thankful to those colleagues and family of the authors who have lived with the book as long as we have – and who (like us) will be very pleased to see it finally published.

Contents

List of Figures

List of Tables

Chapter 1
Introduction to Great Britain

On Knowing Where You Are

Welcome to Britain. Let us begin with a story. Some friends from Canada on their first visit to Britain arrived exhausted at their destination. The long flight from Toronto had been fine: experienced travellers, they had even slept through large parts of it. What tired them out was not the flight, but the 2 h drive from the airport of arrival. In Canada, they were used to long rides through a landscape that changed little from one region to another, and which had little traffic; but in southern Britain over a short space they encountered urban space, open countryside, more urban space, forest, villages, more open countryside and more urban space, all repeated in quick succession. Their exhaustion was not helped by the overcrowded roads. It was as if they had travelled the equivalent of hundreds of miles while in fact travelling only a few. This is not an unusual effect upon new visitors to Britain. For a small island – a mere 800 miles (1,280 km) north to south and 400 (640 km) from east to west at maximum stretch – containing some 60 million people and so relatively crowded, it offers a wide diversity of landscape types and much more (apparently) uninhabited space than might be expected.

Great Britain sits off the northwest coast of mainland Europe (Fig. 1.1), opposite northern France, Belgium, Holland, Germany and Scandinavia. It is part of Europe in two senses – geographically, in terms of its location; and politically as part of the European Union (on which more below). For clarity, we need to specify that this book is about doing archaeology in *Britain*, not merely England, Scotland or Wales, and not all of the United Kingdom (one part of which is on the island of Ireland). Specifically, we are concerned with the island of Great Britain and its main offshore islands – the Isle of Man to the northwest, which has some autonomy, and the remainder which do not. These include the Scilly Isles to the extreme southwest, the Isle of Wight to the south, Anglesey off the north coast of Wales, the Hebrides Islands to the far northwest of mainland Scotland, and the Orkney and Shetland Isles to the north. In addition are small islands – such as Lundy in the Bristol Channel – and offshore defensive establishments from earlier eras (for more on which see below).

J. Schofield et al., *Archaeological Practice in Great Britain: A Heritage Handbook*,
World Archaeological Congress Cultural Heritage Manual Series,
DOI 10.1007/978-0-387-09453-3_1, © Springer Science+Business Media, LLC 2011

Fig. 1.1 Map of British Isles: location in respect to Europe: also showing EU and EEA countries

Finding Your Way Around

The topography of Great Britain is highly varied – from low-lying areas of wetland such as the Fens of East Anglia and the Somerset Levels of the west – to areas of mountain such as the Scottish Highlands and northern Wales, with lower uplands such as the Pennine Hills running up the spine of the island, Dartmoor, Exmoor and Bodmin Moor to the extreme southwest, and the Yorkshire Dales and Moors to the northeast, among others. Britain's highest mountains are in Scotland and Wales: Scotland's Ben Nevis rises to 1,344 m (a little above 4,000 ft) while Wales' Snowdon reaches 1,085 m (approx. 3,300 ft). Other Scottish peaks rise to 1,000 m or more, while Welsh ones reach up to 1,000 m. English mountain heights are lower and all well below 1,000 m. In contrast, the Fens of East Anglia lie up to 2 m *below* sea level, protected by sand dunes and other barriers at the coast. In this region is also found Britain's lowest Iron Age "hillfort" (Stonea Camp, Cambridgeshire), situated nearly a metre below the current sea level. Although the island as a whole is densely occupied, that density of settlement is highly variable, while a variety of settlement forms including major cities, smaller towns, villages, tiny hamlets and scattered farmsteads are prevalent in different areas. For example, the central spine of England, from Dorset in the southwest up to the northeast, has historically been characterised by nucleated settlements, while to the southeast, northwest and far southwest the pattern is different, with dispersed settlements predominant.

There are a number of excellent atlases and maps of Great Britain. For road users, a valuable atlas is produced annually by the Automobile Association (AA: http://www.theaa.com/). Portable satellite navigation systems ("SatNavs") are increasingly popular, and up-to-date maps can usually be downloaded to the device from the makers' Web site.

At the local level, the most commonly used map is one of those produced by the Ordnance Survey (OS; http://leisure.ordnancesurvey.co.uk/leisure/). This organisation has a history that stretches back to the eighteenth century, and as its name suggests was originally an office of the military responsible for the siting of defensive works. It is the country's official mapping agency, providing maps at a number of scales for a range of purposes. Most popular are the "Landranger" multiple-purpose maps at 1:50,000 and the "Explorer" range for walkers and cyclists at 1:25,000. The maps are based on a grid of kilometre squares which covers all of Great Britain and its offshore islands, further divided into squares designated by groups of letters. Within these squares, locations are identified by grid-square numbers. The OS grid is the UK standard for locating sites and the 1:10,000 range is the standard for county Historic Environment Records, many of which are accessible online. The OS also produce useful maps of particular historic periods, such as Roman Britain, Medieval Britain, etc. For the archaeologist, a knowledge of what the OS has to offer is invaluable and even essential (see also Chap. 5).

What the map will not tell you is what the weather and ground conditions could be like when you get there. Depending on where you are, you will need to dress appropriately for the kinds of weather and ground conditions you may experience, and these differ from area to area and season to season. Although the devil can be in the detail, there are some ground rules. Despite Britain's generally mild climate, upland areas in particular can be bleak and very cold even in summer. Yet to be exposed in low-lying or upland open country in summer can cause serious sunburn and heat exhaustion. In winter, careless exposure in upland and other open areas can be life-threatening, while elsewhere it may mean only a mild soaking in chilly rain. It is often said that we British are obsessed with the weather, so naturally there's more we wish to say on the subject.

Climate, Clothing and Weather

A phrase commonly heard: "Britain does not have a climate; it only has weather". This is why:

Great Britain, although quite far north, lies between warm tropical airflow from the Caribbean and cold airflow from the north Atlantic and polar regions. The lighter warm air rises over the heavier cold air, producing the typical British weather pattern of fronts, depressions and rain. As a consequence, the British climate can be very changeable, and all types of weather may be experienced within a single day. In general, however, the British climate is relatively mild for its latitude, since it is also influenced by the Gulf Stream, a warm transatlantic current from the Caribbean.

Although Britain occupies only a relatively small geographical area of the Earth's surface, marked differences in climate do exist between one area and another. The climate of the western half of Britain is dominated by wetter tropical and polar air, whilst the climate further east is often influenced by drier continental systems. In addition to the major air masses, the strength of sunlight received at different locations, which varies according to latitude, also has an influence on climate. Consequently, the climate can be divided into four quarters. The northwest quarter, including the Isle of Man, the Lake District and the Western Isles of Scotland, is characterised by mild winters (average 6°C) and cool summers (average 15°C), whilst the northeast can have cold winters (average 3°C) and cool summers. The southwest quarter, containing Wales and Southwest England, experiences mild winters and warm summers (average 17°C), whilst the Midlands and Southeast England have cold winters and warm summers. In general, the western half of the British Isles experiences a wetter, more maritime climate during winter, whilst the east receives influence from the drier cold air streams from the continent. In summer, climatic differences depend more upon latitude. The greater influence of maritime air in the western half of Great Britain means that it receives considerably more rainfall than in the east. The generally higher ground in the west forces incoming Atlantic air to rise, causing further rain. Parts of highland Scotland, for example, can receive over 250 cm (100 in.) of precipitation per year. The east, by contrast, is lower and flatter, lying in the rain shadow of the Welsh Mountains, the Lake District and the Scottish Highlands, and is consequently much drier. Some parts of the southeast of England may receive only 50 cm (20 in.) of rain per year.

There's no such thing as wet weather; only the wrong clothes (Billy Connolly, Scottish Comedian)

The generally mild climate of Britain is generally good news for archaeological work, as the only time it gets really uncomfortable is when it is wet. Not many archaeological projects require its staff to camp anymore, so even the effect of rainfall, in dampening bodies and spirits, has diminished. For hot weather the best advice is to apply high factor sun cream and wear a hat. You should also have a good supply of fresh water and drink this regularly. If you begin to start feeling the effects of the sun, head for the shade and stay there until you feel better. A 10 min break may be enough to quell the effects sufficiently to return to work.

In cold weather you will know what you can withstand, and how well you need to prepare. Some people have much higher pain thresholds than others! But always good are thermal underclothes, and to keep the extremities warm: good gloves and – especially – a good hat. We are told that you lose 40% of body heat through your head (a figure that presumably increases as one gets older!). Another piece of advice from childhood is to stay warm, because once you get cold it is very hard to warm up again. So, even if you do start to feel warmer, keeping the hat on may be a good idea.

A popular presenter of "survival"-type television programmes, Ray Mears has produced some excellent survival guides, some for extreme environments (mountains and jungles) and some for the calmer, temperate zones. In his *Essential Bushcraft* (2002, 20) Mears describes his clothing of choice for the temperate zone, noting that at some times of the year, and notably spring, the conditions can often range from arctic to arid! Mears notes the importance of strong, leather hiking boots that come half-way up the leg, to provide protection in soft ground. He also notes the benefits of gore-tex lining or waterproof socks to prevent the feet getting moist and cold. Waterproof gaiters are also good for giving protection from rain. Ex-military trousers are good, being comparatively cheap, warm and comfortable, although in exposed areas windproof trousers might be better, such as those with Ventile fabric for added protection. Mears describes his preference for cotton or wool thermal shirts rather than modern fibre thermal tops, and then a wool or tightly woven shirt and larger, thicker shirt (for woodland) or windproof jacket (for the open). We will return to clothing in Chap. 8.

Mears also provides valuable lessons in building shelters, catching and cooking food, and first aid. Quite often field archaeologists use the experience of an excavation as an excuse to "go native". Diggers on excavations have been known to head off before work to set traps and then gather rabbits and foods from the hedgerows on their way back to camp. Any of Ray Mears' books will cover much of this ground, so there is no need to repeat it here. One can live on a diet of "wild food" in Britain, as numerous reports in the press have described. One man finds all his meat in road-kills, and has been on television demonstrating the appeal of badger casserole and Ris-otter!

The British are obsessed with the unpredictability of the weather and inhabitants of Britain are always keen to discuss it, as you will soon learn on coming here (but see Fox 2004, 25–36 for one explanation of what such weather-talk really means). As indicated, Britain has a temperate climate with some regional variation: mild winters in the south, colder in the north, but with some isolated cold "snaps"; and warm (occasionally hot) summers, with higher temperatures in the south. It is also a pattern that is increasingly unpredictable, with unseasonal extremes of temperature, and freak events, such as flooding and storms. The unpredictability of the British weather may be frustrating, but it is never dull.

The general message of this section is as follows: listen carefully to weather forecasts, especially those for your own part of the country. When going on fieldwork ensure you have a range of appropriate clothing: both for warm conditions should they develop, and fully weatherproof gear as well (and for more on this, see Chap. 8).

British Life

The people of Britain are as varied as their weather. Britain has an imperial past, and our population reflects the wide ethnic, religious and cultural diversity of that former empire. At the same time, we are part of the European Union, comprising most countries of western and central Europe, with formal trading and other links with others. Accordingly, Britain's population also includes long- and short-term residents from all over Europe. This ethnic and cultural diversity is most evident in our major cities – with either Leicester or Birmingham likely to become Europe's first city to have a majority of its people from otherwise minority ethnic groups. Although less prevalent, this diversity can also be encountered in some rural areas. At the same time, our traditional concern with the divisions between classes – a classic stereo-type of the British, much loved of television and film writers, and some non-British authors who set their fiction in Britain – has become less noticeable. The rise of "(Thames) estuarine" English – a common accent shared by people in all parts, of all social groups – is a noticeable phenomenon. On your first visit, and depending on your preconceptions, Britain may be much as you imagined, or totally different. As one student of British identity puts it:

> Britain may be a country, but it is not really a place…. Britain is a composite nation, a patchwork of anomalies, mistakes and inconsistencies. It has a standing army but not a football team. It has an anthem, a flag and a queen, but there is no patron saint [of Britain] and no founding date of an original constitution to be celebrated with even token formality (Ware 2007, 1).

Such is the Britain you may encounter as you explore its towns and countryside, and the diversity of the people who live there.

Political Boundaries and Related Matters

The UK is a member of the European Union (EU), and many of the laws and prac-tices of our European neighbours are finding their way into British life. Within this international Union, and as indicated above, the island of Great Britain and its offshore islands do not consist of a single polity but four: three of these are compo-nents of the four-part United Kingdom (UK) of England and Wales, Scotland and Northern Ireland and the fifth (the Isle of Man) is ruled by the monarch as a Crown Dependency but exists independently from the UK. The UK is a constitutional monarchy, so although nominally ruled by its Queen, the real seat of power lies in elected representative assemblies. The most important of these – the UK Parliament – sits in London, but certain powers for internal affairs have also been devolved to similar assemblies in Wales and Scotland and are exercised by the so-called Tynwald in the Isle of Man.

The largest of the four countries is England (its people are English), the dom-inant country and seat of central government in its capital London. To the west lies Wales (its people are Welsh), allowed a certain amount of independent authority through a devolved assembly that sits in the capital of Wales, Cardiff. To the north lies Scotland (its people are Scots or Scottish), with a larger measure of devolved authority and its own Parliament which sits in the capital Edinburgh.

The Isle of Man (its people are Manx) sits in the Irish Sea off the northwest coast of England or, if you prefer, the southwest coast of Scotland, and its main town is Douglas. The political boundaries – between England and Wales, and England and Scotland, and between all and the Isle of Man – are no more than lines drawn on a map: the only indicator that you have passed from one country to another may be a wayside welcome sign, and (in Wales and Man) the fact that all roadside signs will be in two languages: English and Welsh in Wales, English and Manx in Man. A confusing factor is that areas of England that would like to claim a measure of independence – such as Cornwall in the far southwest, once an independent kingdom in its own right – may also have their road signs in two languages (Cornish is related to Welsh but different from it). It is worth noting that there are well-established independence movements in Wales and Scotland and a small one in Cornwall, although only those in Wales and Scotland carry sufficient authority to have achieved political devolution: the Isle of Man was never legally part of the United Kingdom.

Apart from topography, and occasional language differences, there is little indication of separation between the component parts of Great Britain. It is worth noting, however, and as will be further explained in Chaps. 4 and 7, that each represents a distinct legal jurisdiction. The law as it applies in England also applies to Wales and largely to the Isle of Man, but is exercised through separate agencies in the three countries. Although some laws apply to all of Great Britain, the basis of Scottish law is very different from that in England and Wales and is therefore applied differently and through entirely separate agencies. This makes it important that you know where you are: in England, in Wales, in Scotland or on the Isle of Man. Depending where you are, the rules may be very different and exercised by different types of authority.

The map of Britain is further complicated by its administrative subdivisions, creating a patchwork quilt of confusion even for long-term inhabitants. England and Scotland were until recently divided into counties (46 in England, 34 in Scotland) while Wales was divided into 22 administrative areas. Some counties and Welsh administrative areas owe their names at least to past history: the origin of the English county lies in medieval government practice, and some have kept their ancient names even though the borders have been adjusted: Essex (originally an independent kingdom in the seventh century AD) is one example; Dyfed, Gwynedd, etc., in Wales take the names of ancient provinces of that country. Reorganisation for administrative convenience took place in the early 1970s. Some counties were merged, such as Hereford and Worcester, or Cambridgeshire in the east of England, which comprises historic Cambridgeshire, historic Huntingdonshire, the so-called Isle of Ely, and for a while the city of Peterborough which was previously part of Northamptonshire. Elsewhere, entirely new counties were created – such as Avon, Humberside or Teesside (named for their major rivers). Many of these no longer exist: Avon was known for a time as CUBA – the County that Used to be Avon – and Herefordshire and Worcestershire are once again separate counties.

While some counties in England and Scotland are further subdivided into Districts, others comprise numerous "unitary authorities". These are usually former districts which now have responsibility for all the combined functions of a local authority at county or district level, including education, roads, healthcare and environmental issues. Where a division into districts applies, the district is primarily responsible for matters such as planning and development control among other things, and the county acts as a strategic overseer while retaining responsibility for issues such as education and planning. To help support these activities, and planning in particular, each authority (whether unitary or under the old County/District structure) maintains its own Historic Environment Record (HER – formerly Sites and Monuments Record or SMR), comprising information on archaeological sites, historic buildings, landscape and ancient monuments (see Chap. 4). Some authorities have these records online, and available free of charge.

The offshore islands represent different degrees of inclusion in this structure: the Isle of Man is, as we have seen, entirely independent; the Orkney and Shetland islands off the north coast of Scotland, Anglesey off the Welsh coast and the Isle of Wight off southern England are each administrative areas in their own right; while the Scilly Isles are part of the county of Cornwall. (To add further confusion, certain places designated as "Isles" are in fact inland, such as the Isle of Ely which is part of landlocked Cambridgeshire: it is called an "Isle" for historic reasons, connected to its status prior to the drainage of the surrounding wetland.)

Myths of British Identity

Collectively, although we may sometimes choose to distinguish ourselves by reference to our separate nationalities, the people of Britain are "British". However, despite a recent revival of interest in issues of identity among our politicians – in part a response to the perceived threat of divisions along ethnic and religious lines related to the "war on terror" and devolution of power to Wales and Scotland – and among some groups whose recent ancestors came from other lands, the people of Britain are not generally overly concerned with issues of "who they are" (for an interesting review of perspectives on this issue, see Ware 2007). Although there are a number of myths about the British character to which people may apparently subscribe, they generally do so with a keen sense of irony, and occasionally outright and blatant silliness.

The British are known – among other things – for their love of freedom and independence. One island off the southwest coast, Lundy, tried to declare independence in the early twentieth century, going so far as to mint its own currency and produce its own stamps. But the perpetrator, Martin Coles Harman, was prosecuted. He protested to the last, however, claiming that the English judicial system had no authority over Lundy. Another typically English tale of island independence is the Principality of Sealand, an old Second World War fort off the Essex coast (southeast England) where Roy of Sealand proclaimed the constitution in 1975.

Britons and the Second World War

One thing of which we are aware is that we have never entirely outgrown the Second World War, despite its end over 60 years ago. References to "the Dunkirk spirit" (a sense of shared hardship deriving its name from the rescue of defeated British and French soldiers from the beaches of northern France in 1940) and to Britons being able "to take it" (i.e. to withstand adversity, especially related to the bombing of civilian population centres from 1940 to 1944) can still be heard in conversation among those who were not directly involved. Many of our words and phrases are of this time: we still talk about rationing, and "digging for victory" for example. Our television regularly repeats old war films, which retain their popularity. In general, we often behave as if we were recently victorious in the Second World War and would have been so without the help of our allies, although in day-to-day practice we are aware of Britain's role as one of a coalition heavily reliant on outside support. (It may be worth noting, however, that if pressed on the point, especially by Americans, we will argue with vehemence how Britain "stood alone" against the Nazi evil!)

The next chapter will chart the development of archaeology as a field of enquiry in Britain to show how attempts at a serious understanding of our past has deep roots, but it is also worth gaining a sense of the more popular ideas of the past that contribute to a British sense of "Britishness". It is not that people generally believe these myths to be true – although some may be – than they are part of our childhood introduction to ourselves that we carry into adulthood: much as citizens of the USA may carry an image of the "pioneer" or cowboy, or Australians an image of the convict past and the bushranger or "wild colonial boy", even though this is nothing to do with their own or their family past.

National heroes abound in Britain, and, as might be expected, these are not always "British" national heroes, but reflect the heroic resistance of one part of the British Isles to another. So the Scots have Robert the Bruce, who was inspired to persevere by the activities of a spider, and William Wallace, both of whom fought for Scottish independence from England. Wales has Owain Glyndwr (Shakespeare's Owen Glendower of *Henry IV Part I*), who fought for Wales against the English. The English have Robin Hood, well known across the world as one who stole from the rich to give to the poor in defence of the legitimate king. Only Robin Hood may be an invention: the others are historical figures, although they may not have lived quite as legend would have it.

One figure is claimed by all three mainland countries: King Arthur has places in the ancient traditions of England, Wales and Scotland. As a defender of British (pre-Anglo Saxon) civilisation against Germanic invaders, his legend is a relatively late invention. He begins life as a Welsh bandit, reported in the eleventh century *Mabinogion* (a collection of tales from earlier periods) as a jovial stealer of pigs and cattle. By the thirteenth century – in Geoffrey of Monmouth's *History of the Kings of Britain* – he has joined others in a line that descends from the last rulers of Roman Britain, and the tale of his war against the Saxon invaders becomes a justification for the adoption of new rulers from northern France who displace the Saxons in 1066. The greatest of all these early kings, Arthur wields the sword Excalibur, is advised by the great wizard Merlin, who magically brings a great ring of stones (probably intended to be Stonehenge) from Ireland, and establishes the Knights of the Round Table at his castle of Camelot, only to be brought to ruin by his own pride. By the fifteenth century, and Thomas Malory's *Morte D'Arthur*, he is a model of good kingship in a time of trouble, the one who pulled the sword from the stone to prove his kingship, and an ancestor of the new King whose own ancestors are Welsh. As "The Once and Future King" he is promised to return when Britain faces adversity once more. The power of the Arthur story persists: a number of tellings from the second half of the twentieth century into the 21st attempt either to put him into some kind of historical context or to recreate the sense of myth (for attempts at historical versions, see Sutcliffe 1963; Stewart 1979; Cornwell 1997; and for a more "mythical" treatment see White 1958).

Arthur's place as a pan-British hero reflects one of our more persistent historical myths: that of successive "waves of invasion" in the past that led to the development of a distinctive British character that is an amalgam of the best qualities of them all. In this view of our history – one still encountered in popular imagination and even some school texts (although for a more critical consideration based on archaeological evidence, see Miles 2006) – the best qualities of each population become debased over time and need to be restored by the infusion of new blood. At base lies the "Celtic" character, still supposedly evident among their Welsh and Scottish descendants: although wild and free, and somewhat unruly, it is offset by a sensitivity to art, literature and especially music. This was overlain by Roman traits briefly during Roman rule: especially a love of discipline and order, but these were lost again with the supposed departure of the legions in 410 AD. British resistance – led by Arthur – to incursions of Angles, Saxons and Jutes from northern Germany and southern Denmark reinstated Celtic culture once more, but with the final victory of the Anglo-Saxon peoples their traits too were ingrained in the British character: physical courage, a different kind of artistic sensitivity from the Celtic which is more down-to-earth, a strong sense of individuality and a yearning for freedom. As the Saxon people became civilised, and especially Christianised, they lost their essential strength of character and were in part overcome by Vikings from Denmark and Norway, people of similar descent and representing many of the characteristics of the first Saxons. But they too fell prey to civilisation's decadence, were ultimately dismissed from the land and both they and the Saxons fell to the rule of the final invaders from Normandy, originally also descended from Viking stock but retaining their vigour in conjunction with a capacity for organisation and order. Out of this mixture of sensitivity, independence and a sense of order arose – according to such myths – the modern British identity: its strength and authority is evidenced by the supposed lack of further conquests. So too does British opposition to rule from outside – leading in turn to British resistance to the regimes of such figures as Louis XIV, Napoleon Bonaparte, Kaiser Wilhelm II and Adolph Hitler, as well as an apparently ambiguous membership of the European Union.

A number of further myths of British identity derive from this model of Britain as a nation made by invasion. One of these myths has fed two alternative models for political organisation and structure, and a close look at political debates in Britain will often reveal traces of these. On the one side is a harking-back to pre-Norman ways, with Anglo-Saxon (and sometimes Celtic) society envisaged as one where the individual carried more authority than the state and was afforded greater freedom: this changed, according to this myth, with the Norman conquest of England and the assertion of a form of royal authority which was alien to the British way of life. On the other is the assertion of Norman hegemony establishing security, order and control over an unruly population. The history of Britain can be read as a battle between Anglo-Saxon freedoms and the oppressive "Norman Yoke": civil wars as efforts to assert the individual against the state, foreign wars as efforts to preserve a British way of life against foreign threats, the rise of capitalism as an assertion of independence from royal monopoly, the socialist response as an assertion of ancient freedoms against economic dominance. Alternatively, it can be read as the search to find a compromise between anarchy and tyranny: civil wars as bids to limit the power of certain groups, the rise of rule by law and Parliamentary government as a counterpoint to royal authority, the emergence of a mixed economy (partly free enterprise and partly state-control) as a middle-way between socialist control and unbridled capitalist exploitation; all of these trends are summed up in the idea that "the British have riots (or sometimes merely satire) but not revolutions" (in contrast especially to our Continental neighbours who of course have both).

The idea that the British population is made up of different elements – the Celtic, the Anglo-Saxon, and the Norse – fed into scientific discourse in the nineteenth century and persists in ideas about the make-up of British populations. The success of the Roman, Anglo-Saxon and Norse conquests, it is said, forced the native Celtic population to retreat westward into the more mountainous regions of Wales and Scotland, and to the far west of England in Cornwall (as well as to Ireland over the sea). Accordingly, these regions are assumed to be dominated by people of Celtic descent and are sometimes called "the Celtic fringe". By contrast, the remainder of England and southern Scotland – largely lowland areas – are held to be peopled by those of Anglo-Saxon descent. The northwest of England and northern Scotland was also deemed to contain a significant proportion of people descended from the Norse invaders. These groups (in this scheme – not to be confused with historical reality – the Roman population is deemed to have departed with the fall of the Roman Empire in 410 AD) thus make up distinct populations within Britain. Such ideas were prominent in the nineteenth century, and took their place in political debate about the relationship of England to Scotland and Wales (as well as Ireland). By this theory, Wales and Scotland – although politically distinct – were nonetheless subordinate to England by right of conquest (in the case of Wales) and by Union through the common monarch (in the case of Scotland); they could assert no claim to independence as a separate State, however, because the population distribution in each was essentially identical to that in England. An alternative point of view saw Wales and Scotland as historically distinct because of their different Celtic populations, and therefore appar-ently worthy of a measure of self-rule (the argument was actually about Ireland, but the distribution of populations was a part of the argument mobilised by both sides, Patton 2007, 6). Both sides in the debate, however, took the distribution of different populations – based upon the myth of successive invasions – as true, and it survives in some discourses today, especially as the notion of "the Celtic fringe".

The twentieth and twenty-first centuries have seen further developments in the notion of what it means to be "British". The fall of the British Empire and related decline in British influence across the globe – especially as represented by the grant of independence to large parts of Africa, Asia and the Caribbean – meant a significant rethinking of the role of Britain in the world during the second half of the twentieth century. At the same time, influxes of people from the former Empire have undermined the idea that the British population is predominantly White and supposedly Christian. As we have seen, cities such as Birmingham and Leicester vie for the position of the first European city to host a minority White population: the majority will consist of those of Asian, Caribbean and African descent. Recent political initiatives have asserted that "Britishness" lies not in a particular ethnicity but in the adoption of shared values – among them traditions of toleration, of fair treatment for all and of respect for others. These values, which are perceived to operate across ethnic, religious and other barriers, are offered as the providers of a unifying bond to all inhabitants of Britain. In addition – or by contrast, or counterpoint – the notion of Britain as an inevitably "multi-ethnic" society has also been proposed: the problem here, though, is that the term is vague and ill-defined. For some it means separation though parallel ethnicities, so that those of Muslim and Hindu descent from southern Asia, for instance, need not mix, and nor need they with those of Afro-Caribbean origins or with the White population. For others, it means the promotion of an active mixing of traditions, so that elements of Asian, Afro-Caribbean and White "cultures" can be accessed by all. A drive around any major city in Britain can be instructive: on the surface, multi-ethnicity as cross-cultural communication may be actively endorsed, and this will involve music and food festivals, for instance, that bring all the communities together in celebration. But as you travel through the city's various areas, it will become clear that while one section is dominated by a Muslim population, another is primarily Afro-Caribbean, another largely White, another predominately Hindu, and so on. It is a sad truth that the vast majority of archaeologists in Britain are White, and despite efforts at recruitment from other sections of the population, exclusively English-speaking White people continue to dominate the field (Everill 2006).

Class is an issue that is less important in Britain than might be expected (although for a contrary – and quite subtle view – see Fox 2004). Historically, at least until the nineteenth century, the British class system was relatively fluid and allowed a reasonable degree of movement. Two world wars in the twentieth century served to provide a context for the mixing of the social classes that reinstated a measure of fluidity despite official efforts to re-establish the nineteenth century norm of class rigidity: a series of social experiments during the "swinging sixties" and subsequent decades has led to a further erosion of class consciousness. Nevertheless, we retain a discourse of class which can emerge during conversation. Other popular myths – particularly English, Scottish and Welsh – have been subject to critical study especially by historians; these serve to usefully "debunk" such ideas as the "friendly British Bobby" (police), the "ancient" Scottish tradition of highland dress, popular images of Wales, and our perpetual love of the monarchy, all of which are shown to be inventions, and usually recent ones at that (see, e.g. Hobsbawm and Ranger 1983; Porter 1991).

Some Points About Verbal Exchanges

British accents can vary considerably, so it may depend on where you are as to what your colleagues sound like. Most British archaeologists are (despite any claims they make) fairly well educated and probably represent the liberal middle-class in attitude: many will therefore speak in a form of "standard" estuarine English. Some archaeologists, however, as well as the landowners you might encounter – especially in regions such as the far southwest of England, Wales, Scotland or northern England – will speak in a regional accent that may be difficult at first to understand. Some will use their dialect deliberately, perhaps as a form of irony (see below), and will treat it as either offensive or as a huge joke (sometimes both simultaneously) that you do not understand what they say to you.

The form of English used in Britain is not only different from that in other parts of the world, but also varies across the different parts of Britain, so be aware that certain words and phrases may not mean what they mean to you. Typical examples where confusion may arise (especially for citizens of the USA) are references to "[sometimes sticky] buns" – which in Britain refer to a form of pastry, "fags" – which in Britain mean cigarettes, and "to go like a bomb" which means to be greeted with acclaim. Other examples and their translations may be found in convenient publications with a humorous approach (e.g. Long 2007; Fox 2004) and on Web sites (e.g. http://www.peak. org/~jeremy/dictionary/dictionary/dictionary.php; http://www.effingpot.com/ index.shtml; http://www.uta.fi/FAST/US1/REF/engtran.html).

Be aware that the British will happily use irony – sometimes bordering on sarcasm – in their conversation and even in professional exchanges. This may be something some visitors from overseas may be unused-to, especially when speaking to a person in a position of authority. If uncertain, do not try to join in: the rules of such exchanges are complex and vary from group to group and context to context.

The British have in general abandoned calling each other by title (Mr, Mrs, Dr, Professor, etc.) and surname in the workplace, and have adopted in recent decades the practice of calling each other by first or familiar names: this applies both up and down the formal hierarchy. This means that you will normally be addressed by your personal first name and you will be expected to do the same to superiors unless it is made very clear to you that this is inappropriate. This does not necessarily encourage familiarity: some bosses will remain stand-offish. If you are unhappy at being called by a personal name, by all means offer another to be called by at work: it is quite a common practice.

In general, and although outright hostility is to be avoided in the workplace, the British are not averse to arguments about politics or religion. These can – especially when fuelled by alcohol – become quite noisy and apparently acrimonious, but hostility will only rarely accompany the discussion: if it does, it means that someone has broken a rule of social interaction. It may not be you: but if you are uncertain, ask a colleague who was neutral in the exchange.

Archaeology as Part of British Life

Archaeology and "heritage" are popular in Britain as attested by viewing figures for factual television series such as "Meet the Ancestors" and "Coast" (BBC) and "Time Team" (Channel 4), as well as single documentaries on archaeological themes and more recently a drama series called "Bonekickers" (BBC) concerning a fictional archaeological team based in the west of England. This general popularity is endorsed by the manner in which the Press and TV regularly seek out archaeological and heritage news stories. However, as suggested in the brief discussion of "multi-ethnicity" above, this popularity belongs largely to the majority White population, since the past accessed by archaeologists working in Britain is inevitably generally that of the majority population, whether from prehistory or more recent times: this is a major difference of working in any country of Europe with, e.g. Australia, the USA, Canada or New Zealand, for instance. The consequence is that while the work of archaeologists is in general of interest to any audience, the type of interest may be divided: for some, the interest will be primarily in the techniques of investigation used, especially the process of excavation; for others it will lie in the specific findings about "their" area or "their" (supposed) ancestors. Such interest in archaeology rarely develops into claims of ownership or of control over the past: the British past is generally deemed to be so long ago that it no longer matters to those alive now. However, there can be exceptions, especially where issues of identity and of local prestige are concerned. Disputes may sometimes arise over human remains where these are claimed by particular groups or over the fate of ancient monuments that face removal to a museum (as in the case of the Hilton of Cadboll Pictish cross-slab: Jones 2004).

Archaeology (as will be discussed in Chap. 2) has a long history in Britain and is founded upon a tradition of amateur investigation. British archaeologists therefore represent a specific subculture of the British population. They fall into three main groups: dedicated amateurs, usually locally based; academics and students undertaking research and training work; and professionals conducting archaeology as part of the development control and planning process. Accordingly, although within the archaeological profession – including academic circles – the term "archaeologist" is reserved for those with appropriate training and experience, there are in Britain no specific regulations governing archaeological work except those voluntarily accepted by the archaeological community (see Chap. 4). Accordingly, anyone in Britain may call themselves an archaeologist, designate activities they undertake as archaeology, and – except on sites and areas specifically protected by law and so long as they have the landowner's permission – undertake work of an archaeological kind. This includes local archaeological and historical societies, individuals investigating particular areas or features, and the users of metal detectors (see Chap. 4 for limitations on metal detector use). In some areas, professional archaeologists – whether academics or working in development control – have established very good working relationships with both amateurs and metal detector users; in others, relationships are more strained. It will depend on where you are working – and who with – as to the attitude you will be expected to entertain towards these others.

British archaeologists are professional, hard-working, generally affable and friendly people of both sexes, many of whom exist on low pay moving from job to job, rather than having a single employer. The last point reflects the nature of archaeological employment in Britain, which is based on a system of developer-funded work (see Chaps. 4 and 8). Recent work to characterise and understand the attitudes of site staff has produced some interesting results (Everill 2006). While approximately 65% of site staff are male, a majority of younger staff – below age 25 – tend to be female. There is a marked fall-off after about 5 years experience in the field, indicating that a majority of staff will seek other opportunities: those with lower educational attainment tend to stay longest in the field. One thing that emerges from the study is the importance of a feeling of "camaraderie" among professional archaeologists: although many may wish to see changes in the structure of archaeo-logical careers, more pay and generally better conditions, and even though the majority leave after less than 10 years, there is a strong feeling of fellowship which ties groups together. It is these common bonds, so often also part of the social life of archaeological work, that provide much of the attraction of archaeology.

Membership is increasing for a whole range of heritage organisations (see Chap. 8). But the most detailed insight came in a MORI opinion poll conducted in England in 2000. A key finding of this survey was that the vast majority of people agree that heritage plays a valuable role in the life of the country. Similarly, around three-quarters agreed with the statement that "what I love about Britain is its heritage". What's more, they are happy to see public funding (84% agree), and do not think that we preserve too much already (although some group participants did question whether investment in the heritage does represent money well-spent, when there are perhaps more urgent problems in society). Heritage is clearly an important issue in people's minds, even if they are not thinking about it all the time.

Support for heritage is especially strong among the English public on certain issues:

- *98% think the heritage is important to teach children about our past* and that all schoolchildren should be given the opportunity to find out about this country's heritage.
- 96% think the heritage is important to teach us about our past.
- *95% think heritage is important for giving us places to visit and things to see and do*, for encouraging tourists to visit, (94%), and creating jobs and boosting the economy (88%).
- 77% *disagree* that we already preserve too much of this country's heritage.
- *Three-quarters of people (76%) agree that their lives are richer for having the opportunity to visit and see examples of this country's heritage.*

One conclusion to emerge strongly from this research is that the heritage is very much a *personal* thing. Everyone has a different view of what represents their own heritage, and people have different priorities for how heritage should be preserved. When asked how they would spend £100 on the heritage, there was a wide-range of responses (from a pre-coded list), but issues of access, conservation, and education were split roughly equally.

The personal nature of heritage is a matter of some interest, as it determines how heritage professionals think about their role in society. It does seem, for example, that for all our hard work and good intentions to promote a wider, more diverse heritage, historic buildings and palaces do still dominate popular thinking. Non-white respondents to the MORI poll took a different view, however. They tended to bring out more non-built, cultural issues (such as ways of life, types of food, hair braiding, etc.) as being part of the heritage. For those whose roots lie elsewhere, it is perhaps not surprising that their perceptions of heritage are more focused on things which could more easily be transported to a new country. For some of the group participants, the "traditional" English concepts of heritage, like country houses, monuments and so on meant very little indeed.

Politics and the Past

As mentioned above, there has been some recent debate in Britain about national identity and this inevitably involves consideration of the past. The nature of what should be taught as "British" history has also been the subject of some debate over the past two decades, especially in relation to formulating a National Curriculum for schools. In general, however, the past has not been a matter for party political dispute, and there has been in place a general consensus about what constitutes a "British" past for some decades. That this is also a political construct, however, is nicely illustrated by the use of that past regularly made by politicians and their frequent appeals to "the British way" and "tradition".

Since the 1980s, however, and especially within the context of developing the National Curriculum and classifying the heritage as "national", this consensual past has come under criticism for presenting a biased and partial view of what it is to be "British". In general, the critique boils down to a view that a focus on the big, spectacular and especially elite types of heritage object – especially the typically "English" country house, the castle, large prehistoric sites such as the Stonehenge stone circle or the Maiden Castle Iron Age hillfort – denies much of the truth of the past which for most people and their ancestors is nothing to do with such places except maybe that they found them symbols of oppression. Hewison (1987) for instance denigrated the growth of a "heritage industry" which saw museums opening at an unprecedented rate throughout the 1970s as symptomatic of the decline of Britain's industrial base, and highlighted in particular the re-use of closed factories as "heritage" sites which recreated for tourists an image of what had previously been done for real. In like terms, Wright (1985) criticised the emergence of a "national" heritage as the attempt to impose a particular vision of Britishness on a much more diverse population, and one that denied large sections of the population access to their own past. More recently, Smith (2006, 11) has identified the "authorised heritage discourse" which "promotes a certain set of … elite cultural values as being universally applicable". Her work goes on to highlight the attitudes generally held to elite sites such as country houses and the construction of "alternative" heritages based upon lived experience (Smith 2006, 237–275).

The political nature of the past as constructed in Britain, as elsewhere, usually only becomes visible in contexts of specific exclusion. Efforts to deny access to Stonehenge to modern Druids – even though based upon solid historical reasoning – has led to a series of disputes around that site (Chippindale et al. 1990). Similarly, the discovery of a circle of wood off the coast of Norfolk in 1998 led to a major debate between archaeologists, Druids, other "New Agers" and the local community as to its future (Skeates 2000, 69–70). Such disputes are never really about the past – they are about the nature of the present, using objects from the past as a rallying point for excluded groups.

Social Aspects of Archaeology in Britain

Once you get on site and start working you will notice one thing: the work regime can be hard and long hours are common, especially in summer. At the end of the working day, the immediate need is for the removal of accumulated grime and sustenance. Recreation takes place in the most convenient location dedicated to enjoyment, and (in the UK at least) the most available such place is likely to be a pub (short for "public house"; and for advice on pub behaviour for those unfamiliar with them, see http://www.sirc.org/publik/ptpchap2.html). Here, the choice is most commonly for beer to wash away the taste of soil. Beer has advantages: it is a relatively inexpensive alcoholic drink per unit of quantity; it quenches thirst effectively; it is *par excellence* the drink of the physical labourer; and it is easy to order. It can also make a useful topic of conversation in its own right, especially among those who claim detailed knowledge and expertise, which involves none of the complications that may arise from discussions of politics or religion. The typical conversation on any site and in the nearby pub, however, is of excavation itself. This is not usually of the current excavation but, instead, of other excavations elsewhere. Tales will be told of famed archaeologists or sites, of gross errors of practice or interpretation, and of the peculiarities of memorable colleagues encountered. Such talk has two purposes: for the speaker it confirms their right to discourse upon the practical aspects of fieldwork, since it serves to emphasise their breadth of experience and the professional contacts they have made; for the novice, it acts as a device to broaden their vicarious knowledge and experience of fieldwork practice. Comparisons in such talk are usually odious, but where reasonably large quantities of beer have been drunk and the site director is well out of earshot, the talk may ultimately turn to the shortcomings of the leader of this particular enterprise.

Especially, on sites where a high proportion of students or volunteers are employed (but not usually on commercial excavations), play on site can be as hard as work, and here the physicality of archaeological practice is particularly emphasised. On-site parties (held perhaps to mark the departure of one team and the arrival of a new one, or to mark the end of this season's work) may be quite cheerfully ribald affairs. Aspects of the close physical intimacy of shared accommodation and heavy labour in close proximity typical of this kind of work can be drawn upon to be reflected in a diversity of games and frequent parties. One party even left an archaeological trace. An unusual archaeological project in 2006 "excavated" (in the sense of forensically dismantling) an old Ford Transit van, used by the Ironbridge Gorge Museum Trust for archaeological work. One of the more obvious features of the van was a dented roof, which oral historical sources revealed to be the legacy of a party, whereby the van was parked alongside a "bouncy castle", onto which revellers jumped from the van roof! Inevitably in games and parties, the formal hierarchy of the team may be challenged or inverted so that the (otherwise serious and responsible) site director emerges as the chief joker. Such activities can be related to the kinds of fun and games seen on, for instance, building sites, but the particular affinity of on-site jollification is also with those ship-board parties celebrating events such as "crossing the line (of the equator)". Archaeologists thus frequently present themselves to each other as a band of siblings apart from the rest of the world – and privileged in being so. A bit like pirates!

The Tea Hut

In any archaeological excavation of any size there will be a tea hut. Tea breaks are an essential part of archaeological work. Usually the archaeological working day will be from 08.00 until about 16.00 h with breaks in the morning and at lunchtime and sometimes a break in the afternoon. However, the tea hut is traditionally a very democratic institution with a rota for making tea and washing up (woe betide the poor person who forgets to put the kettle on 20 min before tea break) and a generally convivial atmosphere in which aspects of the site are discussed and the shortcomings of any supervisors out of earshot may (again) be analysed. Unlike non-archaeological tea huts the main newspaper will be a broadsheet, traditionally the left-leaning *Guardian* but no longer universally so. Tea huts on smaller sites will contain all facilities in one damp and fetid room; however, increasing professionalisation means that facilities are generally improving – often with separate drying rooms and canteen areas.

In some cases temporary site accommodation might be shared with non-archaeological contractors working on site. Here you will immediately become aware of the English class system, as your middle-class liberal world of archaeology comes into contact with working-class conservatism. Tabloid newspapers such as the *Sun*, *Express* or *Daily Mail* (usually containing an offensive combination of racist statements and pictures of semi-naked women) will vie with the *Guardian* for your attention. Whilst most non-archaeologists are politely interested in your work, if often woefully unaware of the status of the profession (ill-informed comments such as "it's a waste of public money", or "are you a student?" are still surprisingly common), some will be openly rude ("so you're the ones who are holding up the work"). In such shared accommodation it is sadly not uncommon still to find offensive and lewd remarks being made towards women in archaeological teams, despite legislation banning it; the best response is to ignore it unless it is particularly offensive in which case seek the support of your supervisor in approaching the management of the non-archaeological contracting firm. Usually such matters are best resolved informally.

Smoking is no longer permitted in any public building, which includes temporary site accommodation, so the atmosphere in the tea hut is usually brighter and more breathable than it was 5 or 10 years ago. If you are smoker you will have to stand out in the rain with the other "untouchables" – however, smokers have their own camaraderie which can offset the physical disadvantages.

Employment Matters

On entering the country, you will need to ensure you have valid travel documents and appropriate permissions to undertake work or other activities. (This is discussed further in Chap. 8.) All citizens of European Union and European Economic Area countries (EU and EEA) are automatically entitled to stay as long as they wish and to undertake work. Others should note that in general you will not be allowed to apply for permission to work once in the country: you will need to attend to the appropriate formalities in your own country or any other country you travel through to get to the UK. If you plan to spend more than 6 months in Britain, you will need a visa although no visa is required for shorter visits.

All people working in Britain require a National Insurance number (NINO). This is a unique identifier to a particular individual used for income tax and some other purposes, such as paying for state healthcare (free at the point of delivery, to which you are entitled) and pensions through compulsory National Insurance payments: unlike tax, National Insurance is not refundable if overpaid. It is not allowed to undertake paid employment (and frequently unpaid volunteer work) without a NINO. The procedure to obtain one is simple, but requires attendance at a Job Centre and the completion of simple formalities including providing evidence of identity and one's residence status. Both tax and National Insurance will usually be deducted at source (i.e. direct from your pay before you receive it) by your employer in accordance with government-set regulations. As an employee, you are entitled to receive a written contract of employment within 2 months (if this is not done, a basic set of terms designed to protect you as an employee will be assumed to apply). You will receive a pay slip each payday indicating your earnings and how much has been deducted for tax and National Insurance. Britain has a National Minimum Wage in operation, and it is illegal for an employer to pay below these rates, which at the time of writing (January 2010) are as follows: £5–80 an hour for those over 22; and £4–81 an hour for those from 18 to 21 (although most if not all archaeological units will pay well over these rates). There are also certain rights no contract can take away from you: to be treated fairly regardless of gender, race (ethnicity), nationality, sexuality, religion or disability; to receive the same rate for the job regardless of gender; to join a trades union if desired; and time off for medical care if you are pregnant and maternity leave after the baby is born.

There are a number of schemes under which you may be able to obtain archaeological work in Britain. The "business and commercial" permit allows a non-resident (i.e. someone from a country outside the EU/EEA) to work in Britain for up to 5 years and needs to be applied for by the employer: it represents a full-time appointment to a particular job. Student internships may be applicable in certain circumstances if the British employer also operates overseas (which is not very likely for an archaeological unit, but may be the case for some) and is relevant for students coming to work to gain experience of British archaeology: again, the employer makes the application while the student is overseas, and is designed primarily for those who are likely to be taken on as more permanent employees once the internship is over.

Be aware that Britain is relatively expensive in comparison to most other countries and this is a factor you will need to take into account in planning to come. While living in the south of Britain is generally more expensive than further north, the good news is that most prices quoted will be the price you will actually pay: no additional taxes will be added. The bad news on buying most everyday things is that such prices may be significantly more than you would pay at home for an equivalent, and in major cities such as London particularly so. This is important if you plan to seek archaeological employment: rates of pay for archaeologists tend to be lower than in other sectors, which means your standard of living may be lower than you have come to expect. If you come from beyond the EU/EEA, find you cannot survive on earnings, and have no other resources, you will be ineligible to apply for any kind of state benefit.

Finding Somewhere to Live

This is not the place for detail of finding accommodation, merely to state the obvious points. First that the two main options are renting and buying. Buying property in Britain is generally considered to be a sound investment, at least in the medium- to long-term, though legal and administrative costs (notably stamp duty) can be high. Unlike many European countries, there are no restrictions on property ownership by non-Britons. You will almost certainly need a mortgage and at the time of writing mortgage lenders are reluctant to offer mortgages for anything more than 90% of the price of the property. So a sizeable deposit may be needed if you are thinking along these lines. Flats (what elsewhere are often called "apartments") are common in cities; houses and cottages are more frequent in the countryside. Costs to be aware of when buying a house or flat are legal fees, fees for financial arrangements, and in many cases additional "stamp duty" (a tax charged on property transactions), and these may accumulate significantly. If you rent accommodation you will find costs involve a significant initial deposit, local taxes (called "council tax"), some kind of maintenance charge over and above rent, as well as charges for water, electricity and gas supplies.

Local estate agents typically have Web sites, making the search much easier from a distance. There are also various free Web sites which can search a particular area, and with specific search criteria. Most of these Web sites also cover rented property, though local newspapers and shops often hold advertisements for private deals, where the owner is choosing to by-pass the agent. The price of renting reflects property prices in general, though there are often cheap places to be had, either because of their size, their location or condition. Whether you choose to buy or rent, do the research. Spend some time in the area, drink in the local pub, use the local shop and engage people in conversation. If there is something seriously wrong with the area you will soon find out.

It is worth adding finally that often employers will help you to find accommodation, and provide the all-important local knowledge. Some employers, and some projects, may even include accommodation, in bed and breakfast establishments for example, which is always a good stop-gap before you take the plunge.

Having (Even More) Fun

As if archaeology is not fun enough, there are other ways one can enjoy oneself in Britain, far too many and too varied to attempt a summary here. The Web is clearly the primary source, as are some of the better and more informed travel guides to Britain. For something leftfield, recent guide books such as *Bollocks to Alton Towers* (Halstead et al. 2006) and *Far from the Sodding Crowd* (Hazeley et al. 2007) provide details of some of our hidden gems. And if you really feel the need to get away, for ever or for a weekend, European travel remains cheap, with Ryanair and Flybe amongst the more popular low-budget airlines to sunnier and more distant lands (although beware of the tendency to offer very low headline prices and charge various "fees" along the way so your final price might not be as low as you were led to believe).

How to Use This Book

Although written in what we hope is an approachable style, we do not assume you will read this book from cover to cover as you would a novel, but rather dip into it as required, more like a text- or reference-book. We therefore hope that the Contents, the Appendix and Index are valuable guides to what you seek. We do, however, also recommend that you do actually read those parts of the book that are relevant to you rather than merely glance through them. The structure we hope is logical. Chapters 1 and 2 are introductory: this chapter provides a basic introduction to Great Britain and some information you will need both before you arrive and immediately on arrival, while Chap. 2 gives you the historical development of archaeology in Britain (which is especially useful for those coming from countries with very different traditions of archaeological work and very different contexts for that work). Chapters 3 and 4 provide outlines of the knowledge you will need to perform archaeology in Britain: Chap. 3 outlines the kind of archaeological material you will be encountering from particular periods of British history; Chap. 4 outlines the administrative and regulatory framework within which most archaeology in Britain is conducted. Chapters 5–7 focus on specific aspects of archaeological practice: the structure within which work is conducted, and the main types of prospection and sources of information most commonly used are covered in Chap. 5; excavation techniques and recording systems are covered in Chap. 6; while Chap. 7 goes through processes of analysis and publication. Chapter 8 – another that it would be useful for you to read before arrival – examines the types of opportunities that may be open to you and how to obtain the necessary funding. The references and Appendix provide lists of other useful publications and Web sites that you may like – or need to – consult.

As well as the authors' own diverse experiences, we have also drawn on help from our colleagues. Scattered throughout the book are several shorter pieces on various aspects of doing archaeology in Britain – what clothes to wear, what an inspector does, how to look after your car and thus keep moving, what sort of trowel is best and so on. Above all this is a practical book – a "rough guide", a "how to do" handbook, a manual for all who seek to come and practice or learn about archaeo logy in Britain. We hope you enjoy the book, that you find what you need within its pages and, more importantly, that you enjoy your experience of British archaeology!

References and Further Reading

Chippindale, C. et al. 1990. *Who Owns Stonehenge?* London: Batsford.
Cornwell, B. 1997. *Excalibur.* London, St Martins Press.
Everill, P. 2006. *The Invisible Diggers: contemporary commercial archaeology in the UK.* Unpublished PhD thesis, University of Southampton.
Fox, K. 2004. *Watching the English: the hidden rules of English behaviour.* London, Hodder and Stoughton.
Halstead, R., Hazeley, J., Morris, A. & Morris, J. 2006. *Bollocks to Alton Towers: uncommonly British days out.* Harmondsworth: Penguin Books.
Hazeley, J., Morris, A., Morris, J. & Halstead, R. 2007. *Far from the Sodding Crowd: more uncommonly British days out.* London: Michael Joseph.
Hewison, R. 1987. *The Heritage Industry: Britain in a climate of decline.* London: Methuen.
Hobsbawm, E. & Ranger, T. (eds) 1983. *The Invention of Tradition.* Cambridge, Cambridge University Press.
Jones, S. 2004. *Early Medieval Sculpture and the Production of Meaning, Value and Place: the case of Hilton of Cadboll.* Edinburgh, Historic Scotland.
Long, S. 2007. *Le Dossier of Hortense de Monplaisir, or How to Survive the English.* Trans. S. Long. London, John Murray.
Mears, R. 2002. *Essential Bushcraft.* London: Hodder & Stoughton.
Miles, D. 2006. *The Tribes of Britain.* London, Phoenix.
Patton, M. 2007. *Science, politics and business in the work of Sir John Lubbock: a man of universal mind.* Aldershot, Ashgate.

Porter, R. (ed.) 1991. *The Myths of the English.* Cambridge, Polity Press.

Skeates, R. 2000. *Debating the Archaeological Heritage.* London: Duckworth.

Smith, L. 2006. *Uses of Heritage.* London: Routledge.

Stewart, M. 1979. *The Last Enchantment.* London, G.H. Hall & Co.

Sutcliffe, R. 1963. *Sword at Sunset.* London: Hodder & Stoughton.

Ucko, P. et al. 1991. *Avebury reconsidered : from the 1660s to the 1990s.* London, Unwin Hyman

Ware, V. 2007. *Who Cares About Britishness? A global view of the national identity debate.* London, Arcadia Books.

White, T. H. 1958. *The Once and Future King.* London, Collins.

Wright, P. 1985. *On Living in an Old Country.* London: Verso.

Chapter 2
A History of Archaeology in Great Britain

Archaeology in Britain spans the entire history of archaeology as a field of enquiry, and it may be no co-incidence, therefore, that Britain is where some of the most significant developments took place in shaping the modern profession. That said, archaeology in Britain has been the domain of the amateur for most of its history and the role of the amateur in an increasingly professionalised field, enabled largely by commercial funding, is a long-standing debate in British archaeology. It is also one of the themes of this chapter. The other two themes we address are, first, the development of archaeological techniques and second, the development of multiple readings of the British past.

Arguably, the origins of archaeology in Britain lie in the mediaeval period with inquisitive monks. It is then taken up as a pursuit for the leisured landed class, and subsequently becomes a subject suitable for university academics, before becoming, from the late 1980s, a fully fledged practical profession. There are no single publications telling the entire story of archaeology in Britain, despite a recent growth in interest in the history of the discipline (but c.f. Trigger 2006), and most reviews are quite old now: the best include Marsden (1983) and Piggott (1989) on the period to 1900, and Hudson (1981) on the period from the Victorians to the 1970s, all of which emphasise the role of the amateur. A short version which focuses specifically on the rise of professionalism is McAdam's (1995) chapter 'Trying to Make It Happen' in Cooper et al. (1995), while Schofield's Great Excavations (2011) summarises the contribution made by notable excavations and excavators to shaping the modern archaeological profession. For critical reviews of how professionalisation came about and its consequences, refer especially to Lucas (2001), Roskams (2001) and Everill (2006).

Before 1800: Seeking King Arthur, Druids and Others

The earliest example of archaeological work in Britain can, perhaps, be claimed by monks at Glastonbury Abbey in 1194, where the supposed burial place of King Arthur was found during the rebuilding of the great church after a fire

J. Schofield et al., *Archaeological Practice in Great Britain: A Heritage Handbook*,
World Archaeological Congress Cultural Heritage Manual Series,
DOI 10.1007/978-0-387-09453-3_2, © Springer Science+Business Media, LLC 2011

(it was most likely the grave of a former Abbott). A more systematic – and less accidental – approach was taken by John Leland, appointed 'the King's Antiquary' by Henry VIII in 1533 and charged with searching England and Wales for antiquities of all kinds. His *Itinerary* was never published due to his death before its completion, but it stands as an example of the early kind of recording, focussing chiefly upon Roman, Saxon and what were assumed to be 'Danish' remains. There is nothing of earlier date as Leland was dismissive of anything pre-Roman (Marsden 1983, 1; Trigger 2006, 85). Leland's leading successor was William Camden, author of the monumental *Britannia* first published in 1586: this work also included pre-Roman and later Saxon material, although with no clear chronology yet established since major prehistoric monuments – among them Stonehenge – were not identified as such (Trigger 2006, 86; Marsden 1983, 2). The sixteenth century also saw the first society of antiquaries dedicated to the study of Britain's past, founded by Camden and others in 1577. This had a relatively short existence: it became a place where lawyers, in particular, could discuss the legal regime then in place, and was finally suppressed by King James in the early seventeenth century for its political activities (Marsden 1983, 2; Carman 1996, 48).

Despite the closure of the first society of antiquaries, however, the seventeenth century would see significant advances in the study of British prehistory. Among those showing an interest were members of the landed classes such as William Dugdale, who identified stone tools as the product of ancient Britons from an era when metalworking must have been unknown. Robert Plot, first Keeper of the Ashmolean Museum in Oxford, and his assistant Edward Lhew undertook comparison of stone tools from Britain with those known to have been manufactured by the inhabitants of the New World to confirm their manufacture by humans, and in Scotland, Robert Sibbald was doing similar work (Trigger 2006, 93–94). The best known of these antiquaries, however, and one courted by King Charles II, was John Aubrey, who among other achievements recognised stone circles as a distinct category of ancient remains, identified and planned the monument at Avebury and (by noting how shadows fell) was the first to see the ring of holes at Stonehenge that now bear his name (Trigger 2006, 107; Marsden 1983, 3). He was also the first to attribute these great prehistoric monuments to the historically attested Druids, thus providing the basis on which a persistent myth has been based. Nonetheless, the work of Aubrey, his contemporaries and his immediate successors, led to an emerging interest among the landed and more leisurely classes in the material evidence of their country's past. By the end of the century, a number of clear traditions had been established to be built upon by others. From Camden came the recognition that buried features would indicate their presence by differential crop growth or by undulations in the ground surface; and from Aubrey and others a tradition of fieldwork, involving the active seeking-out of remains and their careful recording in words, pictures and as plans; and also the grouping together of monuments into similar types.

The eighteenth century saw the emergence of 'the first great English field archaeologist' (Marsden 1983, 5), William Stukeley. Stukeley drew on the established traditions of fieldwork to identify and record 'the Antiquitys of Britain', resulting in his *Itinerarium Curiosum* of 1724 which contained over 100 descriptions and engravings of monuments and objects of antiquarian interest. It was Stukeley's particular contribution to first suggest that certain classes of monument predated the Roman Conquest and that connections with the nearby European continent may have helped shape Britain's past. He was also one of the first to use excavation as a tool of investigation into the past, driving trenches into a number of mounds which he then was able to classify according to type. Although stratigraphy was yet to be developed as a method of analysis, Stukeley carefully recorded the internal structure of such mounds as well as their contents: for those who came after he would leave evidence of his earlier incursion by leaving a memento – usually a coin – in the backfilled trench. His detailed plans and descriptions of Stonehenge and Avebury have proved valuable to modern scholars, and his attempts at relative dating established principles still followed today: in particular, his recognition that Roman roads that cut through burial mounds or bypassed other monuments must postdate them. The consequent inference that such monuments must predate the Roman occupation led to the theory of a long occupation of Britain prior to the Roman invasion. Stukeley's later work, which followed Aubrey's earlier ascription of major monuments to the Druids (Piggott 1989, 143–146), was aimed to defend the (then still relatively new) Church of England orthodoxy against those who challenged it: it was felt that demonstrating the supposed antiquity of the Trinity would give the theology propounded by the Church a greater degree of authority. With the decline of the debates in which these arguments were embedded, a strictly antiquarian interest in Druidism emerged to cloud developments in understanding the early history of Britain: as Piggott (1989, 150) described it, 'Druids in various fantastic disguises persist'.

Stukeley was a founder member of the Society of Antiquaries of London, originally a group of like-minded individuals meeting informally from 1707, then formally constituted in 1717 before being granted a charter in 1754: it remains a leading learned society that has its offices just off Piccadilly Circus in London. The foundation of the Society of Antiquaries of Scotland followed in 1780, and a further Society of Antiquaries for (the city of) Newcastle upon Tyne (northeast England) in 1813. As Piggott (1989, 152–157) (see also Trigger 2006, 118–120) makes clear, however, the period from the early eighteenth to early nineteenth centuries saw few real advances in the study of the material past in terms of understanding: chronological schemes had yet to be developed, and even though Stukeley had shown that the mound at Silbury Hill must predate the Roman road that swerves to avoid it, thus providing a means to attempt relative dating, field monuments were still haphazardly ascribed to various figures of fancy, history and myth. The publications of the various societies accordingly abound with descriptive pieces and such speculative articles.

However, the fashion for excavation was one trend which did see development in this period. Throughout the eighteenth century and into the early nineteenth, a number of individuals – generally referred to as 'barrow diggers' because of the burial mounds ('barrows') they investigated – carried out extensive investigations, usually in the areas where they lived or on land they owned. The majority came from the professions, which in those days meant the Church or medicine, with the occasional soldier also taking part. By the early nineteenth century, however, members of the new professions and the emerging capitalist class were also becoming interested in these relics. Notable among these were Sir Richard Colt Hoare (the son of a banker) and William Cunnington (a wool merchant), who co-operated on investigating barrows in Wiltshire in southwest England (Marsden 1983, 15–20). In all these cases, those credited with the 'digging' were not those necessarily responsible for the actual spade-work: Everill (2006) identifies a father-and-son team of workmen, Stephen and John Parker, as 'the invisible diggers' who actually carried out work on behalf of Cunnington but whose names are generally excluded from histories of archaeology. Drawing upon and extending an analogy made by Piggott, he compares the group with modern practice, as an early example of a 'contracting unit' in the service of Colt Hoare.

By the beginning of the nineteenth century, British archaeology had some of its foundations in place. Specific antiquities, including some famous ancient monuments, had been identified and ascribed if not to a specific time period, then at least to a period before written history, and the beginnings of a relative dating methodology were established. They had been surveyed, planned and recorded to a very high standard that serves modern researchers well (see, e.g., Ucko et al. 1991 on Avebury; Chippindale 1983b on Stonehenge). There was also, as a result of earlier work by Camden and others, a broad understanding of the types of antiquity that dotted the British landscape, and although the techniques of the 'barrow diggers' of the eighteenth century left much to be desired from a modern point of view, the key methodology of field archaeology – excavation – was well established. The archaeology of this period was inevitably a pastime for the leisured classes: the idea of a state-sponsored archaeology was yet to emerge and the working poor so far lacked the educational background, the time and the energy to take any part in studying the past. As we have seen with the Parkers, however, it was mostly such people who undertook the physical task of excavation, while their employers stood by to watch, and frequently not even that.

The Nineteenth Century: The Emergence of Archaeology

The main intellectual strands of the development of archaeology in the nineteenth century – those that were to transform earlier antiquarianism and 'barrow digging' into archaeology proper – have been widely discussed by historians of the discipline (e.g., Trigger 2006; Daniel 1967; Daniel and Renfrew 1988). These were aspects widely shared across Europe and North America, and although some major participants in this story were based in Britain, they cannot be claimed as uniquely British contributions. Nevertheless, the efforts of British individuals to disseminate the findings of research and of approaches to dating developed elsewhere did much to promote the internationalisation of the field. These include the adoption by such figures as John Lubbock of the so-called 'Three Age System' for European prehistory developed initially in Denmark and extended by the work of Lubbock and others to all of Europe; the adoption from geology of principles such as that of stratigraphy, allowing the identification of deposits separately, and in sequence; the recognition from the work especially of figures such as Boucher de Perthes and – more pertinently for Britain – the finds at Brixham Cave (Devon, southwest England), of the bones of extinct animals associated with worked stone tools, of the antiquity of humanity. All of these combined in the latter half of the nineteenth century to a recognition that the past – the prehistoric past in particular – was deeper than first thought, and could not be filled either by reference to Biblical or historical sources alone, and that the study of material traces of that past was key to its understanding.

A particularly British contribution, however, was reflected in one significant attempt to fill the void of this deeper prehistoric past. In 1859, Charles Darwin finally published his theory of the evolutionary process, whereby species changed in response to natural selection, favouring those individuals best suited to their environment. This ground-breaking theory was published under the title *The Origin of Species*. Darwin's work was underpinned by the geological studies of his friend Charles Lyell, who published his multi-volume work *Principles of Geology* between 1830 and 1833. Darwin received the volumes as they were published – sent to him during his voyages on *HMS Beagle*. Lyell's main contribution was to formalise the principle of stratigraphy in geology, which was of course later applied to archaeology. Darwin never intended to extend his theory to the development of humanity: a devout Christian, he believed fervently that humanity was a special case. Later, however, he would apply his theory to the physical emergence of humanity – making the crucial links with other primates – but not to human social existence.

Yet figures such as Herbert Spencer took the view that if 'survival of the fittest' was a natural law, then it would apply equally to matters social and cultural as to biological phenomena, and it was this view that took root in archaeological and anthropological thinking to develop the first 'scientific' approach to archaeology. This was developed by Lubbock in his series of publications which were later combined into the book *Pre-historic Times*, first published in 1865 (a mere 6 years after Darwin) and which went through 11 editions into the twentieth century. The book combined several concerns: the extension of the Three Age System of Stone, Bronze and Iron Ages to divide the Stone Age into a Palaeolithic (old-) and a Neolithic (new stone age); the establishment of the antiquity of humanity; and an argument that social and moral development went hand-in-hand with technological development, derived from both archaeological and ethnographic sources. For Lubbock, the last of these – and the most important point of the book – connected to his own beliefs in human progress and betterment in his own society through processes of education, especially in the natural sciences (Patton 2007). It also provided support for the conquest – and even extermination – of other peoples on the basis that their inferiority was the result of a natural inability to better themselves.

Figures such as Lubbock, Darwin, Spencer and their associates, including Thomas Huxley, are frequently depicted as a Victorian scientific aristocracy, and indeed confused with the actual aristocratic class in part because of Lubbock's later career in politics that led to his becoming Lord Avebury. It is true that Lubbock and some others were wealthy (Lubbock was director of a leading bank) and had close connections with the landed class, their wealth having allowed them to buy land and the houses to live in. There was also an established connection between students of the past and the aristocracy through the main London-based societies dedicated to its study. However, many of those involved in scientific study in the later nineteenth century were from relatively humble origins and very frequently self-educated, as was Lubbock himself (Hudson 1981, 50; Patton 2007). The closeness of individuals was a crucial component of Victorian science and has been the subject of some study (e.g., Barton 1990, 1998; Chapman 1989). What is less well studied, but equally important for archaeology, was the rise of local, county and regional archaeological societies from the 1840s onwards: it was the work of these bodies that represent the bulk of archaeological work in the nineteenth century, largely continuing in the tradition of 'barrow digging' from the previous century and also extending the range of interests.

Piggott (1976) addresses the origins of the Victorian surge of archaeological societies, tracing its origin to a number of influences: efforts to reform the official religion; the Romantic imagination; a greater ease of transport; and – paradoxically – the emergence of geology as an organised science. The latter had become 'a developed natural science' by the 1820s (Toulmin and Goldfield 1967, 199), thereby effectively excluding the intermittent efforts of amateurs from making any significant contribution, although its findings were also becoming more widely available. At the same time, an improvement in roads (noticeable especially in Scotland, in part the result of a response to the threat of rebellions now past) and the rapid and increasing development of rail travel allowed more people to travel more easily around the country, and thus gave greater opportunity to explore those features that geologists, antiquarians and others had made prominent in the cultural landscape (e.g., see Hudson 1981, 43–47). The works of Romantic writers such as Walter Scott and poets such as William Wordsworth had a similar effect by focussing the historical imagination upon the picturesque, the local and the traditional. A final function was to loosen the increasingly tight restrictions on social activity that were emerging: the members of these societies could – on the pretext, however true, of studying the local past – mix with people of almost all social classes and both sexes without fear of breaking social taboos: this was especially important for women, who would otherwise be largely housebound.

For Piggott, however, the catalyst that brought about the invention of the local society as an institution was the emergence of a concern to rejuvenate the established Church of England by making it distinct from its Protestant rivals. The Cambridge-based Camden Society (by no means accidentally named after the antiquarian) and the Oxford Society for Promoting the Study of Gothic Architecture were in fact organisations devoted to 'ecclesiology', which meant changing the liturgical practices of the Church by restoring them to what they saw as a kind of mediaeval 'purity' (as the original aims of the Camden Society have been forgotten, this movement is normally referred to as 'the Oxford Movement'). In doing so, they advocated changes to the way the fabric of churches was used: restoring fonts (some of which were used as deposits for wet umbrellas, for instance, or as horse-troughs) to their 'rightful' place inside the church; and removing the altar from perhaps a central position close to the congregation, to the East end and away from them. Such concerns inevitably led to a wider interest in the fabric of church buildings, encouraging antiquarian interests among the clergy in particular. In this respect, Hudson (1981, 18–20) demonstrates the high number of clergy involved in the emerging archaeological societies in the 1840s, while Piggott (1976, 182) provides the reason for this and goes further to indicate the nature of religious disputes that caused divisions within the new societies.

The societies that were formed from the 1840s gave themselves varied names once the area they covered (frequently a county, but sometimes the smaller area around a particular town) was specified: 'Archaeological and Natural History Society', 'Geological, Archaeological, Botanical and Zoological Society', simply 'Archaeological Society' or sometimes more simply 'Field Club', indicating the focus of the group on fieldwork outdoors. These societies were responsible for the great bulk of archaeological research undertaken in Britain during the period from mid-eighteenth century to the 1970s, co-operation and exchange between their members being encouraged and enhanced by the creation in 1898 of the national Congress of Archaeological Societies. Archaeology throughout this period was, therefore, driven not by any official or government interest, nor largely by any form of professional concern, but by keen amateurs who laid the basis for much of the knowledge that would be developed by those synthesisers such as Lubbock later in the century. Nevertheless, the seeds of what would become professionalism were sown remarkably early. In 1851, the first academic Chair of Archaeology, named for its first incumbent John Disney, was established at Cambridge University, followed by others at Oxford and elsewhere. Meanwhile the older societies – such as the Society of Antiquaries of London – continued in existence, and newer London-based national societies, such as the Archaeological Institute were also formed in the 1840s.

A key development that would assist the move towards professionalism, although it was never the intent of its founders, was the creation by William Morris of the Society for the Protection of Ancient Buildings (SPAB) in 1877. This group, dedicated to the philosophy of conservation espoused by such promoters of art and architecture as John Ruskin, included in its membership those such as John Lubbock with an interest in conserving the monuments of the past. The agenda of the society was expressly *contra* to that of the ecclesiologists, whose extreme views on 'restoration' to a pristine state defined by ideology rather than fact they abhorred. SPAB was closely linked to the 'Arts and Crafts Movement' also promoted by Morris following the ideals of architects and designers such as Augustus and Ernest Pugin. Looking back to a vision of the mediaeval period as one where artisans had control over their work and could invest in it some moral and ethical values, Morris and his followers sought to challenge the rise of capitalist industrial production by establishing workshops where works of artistic quality could be produced that would in turn influence those who experienced those works. In the end, Arts and Crafts production would be seen merely as a 'style' rather than an attempt to change society for the better, but the influence of SPAB on the preservation of old buildings and in particular their protection from unwarranted alteration was more profound. Its links with the work of others concerned for ancient structures who would inform the emerging conservation ethic that in turn is applied today.

SPAB was not the only archaeological entity to emerge in the 1870s. The decade also saw the MP John Lubbock's repeated attempts to pass into law a measure for the protection of prehistoric structures (Chippindale 1983a; Carman 1996, 67–91). This story is long and complex. On the surface, and largely in reality, arguments about the law concerned issues of protecting private property from government control, and who were the better custodians of Britain's heritage: government appointed experts, or the landed aristocracy in whose hands the monuments had been held for centuries. Below this, however, were other, equally contentious issues: the role of education in promoting welfare, visions of the nation's future, the need for Britain to be seen as an advanced and civilised nation state in comparison with its European neighbours, and even the future of Ireland (then part of the UK). Despite ultimately gaining widespread support for the measure, the government then in power (Lubbock's own political party) repeatedly failed to give it full support and consequently it repeatedly ran out of Parliamentary time before becoming law. In the end, in 1881, Lubbock forced a vote which required the government to take action in respect of ancient monuments, which in the following year they did, and a version of Lubbock's measure finally became law. The law as passed was concerned only with prehistoric monuments, an indication of the ideological differences between prehistorians (generally Liberal or Conservative) and some mediaevalists (such as the libertarian Morris) at the time; it merely allowed landowners to hand over control of their monuments to the State for protection; and although it created a post of government Inspector of Ancient Monuments, it gave the holder very few powers. The law would stay in place until the early twentieth century.

Lubbock's choice for the position of first Inspector was Augustus Henry Lane Fox Pitt Rivers (Bowden 1991), a close ally in promoting prehistoric study. Pitt Rivers (originally named Lane Fox: he took the additional names on inheriting land at Cranborne Chase in southern England, which was required as part of the bequest) was by profession a military engineer, but he also had a strong interest in archaeology. On inheriting Cranborne Chase, he retired from the army and took up residence as a member of the landed classes and began the work of investigating the archaeological monuments of his estate, covering periods from prehistory to the Romans (Bowden 1991; Marsden 1983, 79–80). The publication of these researches is his lasting monument. Although by no means an innovator in terms of technique (see Lucas 2001, 19–26), he was a believer in 'total excavation' as a method and in detailed recording of stratigraphy and of finds. As testimony to its success, those he trained in this technique continued to use his approach after his death in 1900. As Inspector of Ancient Monuments, he regularly exceeded his legal authority, persuading landowners to part with their monuments rather than waiting for them to volunteer them, and carrying out survey work on other people's land to establish the condition of monuments. He also employed assistants to carry out investigative work in his capacity as Inspector and subsequently claimed the costs of doing so from the relevant government office, despite the fact that the post provided no such authority.

By the close of the nineteenth century much of what we would recognise as 'archaeology' had emerged. The work of Pitt Rivers had established a system of excavation that provided a solid basis on which to build interpretations and one that allowed the identification of multiple phases within a site to be identified. In conjunction with – and partly derived from – an evolutionary model of social development, it also allowed interpretations of long-term change to be developed that had meaning for contemporary society. The establishment of the first Chairs in Archaeology at British universities from the 1850s gave the field a respectability it had so far lacked, while the rise of the local and county amateur society as well as national interest groups provided a base from which archaeological work and interests could be promoted and developed. The simultaneous development of a concern for preservation, whether of mediaeval and later buildings by the Society for the Preservation of Ancient Buildings, or for prehistoric monuments under legislation, and the work of Pitt Rivers as Inspector of Ancient Monuments, looks forward to later refinement of law in the field and the development of formal structures to conserve and record the material remains of the past.

Twentieth-Century Developments: Archaeology Emerges as a Discipline and Profession

The First World War saw the effective end of the nineteenth-century project in archaeology (Trigger 2006, 294): a generation raised on the social evolutionary principles of Lubbock's *Prehistoric Times* was virtually wiped out. This was not the beginning of the end of archaeology, however, so much as the end of the beginning: in its place would emerge a more mature, more sophisticated discipline. The period to the 1970s would see developments in technique, in outreach to a wider public, the establishment of archaeology as a recognised academic discipline and further efforts to preserve the material record of the past. The period beyond would see the emergence of a fully professional archaeology, with greatly reduced amateur involvement and a system designed to preserve sites that paradoxically allowed more scope for investigation.

By 1900, the 1882 Act was out of date. However, during the twentieth century, a revived interest in old things and their preservation led to new efforts in legislation (see, e.g. Saunders 1983; and for a more detailed outline Carman 1996, 100–111). An Ancient Monuments Protection Act of 1900 went further than Sir John Lubbock's original intent by specifically defining in broad terms what could be considered an 'ancient monument' for purposes of preservation, and this went beyond prehistoric remains to include mediaeval structures. In 1910, a revised Act created the category of 'guardianship monuments' which were those held specifically by the state to allow direct public access. An Act of 1913 extended the range of legal coverage further, consolidating efforts to include mediaeval remains and attempting also to include Church (of England) buildings: this was defeated, but the Church was forced to establish its own similar protective arrangements under its own power to make law.

A series of further Acts to manage ancient monuments have followed over the decades, culminating in 1979 in the Ancient Monuments and Archaeological Areas Act which remains the main law in place at the time of writing, in spite of efforts to overhaul the system in recent years.

From 1944, and in response to the threat of widespread clearance of historic buildings from bomb-damaged towns and cities, Planning Acts have limited the capacity for uncontrolled development and have incorporated historic buildings which remain in use into the protective scheme (a system known as 'Listing' – see Chap. 4). From 1973, named historic wrecks have also had protection, and the 1996 Treasure Act extended protection to portable antiquities of inherent monetary value. The creation from 1949 of the first National Parks extended protection to wider landscapes and the archaeology they contain as part of a programme of land-use policy that provided access to the countryside to the wider population. The result over the past 100 years has been a proliferation of laws to do with archaeological remains, and of bodies of law related to archaeology and historic buildings, which makes the overall legislative framework for Britain very complex. This complexity is one of the motivations behind recent attempts to reform the means and approaches to heritage protection, including the legislation that underpins it.

This rising complexity in the mechanisms for managing archaeological resources was coincident with an increase in the sophistication of investigative techniques. One such technique was the development of aerial reconnaissance from its military origins during the First World War into a valuable approach for archaeology during the peace which followed. Aerial archaeology was notably pioneered by O. G. S. Crawford at the Ordnance Survey: the identification of soil- and crop-marks from the air allowed the recognition of previously unknown buried sites. Excavation techniques also evolved. Between 1921 and 1937, Mortimer Wheeler developed a technique of excavation that went beyond Pitt Rivers' detailed recording of a total excavation. Wheeler's technique involved excavating in grid squares leaving standing baulks between squares ('box excavation') to allow the detailed recording of stratigraphy, with finds recorded in relation to their context and the sections drawn only after interpretation. This focus on the stratigraphic relationships within the site was widely adopted for several decades, but many of Wheeler's successors forgot the final stage, whereby the baulks would also be removed to result in a total-area excavation revealing the overall plan of the site (Barker 1982, 15). As Barker (1982, 15–16) emphasises, the stratigraphic approach was ideal for Roman sites, but the complexities of prehistoric sites, with many intercutting features, required a truly three-dimensional approach to recording that emphasised section and plan in equal measure. This approach – adopted from continental archaeologists and pioneered by Gerald Bersu during the Second World War – was applied by Bersu particularly to a Viking-age site on the Isle of Man where the presence of overlapping buildings from different phases was indicated only by changes in soil-type (Barker 1982, 20, 24–25). Such open-area excavations were used to great effect on mediaeval settlements, both urban and rural, during the 1950s, 1960s and 1970s, as well as at the Roman site of Wroxeter where detailed recording of contours from the distribution of gravel deposits on part of the site allowed the identification of the presence of ephemeral post-Roman structures (Barker 1982, 153).

Wheeler was not only an entrepreneur in developing excavation techniques. He was also instrumental in founding one of the major academic centres for archaeology in Britain at the Institute of Archaeology, part of University College London, a project he began in 1926 and which saw fruition with its opening in 1937. The Edinburgh Abercromby Chair in Archaeology was established in the early 1920s, and at about the same time Cambridge University established its *tripos* (a 3-year undergraduate course) in archaeology and anthropology, although this became a full (stand-alone) course only after the Second World War (Clark 1989, 6). The first British PhD in archaeology was awarded to Cyril Fox at Cambridge in 1922, and a series of others followed, reading rather like a 'Who's Who' of twentieth-century archaeology across large parts of the globe: among them were Louis Leakey in 1931, Grahame Clark (1934), Glyn Daniel (1938), Charles McBurney (1948), Desmond Clark (1951), and John Evans (1956), Brian Hope-Taylor (1962), Ian Longworth (1964), David Clarke (1965), Colin Renfrew (1966), Barry Cunliffe (1967), Paul Mellars and Derek Roe (1968) and Glyn Isaac in 1969 (for a full list to 1986, see *Archaeological Review from Cambridge* 1989). Of these, three would become Disney Professors at Cambridge, including Colin Renfrew, the first archaeologist to be made a peer of the realm (as Lord Renfrew of Kaimsthorn). Other universities would follow suit and establish archaeology departments – sometimes in conjunction with other disciplines such as Art, Ancient or Mediaeval History, Classics, Geography or Anthropology – in the decades that followed.

The London-based Institute of Archaeology and the Cambridge Archaeology department were two of the most powerful locations for academic archaeology during the mid-twentieth century. In London, from the outset, the importance of scientific techniques to the analysis of the past was seen as central and the focus throughout its history has largely been upon archaeological practice and technique, although some significant theorists – among them V. Gordon Childe – have passed through its doors. In contrast, Cambridge has generally been seen as the home of theory. During the 1930s, Grahame Clark and others founded the Fenland Research Committee, an interdisciplinary group carrying out the first major environmental archaeology project in Britain. Clark is also seen – along with Childe – as a precursor of the 'New' or 'Processual' Archaeology (Trigger 2006, 322–326; 344–361) that emerged during the 1960s: the most prominent of those who are identified with processualism are David Clarke, who drew particularly upon ideas from the 'New Geography' of the time (Clarke 1968), and Colin Renfrew, who developed Grahame Clark's 'systems' approach (Renfrew 1979, 39). From the late 1960s onwards, Cambridge became closely associated with the development of archaeological theory. As well as Clarke and Renfrew leading the British processualist movements, Ian Hodder led the emergence of 'postprocessual' or 'interpretive' archaeologies. In 1978, Cambridge was one of a group of archaeology departments – others included Southampton and Sheffield – to organise the first of what would become the annual conference of the Theoretical Archaeology Group (TAG), a conference specifically tailored to emerging postgraduates and held in a different department in Britain each year, extending in more recent years to Ireland, and spawning regional TAG conferences in northern Europe (Nordic TAG) and the USA. Whilst Cambridge and London remain leading institutions for the study of archaeology, alumni from both places have helped to develop important centres of academic research and teaching at Bristol, Bournemouth, Cardiff, Edinburgh, Exeter, Glasgow, Leicester, Manchester, Sheffield and York, for example.

In spite of the rise of archaeology as a specifically university-based academic discipline, until the 1970s, it also remained an area dominated by amateur involvement. However, the idea that the study of the past was a professional pursuit was inevitably sown with the creation in 1908 of the first of several Royal Commissions for the recording of Historic Monuments, and in 1910 the Office of Works (the government department responsible for ancient monuments legislation) was placed on a fully professional footing. With the increase of building and other development projects following the Second World War from the 1950s to the 1970s, the exposure of archaeological remains – especially in urban areas – became increasingly widespread and efforts to investigate them could not be left to amateur groups alone. An early response came from members of the Congress of Archaeological Societies to form a 'Council for British Archaeology' to promote archaeology and co-ordinate research programmes and policy: in 1944 the CBA replaced the old Congress. A number of reports by (largely museum-based) archaeologists working in London and elsewhere emphasised the potential loss of evidence of our past that urban development was causing. The remit of the CBA specifically excluded it from carrying out excavation and other work: its job was to co-ordinate and proselytise. Accordingly, 1971 saw the establishment of the organisation 'RESCUE: the Trust for British archaeology' whose primary role was seen to be precisely that of organising what are now called 'rescue' or 'salvage' excavations on threatened sites (Hudson 1981, 145–148). At first, such excavations were as likely to be carried out by keen volunteers as by low-paid professionals, but over time such projects also attracted other sources of funding and, in times of economic downturn, were used as mechanisms to provide work for the unemployed. 1975 saw the establishment of the Central Excavation Unit, staffed entirely by paid professionals and operating out of the government Department of the Environment (later English Heritage), to take up the inevitable slack in necessary excavation that could not be met from amateur involvement (Hudson 1981, 151–152). The rise of professional, salaried archaeologists also led to the creation of a professional association that would aim to regulate and oversee standards. Initially called the Institute of *Field* Archaeologists (IFA) (some say misleadingly since it also numbered from the outset academic, museum- and laboratory-based staff among its members), this has now been re-branded 'The Institute *for* Archaeologists' or IfA.

English Heritage was established as a 'quango' (an acronym defining a quasi-autonomous non-governmental organisation) by the National Heritage Act 1983, part-funded by but operating at arms length from government, to act as the chief advisor to government on heritage issues in England. Similar bodies for Wales (Cadw) and Scotland (Historic Scotland) followed shortly. English Heritage initially retained the earlier structures of the Department of the Environment with a discrete 'Inspectorate', archaeologists and some historic buildings specialists employed as Ancient Monuments Inspectors (the same job title as Pitt Rivers a century before), each with specific regional responsibility. There was still an element of the 'man from the Ministry' heading out from London to visit farms in Cumbria, pass judgement, and then return to town, causing some local resentment in the process. But in time, and sometime during the 1990s, regional teams were created, which ultimately (and sensibly) were located in the regions in which they worked. Recent new legislation is intended to take ultimate responsibility for managing historic resources away from government itself and instead delegate it further to English Heritage, Cadw and Historic Scotland. Initially, English Heritage also housed the Central Excavation Unit which it had inherited from the Department of the Environment. However, a further shift of policy first rendered the Unit as only a last-resort when all else had failed and finally saw its closure in the 1990s, evolving into what is now Central Archaeological Services.

Running parallel to this were changes in the planning system, by which new development is regulated. *Planning Policy Guidance Note 16 – Archaeology and Planning* (PPG16) of 1990 for the first time made archaeology a material consideration during the process of approving development projects. It was predicated on the principle that those who are responsible for the destruction of historic resources should mitigate this damage: that they should, therefore, pay for any works considered necessary in determining what development, if any, could take place, and often also to pay for the publication of the results. Developers also selected the contractors to undertake such work, usually by competitive tender. This in turn meant the creation of archaeological units working on commercial lines, staffed by waged and salaried professionals who could be relied upon to do work to a high standard. Although PPG16 was replaced in 2010 by PPS5, the basic 'polluter pays' principle remains, and the now mature structure of developer funding and commercial archaeology is unchanged.

With the growth of develop-funded archaeology, and its place within the planning system, another component of the heritage sector saw massive growth. In the 1970s, the Department of the Environment had started to encourage the creation of locally based Sites and Monuments Records, with staff to maintain them and promote archaeology and heritage within a particular geographical area. These areas were either historic counties or cities. The posts generally created were a 'County Archaeologist' and a 'Sites and Monuments Record Assistant (or Officer)'. The records in those days were card indices, with sites cross-referenced onto 1:10,000 Ordnance Survey map sheets. With the growth of aerial photography, aerial photographic transcriptions and their interpretation were added to the record. But with PPG16 and its successor PPS5, and the sharp increase in the amount of work undertaken, and the need for consistent and routine advice to developers and planners, these areas expanded and more staff were recruited, especially in those busy areas of the southeast where more development was taking place. The records are now computerised, and supported by a GIS (Geographical Information System), which means the skills of the archaeologists are very different. Even the name has changed. These are no longer SMRs but Historic Environment Records (or HERs), a change that reflects the wider range of information they now contain. It is worth noting that it is not a statutory obligation for local authorities to maintain an HER or an archaeological officer, and in recent years Northamptonshire is one county to have been without local government archaeological cover.

The argument can be made that the gradual (and in later years not so gradual) professionalism of the field led to significant change in archaeologists' response to the wider public, replacing actual involvement with outreach events, such as open days and seminars. The alternative argument is that archaeology in the twentieth century changed from an essentially dilettante pursuit for the wealthy to a field that had attractions for a much wider proportion of the public. Both views have merit. In 1925, the first journal dedicated to archaeology was founded as *Antiquity* and although it has generally failed to reach the mass market, it has survived as a journal widely read (if not actually bought) by the interested archaeological community (Hudson 1981, 101–104). Archaeology has also found a ready audience among television viewers, since it was revived following the Second World War. The programme *Animal, Vegetable, Mineral?* broadcast on the BBC television channel (the only one then available) during the 1950s was extremely popular: a panel-game based upon models developed on the radio, it pitted senior archaeologists – Mortimer Wheeler and Glyn Daniel in particular – against each other in identifying objects borrowed from museum collections. Equally successful was a series of half-hour documentaries on archaeological subjects called *Buried Treasure*. Successors have included *Chronicle*, which ran from the 1960s into the 1970s and introduced figures such as Magnus Magnusson and Colin Renfrew to a wide audience (Hudson 1981, 115–119), and, in more recent years, *Meet the Ancestors*, and especially *Time Team* which provides both a vision of archaeology in practice and a game-show element by requiring completion of a project in a mere 3 days. Such programmes are now the main way in which non-professionals gain access to archaeology, although recent years have also seen a rise in dedicated community-based projects, normally led by professionals but designed to encourage an interest in the past. Among the more successful have been the Sedgeford Project (a dedicated excavation project in which professionals serve as advisors to a local community; see Chap. 7) and work by the Castleford Heritage Trust (a community-led project which includes archaeology but is not driven by it; Smith 2006, 237–275).

Archaeology in the Twenty-First Century

Archaeology in Britain today is a largely professional pursuit, led by agencies and local authority curators as well as units organised along commercial lines who compete for work on behalf of builders and other developers. They operate within a system whereby the effects of construction on the archaeological record are mitigated at the developer's expense. The main entry into archaeology is no longer through amateur involvement, as it once was – although that route is not yet fully closed – but through formal academic training at university level and then employment, perhaps in such a unit or through a local authority (depending on whether the desk or the trench is where you feel more comfortable). There has been a steady decline in university research excavations and in amateur project work – apart from some notable exceptions such as the Sedgeford Project. The preservation of ancient remains has become the responsibility of quasi-autonomous government agencies rather than that of officers of the government themselves, although the legal basis for that preservation has been steadily strengthened over nearly 150 years. Today's threats to archaeology continue to be urban and rural developments, and the uncontrolled looting of sites by some metal-detectorists. Paradoxically, development also allows access to archaeological remains, enhances our understanding of the past (e.g. Bradley 2007) and generates work for units and contractors. The number of openings for archaeologists will depend largely on economic stability and fortune. At the time of writing things are tough, and archaeologists are out of work, many now returning to take up higher education or Continuing Professional Development (CPD) opportunities. But things will pick up. They always do.

Summary

Archaeology has changed, from being largely an amateur pursuit, the domain of the landed classes, those with sufficient leisure time and money to follow their passion, to one that has become a profession, with procedures, practices, laws, protocols and ethics codes. There is still room for the amateur but it is now a marginal role, albeit with considerable guidance and encouragement from organisations such as the Council for British Archaeology, and funding initiatives including the Heritage Lottery Fund. In reality, projects that actively encourage amateur participation and which truly benefit the sector (as well as being fun to participate in) are few and far between. The (1995–2002) Defence of Britain Project was a guiding light in this area. A significant gap in our understanding of Second World War archaeology was filled in no small part by the 2,000 volunteers who recorded sites the length and breadth of Britain, guided by the CBA and with HLF funding. The lack of opportunities for the amateur is regrettable, as is the fact that archaeology remains largely (as it always seems to have been here) a white, middle class pursuit. Hopefully, both of these patterns can be reversed with time.

Having reviewed the emerging 'professionalism' of archaeology, especially over the past 25–30 years, we now turn our attention to the results of all this endeavour. What have the archaeologists of the past and present created by way of a record of Britain's past occupation and use? What is the archaeological record for the occupation of Britain actually like?

References and Further Reading

Archaeological Review from Cambridge 1989. Occasional Paper 1: Doctoral Research in Cambridge (1922–1987). Cambridge, *Archaeological Review from Cambridge.*
Barker, P. 1982. *Techniques of Archaeological Investigation.* London, Batsford.
Barton, R. 1990. 'An influential set of chaps; the X-Club and Royal Society politics 1864–85'. *British Journal of Historical Studies* 23, 53–81.
Barton, R. 1998. 'Huxley, Lubbock and half a dozen others: professionals and gentlemen in the formation of the X Club, 1851–1864'. *Isis* 89, 410–444.

Bowden, M. 1991. *Pitt-Rivers*. Cambridge, Cambridge University Press.

Bradley, R. 2007. *The Prehistory of Britain and Ireland*. Cambridge: Cambridge University Press.

Carman, J. 1996. *Valuing Ancient Things: archaeology and law*. London, Leicester University Press.

Chapman, W. 1989. 'The organisational context in the history of archaeology: Pitt-Rivers and the first Ancient Monuments Act'. *The Antiquaries Journal* 69.1, 23–42.

Chippindale, C. 1983a. The making of the first ancient monuments Act and its administration under General Pitt-Rivers. *Journal of the British Archaeological Association* 136, 1–55.

Chippindale, C. 1983b. *Stonehenge Complete*. Cambridge, Cambridge University Press.

Clark, G. 1989. Early days in the development of postgraduate research in prehistoric archaeology in Cambridge. In *Archaeological Review from Cambridge*, 6–10.

Clarke, D.L. 1968. *Analytical Archaeology*. London, Methuen.

Cooper, M. A., Firth, A., Carman, J. and Wheatley, D. (eds) 1995. *Managing Archaeology*. London, Routledge

Daniel, G. E. 1967. *The Origin and Growth of Archaeology*. Penguin, Harmondsworth.

Daniel, G. E. and Chippindale, C. (eds) 1989. *The pastmasters: eleven modern pioneers of archaeology*. London, Thames and Hudson.

Daniel, G. E. and Renfrew, C. 1988. *The Idea of Prehistory*. Edinburgh, Edinburgh University Press.

Everill, P. 2006. *The Invisible Diggers: contemporary commercial archaeology in the UK*. Unpublished PhD thesis, University of Southampton.

Hudson, K. 1981. *A Social History of Archaeology: the British experience*. London, Macmillan.

Lucas, G. 2001. *Critical Approaches to Fieldwork: contemporary and historical archaeological practice*. London, Routledge.

Marsden, B. M. 1983. *Pioneers of Prehistory: leaders and landmarks in English archaeology (1500–1900)*. Ormskirk, G. W. & A. Hesketh.

McAdam, E. 1995. 'Trying to Make It Happen'. In Cooper, M. A., Firth, A., Carman, J. and Wheatley, D. (eds) 1995. *Managing Archaeology*. London, Routledge, 89–100.

Patton, M. 2007. *Science, Politics and Business in the work of Sir John Lubbock, a man of universal mind*. *Aldershot*, Ashgate.

Piggott, S. 1976. The Origins of the English County Archaeological Societies. In Piggott, S. *Ruins in a Landscape: essays in antiquarianism*. Edinburgh, Edinburgh University Press, 171–195.

Piggott, S. 1989. *Ancient Britons and the Antiquarian Imagination: ideas from the Renaissance to the Regency*. London, Thames and Hudson.

Renfrew, C. 1979. The Aegean and the West Mediterranean. In Renfrew, C. (ed.) *Problems in Prehistory*. Edinburgh, Edinburgh University Press, 43–64.

Roskams, S. 2001. *Excavation*. Cambridge Manuals in Archaeology. Cambridge, Cambridge University Press.

Saunders, A.D. 1983. A century of ancient monuments legislation 1882–1982. *The Antiquaries Journal* 63, 11–29.

Schofield, J. (ed.) 2011. *Great Excavations: shaping the archaeological profession*. Oxford: Oxbow.

Smith, L. 2006. *Uses of Heritage*. London, Routledge.

Toulmin, S, and Goldfield, J. 1967. *The discovery of time*. Chicago, University of Chicago Press.

Trigger, B. 2006. *A History of Archaeological Thought*. 2nd edition. Cambridge, Cambridge University Press.

Ucko. P. et al. 1991. *Avebury reconsidered: from the 1660s to the 1990s*. London, Unwin Hyman.

Chapter 3
Britain's Archaeological Resource: A Brief Survey

Chapter 2 outlined how archaeology as a practice has a long history in Britain. This chapter provides an introduction to the results of that work: the time-depth of human occupation in Britain, the kinds of evidence from which our understanding of the past in Britain is derived, and some of the current themes which are considered important in each period. For those of you with no previous experience of archaeology in Britain, we hope that this chapter will be a useful – albeit brief – outline of the archaeological remains you may encounter.

The Palaeolithic (700,000–10,000 BP)

The Palaeolithic (literally 'old stone age') has played a significant part in the history of British archaeology. It has long been a fascinating and rich area for research, not least given the frequency of significant new discoveries, the application of archaeological theory to a period lacking in the diversity and quantity of surviving sites that exist for later periods, the application also of hard science to these fragmented remains, and *that* very famous forgery – Piltdown Man, a very British hoax that had everyone fooled, for a while at least.

Palaeolithic research in Great Britain has its origins in the later eighteenth century. Workmen at a gravel pit at Hoxne (Suffolk) found shaped stones that John Frere identified as the work of man. Not only that; he realised the wider implications of his discovery. In a paper, read to the Society of Antiquaries of London in 1797, he described these finds as:

Weapons of war, fabricated and used by a people who had not the use of metals ... the situation in which these weapons were found may tempt us to refer them to a very remote period indeed; even beyond that of the present world.

The scientific world was unprepared for this discovery, so the finds were put away and forgotten and Frere's interpretation ignored. It was not until after 1860, and the contributions of biologists like Charles Darwin developing theories of

J. Schofield et al., *Archaeological Practice in Great Britain: A Heritage Handbook*, World Archaeological Congress Cultural Heritage Manual Series, DOI 10.1007/978-0-387-09453-3_3, © Springer Science+Business Media, LLC 2011

animal (including human) evolution by natural selection and thereby challenging the Genesis account of the Creation, that discoveries of stone implements were at last received more favourably.

Since that time, studies of the Palaeolithic have escalated, at times almost exponentially (cf. Gamble 1999). The distance in time and unfamiliarity of the Palaeolithic has always ensured its popularity amongst archaeologists and increasingly the public. The idea of cave dwellers butchering long-extinct animals is the stuff of children's fiction. And there is also that oft-quoted statistic – that for over 99% of the time that human communities have occupied Britain, hunting and gathering formed their subsistence base. These people were mobile, moving with the seasons, heading north with the warmth of summer; then retreating as the winters closed in. The more theoretical focus of 'new archaeology' in the 1960s gave a close impression of how this mobility might appear in the archaeological record. Lewis Binford's ethnoarchaeological research (1983), for example demonstrated how archaeological and palaeo-environmental deposits might form at waterholes, what archaeological traces (or 'signatures') seasonal hunting might produce for archaeologists to uncover across the landscape and – at specific sites such as hunting stands – what the artefact distribution might tell us about the human activities taking place there, while waiting for the hunt to begin.

Chronology

What is a hominin? Where once we talked about hominids, the favoured term now is 'hominin'. This change in terminology comes from recognising our close relationship to the African great apes which are also now included as hominids. Hominins are creatures on our side of the branch, but after the split from the Chimpanzee (Parfitt and Stringer 2006: 25).

The earliest evidence for hominins in Britain is currently at Pakefield (Norfolk, eastern England) where 700,000-year-old stone artefacts associated with animal remains were found in 2000 (Parfitt and Stringer 2006). By 2006 some 32 artefacts had been recovered, mostly small flint flakes and a single flint core. All are in fresh condition. The distribution of artefacts across four distinct contexts suggests humans were regular visitors here.

Some years earlier 500,000-year-old remains were found at Boxgrove (West Sussex, south-east England). An astonishing excavation ensued, and a large area of pristine ancient land service exposed over several years. Here, the evidence suggested, hominins had gathered around a water hole, perhaps hunting, making flint tools and butchering animals like rhino and cave bear. The finds at Boxgrove pushed the date of human occupation of Britain back from c. 400,000 years old, and highlighted the archaeological significance of the Sussex raised beach in which the site was discovered. Boxgrove also brought 'Roger' to the world's attention – being a legbone, named after its finder, and the earliest contexted hominin from Europe.

After these earliest traces, finds associated with early hominins in Britain are indicative of seasonal visits during the warmer periods within the Anglian glaciation and the early Hoxnian interglacial. During this phase were two traditions that dominated British Palaeolithic research for decades: the Clactonian, and the Acheulian, the two distinguishable on the basis of tool-making technologies. John Wymer (1982) believed the Clactonian was the earlier of the two, while recognising some overlap. The Clactonian – after the type site of Clacton (Essex, eastern England) comprises mostly tools made from flint flakes struck off the core. Some of the cores were roughly worked as chopping tools. Distinctive Clactonian artefacts were found at Swanscombe (Kent, south-east England), probably from a campsite beside a river. The Acheulian by contrast is characterised by hand-axes or bifaces – tools made by reducing and shaping the core, and used as knives and choppers. In addition to the riverside locations, users of Acheulian industries also frequented caves. Kents Cavern (Torbay, south-west), for example, was excavated in the 1820s, with hand-axes found in the lowest levels of occupation, along with the bones of sabre-toothed tiger.

As the climate warmed, a major expansion of human occupation occurred. The Hoxnian interglacial had a mild oceanic climate with deciduous mixed woodland and grasslands in the river valleys. Herds of large herbivorous mammals were plentiful. For much of this period Britain was also attached to the continent, so a mobile existence, with communities moving between Britain and the North European Plain seems likely. Hoxne (Suffolk, eastern England), discovered first by Frere in the late eighteenth century, gives its name to this interglacial and is characterised by Acheulian industries, as is the case at Swanscombe where Acheulian industries overlie the earlier Clactonian artefacts. At this time the extent of occupation expanded, for example to the cave of Pontnewydd (Clwyd, north Wales), occupied after the Hoxnian at c. 225,000 years ago. Settlement was at the cave mouth, and the artefacts of late Acheulian type. Human remains found at the cave include teeth of *Homo sapiens neanderthalensis*.

Throughout this period, technology continued to develop. The late Hoxnian/ early Wolstonian period, for example saw the introduction of the Levallois technique – removing flakes of a predetermined shape and size to produce a tortoise-shaped core, from which distinctively shaped flakes could then be removed. Mousterian industries were more prominent on the Continent than in Britain, while anatomically modern humans – *Homo sapiens sapiens* – appeared during the middle stages of the Devensian, perhaps living for a time alongside Neanderthals. The range of items in the tool-kit increased dramatically now, with the long tradition of hand-axes finally replaced by bespoke tools, including a blade-based technology and the 'leaf-shaped point'. This is also when burials first appear. The mis-named 'Red Lady of Paviland', for example was discovered in Glamorgan (south Wales) in 1823, and is in fact an adult male, apparently smeared with ochre.

Climate change, and the glacial advance, meant that virtually no traces of Palaeolithic settlement in Britain are found after 25,000 years ago, although for southern Britain, conditions fell short of full glaciation. Resettlement seems to occur some 14,000 years later, from which point on Britain was continuously occupied. The earliest sites for reoccupation lay in the warmer south-west as well as the southern Pennines, with caves providing some protection from the cold.

Although cave art of the type found in France and Spain is unlikely to be found in Britain, there is at least one example now to prove the presence of art during this period. After some false dawns, the discovery of parietal (i.e. on walls, as opposed to mobile) art was finally confirmed in 2003 at Cresswell Crags (Derbyshire, Midlands), dating to the earliest phase of resettlement, c. 12,500 years ago. Two areas containing incised figures were found: one features what may be a male ibex, and the other two birds. Not the most spectacular representation you'll ever see, but following in the long tradition of Palaeolithic research in Britain, our horizons continue to expand and to add colour to the deeper past.

The Mesolithic (10,000–6,000 BP)

The Mesolithic was for a long time the 'in-between' period of British prehistory, and for some the forgotten period between the cave-dwelling hunters of the Palaeolithic, and the revolutionary farmers of the Neolithic, with their cultivated fields, stock, and sophisticated ritual and burial practices (Conneller and Warren 2006). But the Mesolithic has become vogue, partly due to the enthusiasm of young researchers to correct this imbalance, some high profile projects and discoveries, and reinterpretations of the classic site of Star Carr (Yorkshire).

As the ice melted away and post-glacial conditions advanced, the landscape changed significantly, notably with the emergence of birch and pine woodland across most lowland areas. These were not managed woodlands but wildwood, self-regenerative woodland, highly variable in density and cover. It was a wildwood in another sense too – wild ox, deer and wild pig were commonplace. For the early part of the Mesolithic, Britain remained attached to the continent via Doggerland under what is now the North Sea (see below). From about 8,000 years ago, Britain became the island that it remains today.

With the landscape transformed, with animals roaming the woods and with nuts and berries in the trees, the subsistence strategy and the tools needed to implement it also needed to change. Some universal tools – characteristic of the later Palaeolithic – were made, although composite tools became the tools of choice, comprising small blade-like 'microliths' set into wooden shafts, providing the tips and barbs for hunting weapons. Bows and arrows had now replaced spears, while the adze had been developed for carpentry, an important skill now, given the close proximity and usefulness of woodland for just about everything.

Most sites of the earlier Mesolithic are open sites, with riversides generally favoured for the plethora of resources they contain and support. Some sites were on the coast, perhaps home to what Lewis Binford referred to as 'strand-loopers', while occupation also extended into the hills.

Star Carr is synonymous with the British Mesolithic (Fig. 3.1). One feels drawn to the ambiguity of the deer antler head-pieces and the timber 'platform', and the idea of a project in the immediate post-war years, run by Grahame Clark, whose writings dominated archaeology reading lists for years. Star Carr also had the

Fig. 3.1 Star Carr under excavation. (Photo: Chantal Connellier)

benefit of being a wetland site with excellent preservation of waterlogged deposits. In short summary, Clark's excavations revealed a 9,500-year-old birchwood platform on the side of a lagoon. The site's occupants were hunters, their evidence revealing a fauna comprising: red deer, wild pig, wild cattle, elk, fox, wolf and pine marten; birds included crane, white stork, grebe, lapwing and duck. Flint tools were found in abundance, including some microliths with resin still attached, the conditions for preservation were so good. Clark also found evidence for adornment, with the discovery of shale and amber beads from local raw materials, and 21 stag frontlets, with evidence for modification including perforations around the edge of the bone. Suggested uses included some form of head-dress, and a disguise used in hunting or ritual activities.

Since the completion of the post-war Star Carr excavations, a landscape survey has been conducted in the area, producing further evidence for the exploitation of the Lake Flixton region during the earlier Mesolithic.

Upland areas were also settled at around this time including the Mendips (Somerset, south-west), and the Pennines and North Yorkshire Moors (northern England). The evidence survives typically as artefact scatters containing microliths, and generally in places with good visibility and probably in areas originally above the tree-line.

Despite the abundance of resources, and the warming climate, communities remained mobile and reliant on exploiting seasonal variations in the available resources. Evidence from Star Carr strongly supports the seasonal use of resources, though precisely which season remains uncertain: the evidence of antler has now been discounted since this is thought to have been curated; analysis of tooth eruption suggests late spring/summer (Legge and Rowley-Conwy 1988); but more recent work on red and roe deer tooth development is pushing this back towards winter again (Carter 1998). Tools also suggest seasonal variation in the way the landscape was exploited: upland assemblages typically contain microliths, while at lowland sites the majority of tools were for meat processing and manufacturing activities.

There are few burial sites from this period, though two – at Gough's Cave and Aveline's Hole on the Mendip Hills (Somerset, south-west) – date to around 9,000 years ago. Aveline's Hole is the only major Mesolithic cemetery in Britain. Between 50 and 100 bodies were recovered from the cave in the late nineteenth and early twentieth century. Recent dating work suggests the cave was in use for only a few generations (Schulting and Wysocki 2005). A television programme a few years ago conducted analysis of DNA on the Gough's Cave remains ('Cheddar Man'), and found a descendent still living in the village (Barham et al. 1999)!

Glacial retreat caused the sea level to rise, thus finally at c. 8000 BP removing any land bridge and creating the island that Britain has remained ever since. But that was not the only change 8,000 years ago. The woodlands closed in, with oak, alder, elm and lime becoming predominant. Stone tool technology continued to change, with isolation from the Continent curtailing the diversity in material culture. Bone points appear no longer to have been used, while the range of microliths extended and their size reduced. Settlement extended into Scotland and the north. The coast was also exploited more consistently, the sites characterised by large shell middens, such as those on Oronsay which contain evidence for sea-shore exploitation, including crab, limpet, periwinkle, dog whelk, oyster and lobster, as well as shallow water fishing. Studies of the fish and shellfish also indicate another trend: that people were settling down for longer periods. Some areas, such as Wessex, had become quite heavily populated by 6,000 years ago.

The size of Mesolithic hunting bands, and the distances they travelled, can be suggested from archaeological evidence from excavations and field survey. Distances of up to 80 km have been suggested for seasonal migration, while the size of groups making these trips could be up to 25. These groups have been aptly described by Tim Darvill (1996) as 'bands on the run'!

What's Great About the British Mesolithic

Chantal Connellier (University of Manchester)

When I first encountered the Mesolithic as an undergraduate, I was not impressed. After learning about the spectacular art, architecture and burials of the Upper Palaeolithic, the Mesolithic was something of an anticlimax. And in contrast to the exciting new post-processual theories that I learnt about in other courses, where politics, symbolism and individual experience were emphasised, the theoretical approaches to the Mesolithic (which emphasised economy and ecology) seemed very old-fashioned.

So why have I chosen to devote my life to something I initially found rather dull? Well, when I examined the evidence in more detail, and from these new perspectives, I found a rich, exciting, varied body of material. The work of the Swedish archaeologist Lars Larsson on the Skateholm cemeteries was particularly important in making me realise that the Mesolithic was a strange and different time. At Skateholm there was a huge variety in burial practices: dogs were buried with rich grave goods, people were chopped up and put into graves, graves were reopened and bones retrieved.

Furthermore, as a student I was lucky enough to work on some fantastic landscape projects with some inspiring archaeologists: Penny Spikins' work at March Hill, West Yorkshire, and Tim Schadla-Hall's project in the Vale of Pickering, North Yorkshire (both northern England) have been pioneering projects aimed at understanding human action in its landscape context. The work in the Vale of Pickering (also northern England) has been going for 30 years and excavation has always been undertaken in conjunction with detailed palaeo-environmental survey, yielding a remarkable picture of a Mesolithic landscape.

An understanding of what the environment was like is vital for thinking about how Mesolithic people understood past landscapes and experienced environmental change. And so, many years after I derided it as an undergraduate, I have come to appreciate the strong environmental legacy of Mesolithic archaeology. New approaches to the Mesolithic, I think, share a 'groundedness' in environmental archaeology or artefact studies, yet are prepared to investigate ritual practices and world-views.

Star Carr, the site on which I now work, has reflected these changing approaches to the Mesolithic. Once thought to be a typical base camp, or a hunting camp, where a small group of men whiled away their time awaiting their prey, more recent interpretations have drawn attention to the unusual array of material culture at the site. Grahame Clark found 21 antler frontlets, 19 beads and 191 barbed antler points. In 30 years of excavations in the Vale of Pickering in which Star Carr is situated, no more frontlets or beads have been found and only one more barbed point. It appears that Star Carr is actually very unusual in its local landscape. People were placing objects made from animal remains in the reed-swamp or shallow water of the lake edge. This can perhaps be seen as a reflection of attitudes of respect towards animals known amongst recent hunter–gatherer groups. This is often associated with the careful deposition of their bones so that animals would continue to give themselves up to the hunter. At Star Carr these rituals seem very much focused on red deer antler, suggesting that this species was spiritually important and that the antlers perhaps stood for the rest of the animal.

These new approaches paint a picture of the Mesolithic where people had very different attitudes to animals, to death, and to the landscapes they inhabited; even very different understandings of what it meant to be a person. This is no longer a dull period; it is a very exciting time to be working on the Mesolithic.

The Neolithic (6,000–4,000 BP)

One of the things that interests archaeologists most is change – why it happens, what form it takes and how it affects people's lives. Seen from our perspective, some 6,000 years later, the introduction of agriculture and animal husbandry at the beginning of what we now call the Neolithic appeared as a major change of lifestyle and subsistence, and with it, social structure, outlook, religious orientation and so on. But was it really such a major upheaval? Was it a 'revolution', or a more gradual change that drew people in?

Farming was established on the Continent a few hundred years before it arrived in Britain, meaning that southern coastal communities in Britain must have been aware – perhaps through exchange networks – of this radical and imminent change. By around 6000 BP the fertile loess soils of the major north European river valleys supported such farming communities, growing wheat and barley and raising cattle. These new farming communities lived in villages like that at Koln-Lindenthal (Germany) comprising 21 houses over seven phases of settlement.

But with farmers on the continent, and coastal 'strand-loopers' aware of their existence, how did the change happen? The traditional view of colonisation has been largely discredited, although undoubtedly some colonists did come over clutching their precious seeds and tightly clasping the tethers of their stock. But it seems more likely that hunter-gatherers in Britain adopted farming practices more through 'acculturation', as happened in Scandinavia. Either way, hunter-gatherers are almost invisible in Britain's archaeological record by c. 5000 BP with the exception of a few coastal and northern areas.

The fundamental change to occur at this time involved subsistence activities. The archaeological record shows clearly and consistently across much of northern Europe a move away from hunting and gathering, intended to address immediate needs, towards farming with its reliance on a single harvest for the year, and involving the biological manipulation of crops and animals. People were learning to plan ahead – to devise a longer-term strategy that also benefited from being more reliable and, arguably, less hard work than hunting and gathering. This change of strategy was bound up with a change in ideology. Hunting and gathering was dependent upon the skills of individuals for the most part, while farming relied more on communal effort. The advent of the Neolithic is also significant in shaping the society we have today: not only is much of Britain still farmland, farmed in some cases continuously now for 6,000 years, but also because farming has now supported society over that entire period, and will continue to do so in the future.

The focus for archaeologists is material culture, which for the Neolithic we have in great abundance and diversity. The types of artefacts are almost entirely new. Pottery appears for the first time, for example, as do farming implements: sickles, querns and polished stone axes. And new types of site appear, including permanent settlements such as Skara Brae (Orkney, northern Scotland), communal burial sites (long barrows) and ceremonial monuments such as henges and causewayed enclosures. The trackways of the Somerset Levels (south-west England) have an early date (the Sweet Track is dated to c. 5000 BP), while preserved plough marks found beneath later monumental features provide a clear impression of agricultural practices. Finally, alongside monumental remains and artefacts, is the palaeo-environmental record (pollen, insects and land snails) which provides evidence of woodland clearances and cultivation.

Permanent settlements do appear in the Neolithic period, at Skara Brae for example, where the houses have the impression of structures abandoned not in the deeper past but in the historic period, their furniture (beds and dressers) still in place and objects including personal possessions left where they were dropped. But these more permanent houses came later in the Neolithic. In the generally more stable social conditions of the earlier Neolithic settlements appear to have been temporary. The few recorded houses suggest flimsy post-built structures, suggestive of small communities making seasonal movements between low lying river valleys and higher ground. Much of the evidence for settlement has come from field-walking, an archaeological method that systematically collects stone artefacts from field surfaces, recording artefacts disturbed from their original context by modern farming practices. By 'mapping' these artefacts, traces of settlement are revealed through the density of finds, and the composition of fieldwalked assemblages. Much evidence has now been collected, the general spread and frequency of Neolithic artefacts suggestive of repeated occupation of certain favoured locations. Ethnographic studies of other mobile communities illustrate the types of evidence this settlement pattern leaves behind, and there are obvious similarities. Ethnographic observations in Mongolia also demonstrate that monument building can occur amongst mobile groups (Lawson 2007), and as we will see, monumental architecture is a defining feature of the British Neolithic.

Ritual activities are clearly evident amongst these early farming communities. With one or two earlier exceptions, burial sites appear for the first time in the earlier Neolithic, as well as causewayed enclosures, these two monument types apparently closely associated through treatment of the dead. In its earliest stages, burial was in small mounds however – small round cairns with a central cist in the Cotswolds (west of England); and so-called Portal Dolmens in west Wales and the south-west of England. At around 4800 BP, a change occurred, and communal burial in larger mounds became predominant. Well over 500 of these 'long barrows' have been recorded from England alone, displaying regional variation in form, size and frequency. But they are all clearly monumental tombs, and burial is generally communal. In places the tombs were stone-built (cairns), such as in the Cotswold-Severn region in the west of England; in other areas they were earthen. Often the larger later mound incorporated an earlier one.

The burial ritual was a complicated affair. Evidence from burial mounds and the contemporary causewayed enclosures point to a process by which bodies were exposed on platforms within the enclosures, before the bones were collected for burial. Many people were buried in each tomb, most containing at least 50 individuals, usually without grave goods. Causewayed enclosures and long barrows were the result of significant physical effort, and presumably social organisation: one estimate suggests that a medium to large-sized tomb could take between 7,000 and 16,000 man hours to build.

Monumental construction escalated in the later Neolithic period, in frequency, complexity and diversity of form. Bank barrows appear, apparently in the tradition of earlier long barrows. These are extremely rare nationally with less than ten examples known, few of which have been archaeologically investigated. Cursus monuments are thought to be ceremonial avenues, some associated with the great 'monument zones' of Wessex, at Stonehenge for example, and Cranborne Chase, both in the south-west of England. These cursus varied between the short (700 m long at Springfield, Essex, south-east England) and the very long (10 km, on Cranborne Chase). Henges begin to appear at about the same time as bank barrows and cursus monuments. These are circular enclosures with a bank outside the ditch. As with other monument types, there is considerable variation in size (from 50 to 200 m in diameter), form (number of entrances varies from one to four) and distribution. Some examples have produced evidence for massive open-roofed timber structures, while at Durrington Walls near Stonehenge there is clear patterning in the distribution of animal remains from the site's post holes. This 'structured deposition' of evidence suggests their main function was probably ritual.

So, what *was* the British Neolithic? It was certainly different to what had gone before. The subsistence base was radically transformed, while sophisticated burial rites and associated ritual activities appear in the archaeological record as a matter of routine. The wildwood was opened out, and people gradually settled down with their stock and crops. The great monument zones of the Neolithic can dominate our thinking as well as our research practices, and for good reason. There is still much to be learnt about the Stonehenge and Avebury landscapes in southern England for example, and Orkney in Scotland where the Maes Howe chambered tomb, the Stones of Stenness and other monuments occur in sufficiently close proximity also to warrant World Heritage Site status. But other areas also continue to yield their secrets, more often now through archaeological work required as part of the development control process (Bradley 2007; Chap. 4), than through research projects in the traditional sense. The Neolithic is a well-documented period of prehistory, yet much remains to be learnt.

Stonehenge, Avebury and the Phenomenon of the Megalithic

Joshua Pollard (University of Southampton)

The great megalithic monuments of Stonehenge and Avebury have captivated the academic and popular imagination since they became the subject of antiquarian research during the sixteenth and seventeenth centuries. An enduring fascination of these sites has operated at several levels: for many visitors it resides in their perceived sublime, mysterious and romantic qualities; while for archaeologists these monuments offer critical windows into a culturally different prehistoric past. Through the early work of John Aubrey, William Stukeley and others, the very process of research has even reinvested Stonehenge and Avebury with a religious significance that has been promulgated through neo-druidic and latterly neo-pagan movements (Fig. 3.2).

Fig. 3.2 Excavating a henge monument. (Photo: Joshua Pollard)

Through programmes of excavation and fieldwork during the twentieth and early twenty-first centuries, our academic knowledge of both monuments and their surrounding landscapes has increased greatly. We have a better sense of chronology, of regional sequences, the extent of these complexes, and the kinds of practices associated with them. We now know they were created in a series of stages during the third and second millennia BC (i.e. during the later Neolithic and early Bronze Age), as components of extensive monument complexes which include other henges, palisade enclosures, timber and stone circles and giant mounds (as in the case of Silbury Hill, near Avebury). Such 'ceremonial centres', which also acted as foci for contemporary settlement, are known from many regions of Britain and Ireland; although, whether for reasons of sacred and/or political pre-eminence, the scale of construction seen with the Wessex chalkland complexes is rarely matched elsewhere (exceptions include the remarkable group of henges at Thornborough, Yorkshire, northern England).

These were not the first monuments to be created in these landscapes, but in terms of architecture and labour input they are certainly the most awe-inspiring. But why were they created? Imaginative images of these sites as the settings for elaborate public rituals – regular mass gatherings, processions and sacrifices – may be misleading. They probably did not operate like medieval churches and cathedrals, as early analogy supposed. Rather, current thinking suggests megalithic monuments of the later Neolithic and early Bronze Age may have been rather quiet, even 'marginal' spaces, being locations for the burial of the dead and the veneration of ancestors (conceived as a critical supernatural power during the period). The contrast has been drawn with contemporary timber monuments where evidence for feasting and celebrations by the living is much more in evidence.

Prehistorians have also stressed that it was the act of construction of these monuments, rather than their subsequent use, which was of paramount importance; serving as means of re-engaging with sacred domains, reanimating the symbolic and mythic significance of places, and venerating spirits, deities and other agencies.

This said, spectacular though they are, we should not be misled into thinking that constructed forms were the features of paramount significance within these landscapes. Ethnography has highlighted the critical importance of natural features (hills, rivers, stones, trees, and so forth) in the mythic and cosmological worlds of both hunter-gatherers and subsistence farmers. It is therefore of interest that Stonehenge and the nearby and contemporary henge of Durrington Walls are physically connected to the River Avon via earthwork avenues; and the Avebury henge and Silbury Hill are located at the source of the River Kennet. Many other later Neolithic monument complexes are sited adjacent to rivers, and especially in locations where southerly and easterly flowing watercourses meet. In this sense, the creation of monuments was perhaps but a response to the existing significance of cosmologically 'potent' landscapes.

The Bronze Age (4,000–3,200 BP)

The Bronze Age was the second of Thomsen's 'Three Ages'. The association of the Bronze Age with the manufacture of Bronze is perhaps somewhat misleading, since culturally the Early Bronze Age has much in common with the Neolithic, and the period of transition at the end of the Bronze Age (from c. 1200 BC onwards) naturally leads into the Iron Age. However the metallurgical developments of the British Bronze Age are extremely important, and have formed the basis for subdivisions of the period which are still valid. On continental Europe the Bronze Age was preceded by an extensive Copper Age. Britain, on the margins, caught up relatively late, and as a result the British Copper Age (if there can be said to be such a thing) was compressed to a 500-year period from approximately 2700–2200 BC. In fact the use of bronze arrived very shortly after awareness of copper. Bronze is an alloy of copper and tin; the effect of the alloying is to produce a much harder material.

Bronze was in widespread use as the principal metal for the best part of 1,400 years. Britain is quite rich in both copper and tin, although the earliest evidence for copper smelting can only be dated to the later second millennium BC. Although the development of ironworking took place from c. 1000 BC, the conventional end-date for the Bronze Age is around 700 BC. Bronze Age metalworking activity is divided into Early, Middle and Late. The Early Bronze Age (c. 2200–1500 BC) is characterised by narrow-bodied axes with wide blades and by long ribbed daggers, as well as awls and halberds. Towards the end of this period spearheads and axes were both socketed and tanged, and chisels and other tanged tools were also in evidence. The Middle Bronze Age (c. 1500–1100 BC) was characterised by palstaves, dirks and rapiers and side-looped spearheads; and in its later stages sickles and socketed axes. There is a notable change in the period c. 1400–1250 (known as the 'Ornament Horizon') when bracelets, torcs, pins and other quite ostentatiously ornamented decorative items are produced. The Late Bronze Age (c. 1100–700 BC) is characterised by swords and socketed axes, with the use of iron-bladed swords evident during the last 100 years or so.

The development of metalworking marked the beginning of cultural changes. One of the most characteristic forms of Bronze Age material culture is so-called 'Beaker' pottery – tall, narrow-necked vessels with incised decoration in the form of bands, lines and cross-hatching. Beakers are usually found as part of an assemblage of grave goods, including arrowheads and daggers. Widespread across Europe, beakers were used in Britain from c. 2500 to 1700 BC. Originally thought to represent an immigrant 'beaker culture', it now seems more likely that the distribution of Beaker culture is more the consequence of extensive trade networks. However, there were certainly high levels of pan-European mobility – strontium isotope analysis of the Amesbury archer, one of the most famous Beaker burials, suggests that he originally came from the European Alps.

One of the most interesting aspects of the Bronze Age in Britain is the transition from large megalithic funerary monuments in use by large groups, to much smaller isolated burial mounds (round barrows) and round barrow cemeteries, which focussed on individual or family groups. Whilst Stonehenge is normally associated with the Neolithic, in fact its construction and adaptation continued well into the Bronze Age. An arc of paired Welsh bluestones was erected in c. 2500 BC, and the sarsen uprights and lintels probably a hundred years or so later. The present form of Stonehenge actually dates to the period c. 2300–c. 1900 BC, and new stone circles were even contemplated on the site as late as c. 1600 BC. Other henges continued to be built elsewhere in the country, such as the wooden 'seahenge' in Norfolk (eastern England), built in c. 2049 BC. In southern Britain, the period c. 2200–c. 1800 BC coincides with the so-called 'Wessex' culture of extremely rich burials with gold artefacts. Funerary practices changed after this. By the middle of the second millennium BC cremations were being packed into ceramic urns which were dug into earlier barrows. These sometimes extensive barrow cemeteries are characteristic of the Bronze Age landscapes of southern and western Britain, and many remain visible today

This later Bronze Age landscape was a firmly agricultural one. Much of lowland Britain had begun to be cleared during the third millennium BC, but this process accelerated rapidly after c. 2500 BC. By c. 1800 BC even the lower slopes of upland areas such as Cumbria and the Pennines (northern England) had been deforested, and there were few trees on the higher moorland by c. 1200 BC.

Essentially the modern upland landscape of Britain – characterised by peat, heather and sheep grazing – is a product of the Bronze Age. This clearance was accompanied by increasing division of the landscape into rectilinear fields and small enclosures, the most famous survival of which is the system of dry stone walls on Dartmoor (south-west) known as 'reaves'. From c. 1800 BC onwards houses were circular structures usually grouped in small settlements of between two and ten; they are usually found in association with other buildings that would have provided shelter for livestock and storage. These houses were laid out in a particular way. The central hearth acted as the focal point of a cycle of activities; from the doorway in the east movement through the day went in a clockwise direction – cooking, working and sleeping. This appears to have symbolised the movement of the sun during the day, as well as making a broader connection with the passage of life itself: burials are characteristically found under the north-eastern part of the house.

From c. 1200 BC the more extreme upland areas began to be abandoned. This was partly due to a sudden deterioration of climate in the 1150s and 1140s BC. The effect of this was to produce larger and more permanent settlements at the centre of complex field systems often known as 'Celtic fields'. For the first time – notably in central southern England and the Welsh borders – enclosures begin to appear on prominent hill tops. These may have been associated with pastoral activity, but represent substantial investment of labour and resources by increasingly large communities.

The Iron Age (3200 BP to AD 43, but Variable by Region)

Although they first appear in the Bronze Age, hilltop enclosures are a characteristic feature of the classic British Iron Age, and by the middle of the first millennium BC they had evolved into substantial fortified structures: hill forts. The other main characteristic of the Iron Age is, of course, the use of iron. Iron was certainly in use from c. 1000 BC in Britain, but does not seem to have been extracted and smelted here until much later. Knowledge of smelting and ironworking probably spread across Europe from the Middle East after c. 1300 BC. Despite the relative paucity of field evidence, it is apparent that in Britain iron was being smelted in bloomeries and worked in smithies by the middle of the first millennium BC.

From c. 800 BC onwards there was an increase in trade and communication with continental Europe; not least through the Phoenician trading settlement at Cadiz which enabled communication with people living in the Mediterranean, Iberian and Atlantic zones. At the same time links with northern Europe across the North Sea began to rapidly expand. The rich mineral resources of the British Isles were certainly in demand – not just iron ore but also other minerals: copper, tin and lead, as well as gold and silver. This export trade was balanced by the importation of a wide range of goods from across Europe, including ornamental metalwork in the Hallstatt style and new weapon types (such as the 'Carp's tongue' sword) and, significantly, horse gear. However, changes in the broader European picture from the middle of the sixth century BC began to have an impact on Britain. A decline in Phoenician power took place as the Hallstatt kingdoms turned away from Atlantic trade, and Britain became somewhat marginalised once again during the period after c. 600.

These continental changes, together with climatic change (which brought about wetter conditions) led to further changes in social structure and the organisation of the landscape. The tendency to demarcate different territories, already evident in the later Bronze Age, accelerated during the Iron Age. From the eighth century BC, substantial ditches were dug – often cutting through earlier Bronze Age field systems – which terminated in large enclosures. Most common in southern England, these landscape divisions suggest an increasing desire to demarcate territories. From the late sixth century and into the fifth centuries, the landscape in most of mainland Britain (except the far north-west and the central eastern regions) was transformed by the construction of hillforts – large bank-and-ditch enclosures, typically on prominent hilltop sites. These early hillforts consisted of a single bank, and were often quite closely spaced. Other parts of Britain saw the construction of defensible enclosures with wooden palisades. The pottery of this period seems to become much more localised in production and distribution. Together, the landscape and material culture evidence points to an increasing number of much smaller territories.

The Middle Iron Age, from c. 400 to c. 100 BC, saw significant further increases in the intensity of settlement and the apparent complexity of social organisation. The system of hillforts in southern and central Britain was rationalised: many sites were abandoned, and resources were concentrated on fewer larger sites. The remaining hillforts were substantially enlarged, both in terms of the area they occupied and in the size and complexity of their defences – often comprising several sets of banks and ditches. Famous examples of these developed hillforts include Maiden Castle in Dorset (south-east) (Fig. 3.3), Danebury in Hampshire (southern England) and Oswestry in Shropshire (west). It has been suggested that in some cases these hillforts were almost urban in character and had a wide range of activities taking place within them – evidence has been found for industry, storage and even places of worship in those that have been excavated. The patterns of organisation represented by hillforts were mirrored in other parts of Britain by the construction of enclosed and defended nucleated settlements. In Atlantic Scotland, for example, an earlier tradition of roundhouses developed into substantial and impressive circular fortified stone towers known as brochs. Hillforts, fortified enclosures and brochs represented continuity of occupation of earlier sites and an increasing desire for defensiveness and visibility across the wider landscape. Throughout Britain these Middle Iron Age settlements made powerful statements about control of the landscape. These settlements were surrounded by an intensively-farmed hinterland containing a dense network of farmsteads, some of which were also provided with defensive enclosures.

The long period of continuity of settlement and trading patterns represented by the Early and Middle Iron Age periods came to an end from the middle of the second century BC, after which most of Britain saw massive social, economic and technological changes. Roman military and trading expansion in the Mediterranean, notably into France, Spain and the Alpine regions, had an impact on the Atlantic

Fig. 3.3 Maiden Castle, Dorset. (Photo: Kate Page-Smith)

trade routes of which Britain was a key element. Roman consumer demand for raw materials and slaves was matched by British and French thirsts for Italian wine. Coins first started to be used in Britain on a wide scale for trade from around 130 BC onwards. Tribal groupings coalesced in southern Britain during the first century BC. A large and powerful 'core' of groups began to develop in south-east England – split between the Catuvellauni and the Trinovantes to the north of the Thames, and the Atrebates to the south. This 'core' area was surrounded by a 'periphery' of three smaller tribal zones – the Durotriges of Dorset, the Dubonni of Gloucestershire and the Corieltauvi of Leicestershire and Lincolnshire. This 'core and periphery' was closely linked to Gaul, and, since by this time Gaul was effectively under Roman occupation, to Rome.

The 'core and periphery' zone in southern Britain saw substantial social and economic changes during the first century BC which were reflected in the landscape. Probably the most marked transformation was in the abandonment of hillforts as central places. They still retained some of their ritual and defensive functions, but the main focus of settlement was transferred to enclosed 'oppida'. These were still enclosed by banks and ditches, but were located at river crossings on trade routes and were effectively small towns. Many of the larger oppida, such as Verulamium (St. Albans), Camulodunum (Colchester) and Calleva (Silchester) were at the centre of large hinterlands which were in some cases marked by linear earthworks; they were clearly substantial administrative centres where leaders were buried and coins minted. The various groups formed constantly shifting alliances, some with allegiance to Rome and some more closely allied to anti-Roman elements amongst the Belgic tribes. Beyond the English 'core and periphery' the earlier Iron Age social and economic structures continued largely unchanged, although there seems to have been a tendency towards more nucleated settlement at the expense of ostentatious displays of defensibility. For example, this period saw many of the Scottish 'brochs' become surrounded by small villages of densely packed stone houses.

For southern Britain the Iron Age came to an abrupt end with the Roman invasion of AD 43. Elsewhere in Britain – notably in Scotland which was never firmly brought under Roman rule despite many efforts – an end-date for the Iron Age is less obvious. However the grouping of several tribes into a broad confederation known (to us, although not to themselves) as the Picts, took place during the later Roman period and was consolidated from the sixth century AD.

For archaeologists from the New World, it is worth remembering that the archaeology of Late Iron Age Britain is an *historical archaeology*, in that for the first time written accounts survive of the period. These are mainly secondhand from classical sources, such as the account by Pytheas of the island of 'Albion' in c. 320 BC. Perhaps the most famous is Julius Caesar's *Commentaries* on the Gallic Wars, which provides a snapshot of the social and political organisation of Britain in the middle of the first century BC.

The Romano-British Period (AD 43–410)

Traditionally, the Roman period begins in AD 43 with Claudius' successful invasion – although as we have already seen, Roman influence was evident for 200 years before this. Julius Caesar invaded (twice) in 55 and 54 BC, forcing the surrender of local leaders, and, ultimately negotiating peace with Cassivellaunus – who had been hastily appointed as supreme commander by a temporary alliance of the normally argumentative groups in the 'core' of south-east England. Nearly 90 years later, the rise of anti-Roman sentiment among the Catuvellauni led to the ousting of the Atrebatean king, who fled to Rome. This provided a pretext for invasion, and between AD 43 and 48 the disunited British tribal groupings were subdued. Some came quietly, negotiating terms (such as the Brigantes from the Pennines and the Iceni of Norfolk); others put up fierce resistance, such as the Durotriges of Dorset and the Silures in south Wales. By AD 52 the Romans were sufficiently sure of their conquest to build an arch in Rome commemorating Claudius' defeat of 11 British kings. However, this confidence was punctured by an uprising of several tribes in AD 61, famously led by Boudicca. Although this rebellion was defeated, Rome itself was entering a turbulent period of power struggles. Following the suicide of Nero in AD 68 there were several rival emperors, and the resulting civil war was ended by the emergence of Vespasian as emperor in AD 70.

Vespasian appointed Agricola as governor of Britain in 78, and it was under this vigorous military leader that Britain was brought more firmly under Roman control. In a series of campaigns, Agricola pushed the Roman advance through north Wales, Yorkshire and into the far north – even briefly getting as far as Orkney – defeating the temporarily united Picts at Mons Graupius in 84. Consolidation took

Fig. 3.4 Hadrian's Wall. (Photo: Kate Page-Smith)

place over the next 20 years, with temporary forts being rebuilt in stone and in some cases forming the nucleus of later substantial settlements – such as at Chester (Deva), Lincoln (Lindum), York (Eboracum) and Gloucester (Glevum). In many cases Roman settlement occupied or replaced former oppida. In 122 the Emperor Hadrian visited Britain, following which Hadrian's Wall was constructed from the Tyne to the Solway as a barrier against the Pictish tribes to the north. Attempts in the following decade to advance further north resulted in the Antonine Wall being constructed from the Forth to the Clyde; however, continuing unrest in the north resulted in a tactical retreat – so the Antonine Wall was abandoned and Hadrian's Wall (Fig. 3.4) became the northern boundary of the Roman Empire in Britain from the 160s. From 197 Britain was divided into two provinces – Britannia Prima in the largely peaceful and settled south, and Britannia Secunda in the still-rebellious north. For the next two centuries Roman rule was fairly firm, although minor uprisings continued to occur, notably when the Romans were distracted by their own divisions – such as the revolt in c. 286 of Carausius, the commander of the British fleet, which led to 10 years of conflict in northern Gaul and Britain. When order was restored by Constantius (later to become emperor), Britain was reorganised into four provinces as part of a much wider reorganisation of the Roman Empire. Further radical changes to imperial organisation took place under Constantius' son, the emperor Constantine during the early fourth century – and by the late fourth century the empire was divided by internal squabbles and came under attack on many of its extensive borders (including further serious attacks by the Picts in northern Britain during the 360s). After the death of the emperor Theodosius in 395 the once great empire was divided into east and west; the Visigoths captured Rome in 410 and the last Roman legion left Britain to its own devices.

This chronology says very little about the impact of Rome on the inhabitants of Britain – an impact which was to last a great deal longer than the occupation itself. Indeed various legacies of the Roman period are still a part of life in Britain today: many roads, several administrative boundaries, and the location and layout of numerous towns and cities (including, of course, Londinium). Despite first appearances there are substantial upstanding chunks of Roman buildings still extant in Britain, notably large parts of Hadrian's Wall (now a World Heritage Site) and parts of the baths basilica at Wroxeter in Shropshire. Many more have been used as the basis for medieval or later structures, such as city walls in London and elsewhere.

The archaeology of the Roman period is well-studied, and several excavations have taken place in cities (notably London, Silchester and Wroxeter) as well as on individual settlement sites and farmsteads – known as 'villas'. Essentially these villas formed the nucleus of large country estates, and were occupied by the Romanised native elite. Following an initial phase of post-conquest construction in timber, most villas were lavishly rebuilt in stone and brick during the second and third centuries. As well as agricultural storage and processing, villa complexes also housed industrial activities and accommodation for labourers and servants as well as the owners, usually arranged around a courtyard. All had underfloor heating systems, and some had their own bath-houses and central heating systems – all of which have left tangible remains. Mosaic floors are a common find, and many villas have extensive remains which are now visitor attractions – such as Cogidubnus' palace at Fishbourne (Sussex), Brading (Isle of Wight), Lullington (Kent) and Chedworth (Gloucestershire).

It is perhaps not surprising that much of the archaeology of Roman Britain is military in nature. Many of the temporary and permanent camps and forts still exist as archaeological sites. Of these the most basic were marching camps, often used by a single army unit for an overnight encampment, with a single ditch and bank. More substantial were the auxiliary forts, often with several ditches, and rectangular in form with internal roads. The most spectacular were the legionary fortresses – permanent and substantial fortified settlements occupied for decades or even centuries. Several such military sites are open to the public, such as the impressive legionary fortress at Caerleon in south Wales, and the forts associated with Hadrian's Wall at Birdoswald (Cumbria), Vindolanda, Housesteads and Chesters (Northumberland); as well as spectacular remains of the coastal defences at Richborough (Kent). Forts and cities were linked with an extensive road network radiating from London, and fragments of this system survive in present-day English roads which follow the routes of their Roman antecedents.

Traditionally the 'end of Roman Britain' is marked by the departure of the Roman army in AD 410. However, the inhabitants of southern England had already become used to Roman manners and customs before arrival of the Romans themselves, and the 'Romanisation' of Britain did not suddenly end overnight. Of course, some aspects – such as the central appointment of officials and troops, and the issue of coinage – did come to an end. But the largely Roman culture continued: Britain was still divided into four provinces, Latin remained in use for elite and official purposes, and Christianity continued as the principal religion. Despite the traditional archaeological view of the post-Roman period as the 'dark ages', it is clear – from evidence of burials, buildings and landscapes – that a culturally sophisticated and well-connected hierarchical society continued to flourish.

The Post-Roman Period (AD 410 to c. 1000)

Somewhere between about ad 400 and 600, people of Germanic origin established settlements in southern Britain and their distinctive material culture came to dominate that of the previous population. During the same period further north, invaders from Ireland established new kingdoms. By the end of the ninth century (AD 800) the invaders were sufficiently well established that we can begin legitimately to call much of southern Britain 'England' and the Irish 'Scots' are sufficiently dominant that we can call the northern part 'Scotland'; the territory of modern Wales was divided into several polities, the names of which have reappeared as the names of modern administrative areas. From around 800, however, a new invading force was on the scene in the form of Vikings from Scandinavia. Much maligned in popular imagery, they also played a significant part in the story of Britain.

The earlier part of this period – mainly because of the lack of historical reportage, in contrast to the Roman period – was for a long time called the 'Dark Ages'. The efforts of archaeologists have made them significantly less dark, but there is much still to learn. In particular, there is a reliance upon certain types of evidence, and certain themes which dominate debate.

A lack of clear settlement evidence means a reliance upon burial practices to identify different groups within Britain at this time. While burial evidence is generally lacking for northern and western Britain, what evidence there is indicates continuing practices from the Iron Age and Roman periods, and as time goes on the inclusion of specifically Christian elements. Further south, cemeteries attributed to Anglo-Saxon immigrants are widespread showing practices that have closer connections with areas on the other side of the English Channel. However, since there is a lack of burial evidence from the later Roman period, it is not clear to what extent these really differ from Romano-British practices. Regional differences complicate the picture. There is a preference for cremation in the east and northeast of England, and for inhumation, usually without grave goods, further south. After about 600 AD inhumations are arranged in large groups with a clear gender distinction evident in the inclusion of weapons with males and jewellery with women. From the later ninth century, burials showing the characteristics of Scandinavian origin also appear in the east and the Isle of Man, with burials (in some areas cremation) under barrows, burials within ships also under barrows, and – with the arrival of Christianity among the Vikings – the erection of decorated stone crosses.

Pottery styles are always a clear indicator of cultural and other differences. While England provides a range of different indigenous styles from different regions as well as foreign imports, Wales and Scotland are almost entirely aceramic until later in the medieval period, making the identification of sites very difficult. In England, the earliest part of this period is dominated by wares made in the continuing tradition of the late Roman period, augmented by courser handmade wares. By 700 AD, the slow wheel came into use in East Anglia and Northumbria, and by around 900 wheel-thrown wares dominated production except in the north-west of England and southern Wessex. The early eleventh century saw a resurgence of handmade pottery.

Environmental archaeology has established that despite the end of Roman rule and the immigration of settlers from Germany and elsewhere, there was little change in agricultural practice, except perhaps a slight shift from arable cultivation to pasture. New types of settlement did, however, start to appear. In the west of Britain, elite defended sites on hilltops show evidence of construction in this period, especially Dynas Powys in Wales, Tintagel in Cornwall (which also has Arthurian connections according to some traditions), and Dunadd in Scotland. In England, undefended rural settlements show up as scatters of artefacts or from aerial photography. While few have been excavated, the typical structures are a *grüben-haus* (a sunken-feature building used as an ancillary structure) and a larger hall for communal living, possibly of both people and animals. Viking immigrants into eastern and northern Britain introduced different building styles which they brought with them from Denmark, especially the 'bow-sided' hall resembling an upturned boat. In the northern isles of Scotland, Viking settlements are easier to identify: stone-built longhouses replaced the oval and round structures of the original inhabitants.

The general abandonment of urban space at the close of the Roman period is marked by the presence of so-called 'dark earth' – a layer of black material found in most former Roman towns. Frequently ascribed to burning by incoming Germanic invaders, this is now more commonly understood to represent a change in occupation practice. Rather than densely populated centres, distinguished from 'country' by distinctive urban practices such as trade, areas within towns were turned over to garden-plots for agricultural production, effectively transforming urban character into rural. Trade with the near continent required coastal bases where ships could land, and by around 700 AD a number of these were established in Britain: notably outside the walls of Roman London and York, and on the south coast near Southampton. These 'wics' (so-called because the suffix 'wic' appears in so many of their names – Londonwic, Hamwic) were not true towns but had many of the characteristics associated with them. When due to Viking incursions from 800 AD onwards they occupied more easily defended positions – within the walls at London or York, across the river at Hamwic – they become known as 'burhs', and a system of such defended settlements stretched across England by the ninth century. Many of these were created in empty space, and represent planned towns with a grid pattern of streets as well as enclosing earthen banks.

The adoption of Christianity by the early medieval populations of Britain resulted in two types of building distinctive to that religion: churches and monasteries. At the start, already extant halls may simply have been converted to religious use, but continental workers were also employed since the arts of building in stone, with plastering, glazing and tiling, had passed from Britain with the Romans. While few early churches – if any – have been identified in northern and western Britain, others in the south and east show the typical features of this period: tall narrow proportions, round arches, small windows and towers, and, most typically, 'long-and-shortwork' decoration on the corners. Some stone churches incorporated earlier Roman features, sometimes including entire extant Roman buildings, at other times columns or merely the reuse of earlier tiles. Plans were generally simple, but became more complex over time. Not all churches had a related cemetery from the outset: some were added later; and in some the cemetery predates the construction of the church. Monasteries can be difficult to identify from archaeological evidence alone, since so many indicators are also the indicators of a thriving secular settlement. In western Britain, however, a preference for locating them in remote spots may be a useful pointer. Notable sites include Jarrow in northeast England, and Repton in the north.

The Middle Ages (AD 1000–1550)

The dominant image of medieval Britain is perhaps that of the stone castle, of which many examples remain. The introduction of the castle – of earth and wood rather than stone, the first recorded example of which was built in 1066 to assist William of Normandy in his conquest – certainly marks the beginning of the period. William's victory created the first fully united kingdom of England, and a few centuries later Wales would become a vassal principality, while Scotland remained an independent state until the next period of history. The period marks the transition from a distinctively pre-modern society to something we could recognise as having many of the elements of modernity. A key moment for both historians and archaeologists is the mid-fourteenth century, which saw a large proportion of the population extinguished by the 'Black Death' with consequences for urban and rural life. The period's end-date is commonly accepted to be that of the dissolution of the monasteries, marking the end of a distinctive medieval institution in Britain.

The presence in a central band from southern to northeast England of large numbers of former villages – identifiable by earthwork platforms representing where houses once stood and associated linear depressions marking roads and droveways – indicates a sizeable population in medieval Britain, at least within this central region. At Wharram Percy (Yorkshire, northern England), for example, a so-called 'DMV' or deserted Medieval Village has been carefully excavated over many years, including analysis of its population from the close study of medieval burials in the churchyard. It is common also to see fields containing parallel (often elongated S-shaped) banks representing the evidence for medieval field systems, again predominantly in the same 'central' region of England (the south- and north-west regions, and the east being characterised more by dispersed settlement and different farming practices). Further north, field boundaries were marked by drystone walling. The detailed excavation of rural settlements has provided evidence for changes in housing – from earlier longhouses to sets of separate buildings – and the development of some farms to elite manorial estates. It has also allowed the identification of specialist buildings, such as sheepcotes, from other types of building, making it possible to view changes in farming regime through the archaeological record. In particular, the variety of building styles and landholdings that developed – both across regions and between them – has come to light, demonstrating the complexity of medieval life.

The form and structure of buildings gives insight into medieval life, both urban and rural. In towns, the presence of stone buildings testifies to a certain level of prosperity, and the layout of streets and their relation to each other can help distinguish domestic zones of occupation from specialist areas where particular industries were carried out. The interior of buildings reveals changes in room layout and function marking the change from a form of communal living to the development of separate (and often private) functional spaces. The introduction of chimneys allowed and encouraged people to devote individual rooms to specific purposes if they could afford it.

In terms of material culture, the large-scale wheel-thrown pottery manufacture of later Saxon times gave way during the twelfth century to smaller more local industries based around individual towns. The consequent rise in regional variations is useful for dating purposes and establishing trading connections. However, in the mid-fourteenth century this system largely collapsed to be replaced with a proliferation of coarser wares made for domestic purposes. This in turn gradually gave way to a revived industry centred on London and the Midlands, which provided the distinctive wares of early modern Britain.

There are three clear periods of urban rise and decline evident from this evidence. These are: a period of growth from 1050 to 1300; a period of crisis and decline in the early to mid-fourteenth century; and one of recovery from 1350 but which sees increasing dominance of some centres – especially London in England and Edinburgh in Scotland – over others. Towns that were deliberately planned are evident from the earlier period. While the more obvious grid-patterns are rare, other towns saw a castle located at the core of the settlement forcing streets to conform to this outline. In other cases, a central marketplace determines that all streets are subsidiary to it. Planned towns are particularly noticeable in Wales and along the Welsh Marches, following the conquest of that country by English monarchs. Some towns – planned and otherwise – retained former Roman outer limits and defences, while others had new defences built for them which also provided other amenities: public lockups, housing for city officials, and water barriers which also acted as fishponds and provided power for mills. Suburbs would also be planned, their development offering useful insights into periods of growth and decline. Similarly, waterfronts were developed in a number of coastal and riverside towns. The urban archaeology of the Middle Ages overall provides information about towns as social phenomena, and economic and political centres.

The archaeology of medieval churches looks back to their origins in the Saxon period but also forward to redesign and rebuilding that came later. The 'Great Rebuilding' of the period 1050–1150 saw the replacement of formerly wooden structures with new buildings of stone, many in the distinctive 'Romanesque' style.

Later centuries would see their extension and development as new styles became apparent, culminating in 'Perpendicular', the graceful and peculiarly English form of Gothic. Burials were prohibited within churches until the twelfth century, except for founders and priests. After this, prominent local figures may also find their place within the walls. Accordingly, cemeteries are associated with churches from inception. The excavation of cemeteries has provided valuable information on ritual practices, including the 'zoning' of cemeteries to allow different classes of person to be buried in different areas, as well as offering valuable evidence of demographics and health issues. In addition, changes in boundaries and the addition of other features related to religious practice – such as chapels, charnel houses, bell houses and almshouses – provide evidence of local and regional variation.

The period after 1066 and the Norman conquest sees the establishment of monasteries on a Continental model, comprising not only a church and cloister, but also domestic space, industrial facilities, guest housing, infirmary and schools as well as ancillary structures such as fishponds and mills, allowing the establishment to be self-sufficient. Although many were originally constructed of wood, these would be replaced with more permanent stone buildings as soon as funds allowed. Variation is evident across different monastic orders, and dependent on whether they included lay brothers or were more or less dedicated to service outside the monastery itself. Nevertheless, in distinction from those of earlier periods, monasteries are clearly different from other communities, whether rural or urban. The 1500s sees the major change in the religious structure of Britain with the establishment of Protestantism in both Scotland and in England: the latter in particular results in the wholesale closure of religious houses and the removal of material for building work elsewhere.

Town defences, castles and other military architecture form a specific area of research in the medieval period. The earliest castles date from the later eleventh century and were built mostly of wood and earth (generally referred to as 'motte and bailey', emphasising the mound supporting a tower and the enclosing courtyard): some later would be replaced by stone. Periodic periods of conflict – such as the so-called 'Anarchy' of the twelfth century – also saw periods of their building, either as temporary structures to meet specific military needs or to be converted into permanent strongholds. By the thirteenth century, castles, now mostly of stone, were generally losing their strictly military function and instead becoming elite housing. Most castles of this period – apart from those built to control the Welsh border and along that between England and Scotland where frequent raids took place – were built as status symbols by the wealthy and powerful rather than as necessary protection against a subservient population. The distinctive Scottish form was the tower house, with a hall attached and surrounded by a courtyard.

A recent development in the study of this period has been the emergence of battlefield archaeology. Research has sought to identify the locations of major battles from the scatter of materials left behind as a distinctive 'signature'. By plotting the distribution of such material, archaeologists can trace the action through these material remains, often challenging conventional and established historical accounts. Investigation of human remains has also given insight not only into the practices of medieval warfare and weaponry, but also into the age, health and status of soldiers.

Post-Medieval and Industrial (AD 1550–1900)

The post-medieval period (and the one that follows – see below) has traditionally been the outsider in British archaeology: still rarely taught at undergraduate level and often ignored in favour of the rich legacy of earlier periods. However, in the last 30 years the discipline has developed enormously. Archaeologists from the Anglophone New World are used to dealing with 'historical archaeology', and certainly in dealing with British archaeology of the same period, you are likely to encounter similar types of material culture and similar categories of site. However, although British post-medieval archaeology has engaged with the broader global 'historical archaeology', it has many unique characteristics which make it a much more complex – and arguably much more rewarding – field of study. In Britain, the study of this period is crowded by the work of historians, geographers and sociologists as well as archaeologists, and only now is a coherent modern archaeology beginning to emerge. Some practitioners have criticised British post-medieval studies as 'atheoretical' and focussed on material culture at the expense of broader analyses; however, this criticism is no longer valid.

There is a dichotomy between the arguably middle-class, humanities-based origins of 'post-medieval archaeology' and the working-class, science- and engineering-based approaches of 'industrial archaeology'. This has sometimes polarised the discipline and diverted energies away from co-operation in understanding the archaeological remains themselves (Cranstone and Barker 2004). Many see value in the term 'post-medieval', but choose to ignore (or subvert) the expression by the founders of the Society for Post-Medieval Archaeology that the period ends at 'the onset of industrialisation' (Anon 1967, 2). Defining a period by what it is not (post-medieval – not medieval, but what?) does raise issues for some. We think it is misleading to suggest, as Susie West did in 1999, that post-medieval archaeology is the last refuge of 'traditionalist archaeology', operating as an empirical data-gathering exercise without theoretical rigour (West 1999, 6–7). Outlining the scope of 'industrial archaeology' is also fraught with difficulty, and meetings of the Association for Industrial Archaeology have grappled with this subject. Certainly the subject has moved a long way from the days when one of its founding fathers, Kenneth Hudson, could state that 'the very point of Industrial Archaeology … [is] … to provide facts about the history of industry and technology' (Hudson 1967, 9). Instead, its most innovative practitioners prefer to explore 'social transformations … power relations, new systems of control and the creation of a work ethic' (Gould 1999, 153). Marilyn Palmer has written of the 'long pre-history of industrialisation' which preceded the industrial revolution, and has acknowledged that industrialisation was 'one of the key developments in the post-medieval British economy and society' (Palmer 2004, 1). So 'industrial archaeology' is today generally acknowledged as a subset of 'post-medieval archaeology', but with a specific focus on the issues surrounding the process of industrialisation (Palmer and Neaverson 1998).

The period after AD 1550 is characterised by extremely rapid changes in society, technology and landscape. One of the real issues in dealing with this period is the superabundance of evidence in the form of artefacts and sites. It has been successfully argued that the archaeology of this period is to an extent the 'archaeology of capitalism' (Leone 1995; Johnson 1996; Leone and Potter 1998). Matthew Johnson employed a broad definition of the term, which included notions such as the increasing privatisation of social space, as well as conventional material activities such as trade and the consumption of artefacts. Post-medieval archaeology has traditionally been very good at identifying where and how goods were produced and consumed, and in more recent years has begun to use artefacts to tell more complex stories about the people who used them. Archaeologists have been less successful in trying to understand some of the more subtle and shifting nuances of meaning that have been created in our sites, buildings and landscape by the ever-developing processes of capitalism. Johnson and others have used the term 'commodification', by which the notion of capitalism 'embraces other concepts such as privacy, individualism and sentiment' (Johnson 1996, 87–90; Tarlow and West 1999, 265). The development of capitalism was already underway when the dissolution of the monasteries created new patterns of asset ownership from the sixteenth century. This in turn provoked widespread and ongoing adjustment of social structures and power relations. Everything in the new post-medieval age had its social, cultural and economic price, and the continual renegotiation of value is one of the key drivers of the development of the modern world.

One of the most obvious manifestations of capitalism was the process of industrialisation, a process which came first to the British Isles. Mining, pottery manufacture, iron- and glass-making had been taking place since the middle ages, but the protestant reformation of the mid-sixteenth century resulted in substantial shifts in the balance of power. The dissolution of the monasteries effectively privatised formerly large corporate landholdings, and enabled entrepreneurs to buy up land relatively cheaply and exploit it for its mineral wealth. From this followed the massive industrial expansion of the seventeenth, eighteenth and nineteenth centuries, characterised by increasing mechanisation and mass production.

The patterns of industrialisation were to a large extent determined by geology. A great deal of early industrialisation took place on the 'Coal Measures' – a distinctive band of coal, iron, limestone and clay which runs in a broad sweep from southwest to north-east England. The post-medieval iron industry, for example, soon moved from its embryonic beginnings in the Weald (south-east) to the much more productive coal measures of the Midlands and north of England. One influential site was the Ironbridge Gorge (Shropshire, Midlands) (Fig. 3.5), which saw the early development of coal mining and iron making – as well as a wide range of other industries. Similar developments took place elsewhere where mineral resources were close to the surface, but the development of steam power meant that mines could be made deeper and previously inaccessible resources exploited. Freed from the need to use water power, later ironworks became larger and were located as much for their transport links as for their proximity to raw materials. Huge new ironworks were built in the nineteenth century in Scotland, south Wales and the north-west of England. Some areas specialised in particular products – so Sheffield became famous for cutlery and steel and Birmingham for armaments and jewellery.

Fig. 3.5 The iron bridge (Shropshire). (Photo: Paul Belford)

Other metalworking industries also developed rapidly during the eighteenth and nineteenth centuries. Cornwall (south-west) was well known from Roman times for tin, and this industry hugely expanded in the eighteenth century – along with copper mining. These metals (and their by-products, such as arsenic) were so lucrative that massive investments were made in technological advances such as steam engines and drilling methods which were exported all over the world. The manufacture of textiles was also industrialised, with huge steam-powered mills coming to dominate the landscapes of the north-west and Yorkshire. All of these industries became heavily dependent on global systems of trade, both as a source of raw material and as markets for the finished products. As a result, when market conditions changed, such industries often collapsed overnight. This happened to the Cornish tin and copper industries in the later nineteenth century, to the northern textile industries in the mid-twentieth century, and to the iron, steel and coal industries from the 1980s.

The creation of these sorts of capital-intensive production infrastructures required the construction of new physical landscapes, and mental adjustment to new (and continually adjusting) power relations between men, women and children. Landscapes of industrial production and transportation created new types of buildings and structures, and new hierarchies of relations between them. The archaeological remains of industrial sites are often extremely complex and difficult to interpret, and the substantial nature of the remains means that a much more robust approach to excavation needs to be taken – using mechanical excavators rather than brushes and trowels! Of course, excavation is not the only tool in understanding this complex period: buildings and documents also need to be part of the archaeologist's repertoire.

Closely linked with the development of industrialised capitalism was the creation of a consumer society. Increasing consumption of 'stuff' can be seen as a marker of modernity and individuality. However, consumption studies have traditionally had art-historical origins rather than archaeological ones, and have therefore tended to focus on groups and individuals from well-documented sections of society. The archaeology of consumption can be studied at all levels – from the appropriation of medieval landscape features by wealthy landowners, to the use of pub tokens by urban workers. Perhaps one of the greatest strengths of post-medieval archaeology is its ability to look at sections of society traditionally marginalised by (the absence of) documentary records. Changes in the consumption of space are also significant, not only 'private' domestic space but also 'public' spaces such as streets, railway carriages, art galleries and brothels.

The rise of consumerism was assisted by the development of trade, transport and communication links. Improved navigability of rivers and the development of canal, railway and road networks resulted from the need to move raw materials and finished goods around. Improved communication also increased the consumption of ideas. Not only was a new world being manufactured at home, but the New World abroad was being 'discovered', mapped and colonised. The colonial experience for existing and new inhabitants of these places – from seventeenth-century Ireland to twentieth-century Australia – has been extensively studied from a variety of viewpoints, and in all of these places we find the consumer products of the industrial capitalism of the British Isles.

Several key themes – capitalism, industrialisation, consumption and globalisation – emerge from the study of the post-medieval and industrial periods – five centuries during which the landscape, character and identity of Britain was transformed more rapidly than it ever had been before. Sometimes these broad themes are not always apparent on the ground. The superabundance of evidence – including artefacts, buildings, landscapes and documents – can make it very difficult for archaeologists to say something meaningful. Increasingly archaeologists are seeking to tell individual stories about people, artefacts and lifestyles. Present within all of these thematic groups is a number of subjects which will more readily manifest themselves in the archaeological record, or at least in our interpretation of it. These subjects inter-connect and overlap; thus an archaeology of conflict may also be present in a gender-based archaeology of the home; or it might equally be evident in an investigation of scientific developments in the workplace.

The Twentieth Century and Beyond (AD 1900–2011)

Until very recently, most archaeology books would have ended with the industrial archaeology of the nineteenth century – archaeology being about 'the past', and the ancient past at that. But more recently archaeology and heritage have extended their focus into the modern period: archaeology is viewed as a perspective, a way of seeing, interpreting the world through its material remains. In that sense at least, archaeology is just as relevant for the modern period as it is for the deeper past. (Indeed this was the case with the 1st Edition of Hunter and Ralston's staple *The Archaeology of Britain*; the recently published 2nd Edition contains a new chapter on 'The Modern Age' covering the twentieth and twenty-first centuries, cf. Hunter and Ralston 2010.)

But what is the archaeology of the modern world, of the twentieth century and beyond? Above all else, this is the archaeology of 'after modernity' (Harrison and Schofield 2010), even 'supermodernity': of a period in which industry and militarism have been both predominant and closely connected within the context of a so-called 'military-industrial complex'. The archaeology of twentieth-century conflict has been practiced by increasing numbers of archaeologists in recent years, including work on the First World War battlefields and the later German defence, The Atlantic Wall. In Britain much has been done: from surveying and studying Second World War anti-invasion defences, to recording redundant airfields, and excavating crashed aircraft. A huge diversity of these former military sites has been studied and recorded through documentary research. For the first time in the long sequence of human occupation in Britain it can be said, with confidence, precisely how many sites of each type were built, where they were built and why.

The Cold War period presents some very different issues. This was a period in which defence and scientific research and development prevailed. Many sites were extensive research establishments comprising large numbers of unique structures, often not built to last and incapable of any further use, and defence sites related to the nuclear deterrent, and to counter the effects of nuclear attack – early warning sites, civil defence structures including private shelters, and the airfields that supported the V-force whose purpose was to provide the nuclear deterrent. Another dimension was of course the American presence, as it had been in the Second World War – airmen and their families occupying remote rural bases, their provisions and cars flown in from the USA. These bases still remain even though may of the troops have gone: and from the physical remains that survive, the American influence is obvious: baseball courts and wall art are the clearest traces left behind.

Industrial archaeology of this period is equally diverse, from the industries that supported military actions of the First and Second World Wars, to research and development of the Cold War, the road and rail networks and infrastructure, chemical industries, water and sewage, car-making, and the new industries that characterise 'Sunrise Valley' comprising the M4 and M3 motorways and a wider zone on the western side of London. The material culture here tends to be dominated by buildings and structures, and increasingly the spaces where 'recent' buildings once stood.

Domestic housing provision and retail are other prevailing themes. As the twentieth century progressed, public opinion and political will and direction ensured a series of changes to public housing provision. Homes for Heroes built after the First World War remain in many areas, a few of the homes housing descendents of their first occupants; prefabricated bungalows (prefabs) appeared after the Second World War, with council estates and high rise, and now gated communities coming later. Some of the slums still extant in the early twentieth century were replaced by estates in the 1960s, only to be replaced again in the nineties and the noughties.

Shopping has gone from the High Street, where individual shops specialised in particular goods, to the out-of-town shopping centres that now prevail, with their massive car parks merging into one another at motorway intersections (Graves Brown 2007). And in this area perhaps more than most Britain has lost much of its diversity: we have become 'clone town Britain' – we can walk down any high street and could be anywhere: regional dialects have been diluted with greater mobility; and every high street has the same stores, something that is increasingly true on a global scale. In the countryside the changes can also be seen: the effects of the Common Agricultural Policy, for example, and conservation whereby farmers are now paid to preserve and maintain aspects of their historic environment and wildlife. In some areas, such as Areas of Outstanding Natural Beauty and National Parks, the additional constraints on new development are enforced through planning rules and regulations that can discourage inappropriate change. Despite this emphasis in some areas for preserving the historic environment, Britain continues to change as it has done over 700,000 years. It is just that the scale and the speed at which change occurs is faster than ever.

To what extent though is all of this 'archaeological' or 'heritage'? 'Why not?' is a stock response! Archaeology is after all the study of material remains as a means to understanding human behaviour in the past. That 'past' can be 700,000 years old, or seven. Equally, the heritage is our cultural legacy, and that too can be old or recent. The heritage legislation in Britain, unlike some other countries, has no threshold, no cut-off date before which items can be considered 'heritage' or 'historic', and after which they cannot. And one big feature of this modern, contemporary, heritage: we all have strong opinions about it, because it is so familiar. Everything we describe in this chapter matters – because archaeology gives a rootedness in the past, especially at times of increased mobility. But for modern places there is that extra dimension: memory. We have strong views on these places because they matter to us, personally, often for a complex array of personal, intimate and emotive reasons.

My Favourite Twentieth-Century Heritage Site: The Oasis, Endell Street (London)

Sefryn Penrose (University of Oxford)

1951s beauty pageant comedy *Lady Godiva Rides Again* may not be the most remembered of post-war films, but it is packed with lively illustrations of life in Festival era Britain: Diana Dors, Miss Non-Ferrous Metals 1950, picks up two affluent Australians in the Dome of Discovery, one of whom proceeds to nonchalantly win all the top prizes in Battersea Park's Festival Pleasure Gardens, promoting his homeland to potential Ten Pound Poms; Johnny and Janey get engaged for 'the promise of a prefab', and look forward to their week off work, 'getting brown at a holiday camp'.

Publicity stills for the film show Joan Collins, beauty queen, louche, as if on sun-drenched shores. Although black and white, we can still drink in the optimism of London, 1951, a sunny city recovering with the help of 'Miss Norfolk Broads'. She stands beside a swimming pool, over her shoulder the Shaftesbury Theatre. In the heart of London, this outdoor swimming pool, the Oasis, reopened in 1947, remains, now side-by-side with its 1960s indoor neighbour, a gym, an office block, encircled by redbrick council flats, the balconies of which overlook its year-round blue. Could anything be more elementally incongruous in this all-hours congested city in which space must pay to survive?

Water on this site has an almost mystical history: a spring fed baths known as the Duke's Bagnio in the seventeenth century. Today's Oasis may not have the 'pilasters and Inigo Jones style cornice' once attributed to it, or the florid Victorian architecture of the 1852 reconstruction but it is part of the same story. Once administered by the diocese of St Giles and St George, the Holborn Baths offered washing places, wringing machines, mangles and irons, slipper baths, swimming baths, to all of London's residents for a few pence. Work on new first class, second class, and ladies' pools behind a 1930s neo-classical façade and under a glass roof were halted by war, and post-war austerity forgot them entirely. But what remained, although diminished and rumoured to have been used as a water tank during the war, was resurrected after the Education Act advocated swimming for the health of the nation's young. The Dome of Discovery is gone, as has Battersea's funfair, and Joan Collins is better known for shoulder-pads than bathing costumes, but for a reasonable £3.60 you can still back-stroke in all weathers under London's changing skies, and in winter evenings count lucky stars that have allowed such a facility to enter the twenty-first century, heritage intact.

Pulling It All Together: The Idea of Landscape

Having summarised Britain's archaeological resource in terms of periods and places, artefacts and excavations, we end this chapter by emphasising the need to also adopt a wider view. Towards the end of the review we discussed the need to include modern sites within our consideration of the archaeological resource. Here we emphasise the need to place all of the above in the context of a wider landscape, which of course divides into that which is submerged and that which is not.

Underwater Remains, Crash Sites and Wrecks

Some archaeologists prefer to work on dry land, and others at sea, or in rivers and lakes.

Maritime archaeologists concentrate on the evidence of humankind's past use of the sea whether through investigating submerged marine sites or studying port and harbour buildings. Today there is also emphasis on making results available from, and encouraging access to, our heritage, submerged and terrestrial.

Archaeological sites in the sea such as fish-traps, harbour remains, military defences, or even shipwrecks, may not always have been submerged, but may have been affected by rising sea-levels or coastal erosion. Marine archaeologists, specialising in sites that now exist beneath the sea, have typically included diving in their training but increasingly other disciplines are employed such as marine geophysical surveying.

For the marine environment, archaeologists need specialist knowledge to understand what types of site they might encounter, what conservation options might be available to stabilise and protect sites, and what 'formation processes' have influenced the site as it exists today. For a long time maritime archaeology was undertaken largely by amateurs, members of dive groups who specialised in archaeological work, principally ship wrecks. But now it plays a significant part in professional archaeology and heritage management practice. Several British universities have maritime archaeologists on their staff and offer specific courses including at Masters level at the universities of Southampton, Bristol and University College London, for example. Some of the commercial archaeology units have maritime archaeology teams, and the heritage agencies also now have specialists in this area, to provide a professional lead and give expert advice.

The bulk of maritime archaeology work is concerned with ship wrecks. Some of this work is for documentation, to determine their extent and condition, for example. Other work is directed towards statutory protection, public archaeology and outreach, or research into conservation matters such as stabilisation. While ships have been discovered from the Bronze Age period, for example at Dover (south-east England), the great majority of known wrecks in British waters are from the later medieval period onwards (because of the existence of better records), a large number of which date to the Second World War, from the Battle of the Atlantic for example, and at Scapa Flow (Orkney) (Fig. 3.6). A further feature of the twentieth-century maritime

Fig. 3.6 Scapa Flow wrecks of the Second World War. (Photo provided by Ian Oxley)

record are military aircraft that crashed into the sea, mostly off the south and east coasts of England in the Second World War. Quite a few of these crash sites have been recovered by excavation, notably a Spitfire from the inter-tidal zone in Essex (eastern England).

But there are other remains beyond ships and aircraft. For long periods of time during the Pleistocene, Britain was physically part of the Continent of Europe with a land bridge occupied by hunters and gatherers. Part of this area of former land is referred to now as Doggerland, between England's east coast and the coast of northern Europe – Germany and the Netherlands, and beneath the southern North Sea. Recent archaeological work, plotting finds from the nets of trawlers, and geophysical survey, has revealed much about this vast landscape now in an under-water world (see Doggerland text box below).

One of the best known maritime military operations was the embarkation for D-Day in June 1944. A seabed survey of this maritime landscape revealed how many artefacts had been lost along the way – from tanks and other military vehicles, to components of the floating harbours.

Our knowledge of the maritime record continues to grow, and increasingly there are opportunities to conduct research in areas affected by new developments. Newly constructed wind farms are increasingly constructed off-shore, while oil platforms are built, and then scuttled in the marine environment. Equally, a broader view of the marine environment is now emerging through 'seascape' characterisa-tion, a term which simply highlights extension of the principles of Historic Landscape Characterisation (see Chap. 4) to the marine environment – ensuring that any future works within this vulnerable and important cultural landscape take account of the historic dimension.

Doggerland: A Lost European Country

Vince Gaffney (University of Birmingham)

Few people appreciate that the grey waters of the North Sea cover a prehistoric landscape larger than the United Kingdom. This landscape was lost between 18,000 and 7,000 BC when global warming raised sea levels rapidly. One of the most extensive prehistoric landscapes in Europe and, perhaps, the world was then preserved, far beyond the reach of modern archaeological prospec-tion, by the murky waters of the North Sea (Fig. 3.7). In the absence of any practical method to explore this territory, the lands of the North Sea were gradually forgotten except, perhaps, as a land bridge across which Britain was colonised.

That was the situation until researchers at the University of Birmingham used new technology to map and explore this lost world as it appeared around

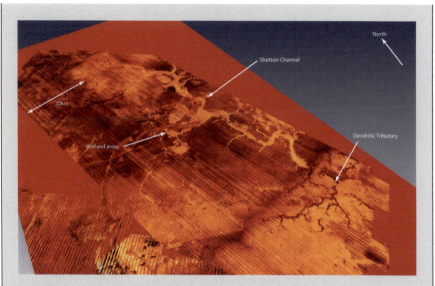

Fig. 3.7 Detail of an extensive river system stretching more than 30 km and provisionally named the: Shotton River (after the famous Birminghan geologist Fred Shotton - http://www.archant.bham.ac.ak/shottonproject/profshotton.htm))

10,000 BP. Seismic data, collected for oil exploration, was used to locate buried features over 23,000 km². Unlike terrestrial geophysics, the extent of data available within the North Sea allows researchers to map this mysterious Mesolithic landscape over an area equivalent to that of Wales. Archaeologists can now trace the rivers, streams, lakes and coastlines of a lost European country. We can also explore these lands using 3D maps of its geography and coastline. We can even use this information to predict where Mesolithic people lived and begin to plan the exploration of this hidden world in detail.

These discoveries are not simply scientific novelties; a very real human tragedy lies behind the loss of this immense landscape. The coastlines, rivers, marshlands and hills mapped during this project were, for thousands of years, parts of a familiar landscape to the hunter-gatherers of Europe. Rivers would have been named and estuaries and low hills associated with ancestral memories dear to these peoples. Insidious and slow overall, but terrifyingly fast at times, inundation must have been devastating for the people who lived here. Whole territories may have disappeared within the memory of generations. Disturbingly, these changes occurred as a consequence of climatic change equivalent to the rate predicted over the next century. As temperatures and sea levels rise today, the fate of the landscapes and peoples of the North Sea may yet be interpreted not as an academic curiosity but a significant warning for the future.

Landscape

Landscape (not landscapes – there is only one!) presents a challenge to conventional approaches to heritage management and archaeology, by virtue of its scale but also its continuity of use, the diversity of landscape types, and the range of techniques by which we can study it. To help disentangle how archaeologists study landscape, we can identify three particular types of landscape archaeology (after Fairclough 2006).

The first is 'archaeology at landscape scale'. This is perhaps the most obvious and conventional branch of landscape archaeology, that involves studying the material remains of the past at large scale using established methods such as regional survey, aerial photography or environmental archaeology. In this case, particular (usually relict) landscapes are studied to find out what the past was like. Archaeological field survey work has taken place in upland areas like Bodmin Moor (Cornwall, south-west England), for example, mapping and interpreting field remains; the Fens in the East Midlands of England; and more recently on Exmoor (south-west England).

Second is an approach that became more popular as the influences of anthropology on archaeology came to be felt. The 'archaeology of past landscape' is an attempt to gain a view of how people in the past perceived areas of land as landscape, how landscape reflected mentality, for example, and how it was used to shape society. Phenomenology is an example of this, and notably the studies of Cranborne Chase (Dorset) and Bodmin Moor (both south-west), in which the connections between sites and monuments and the lie of the land was closely investigated.

Finally is 'the archaeology of landscape', using archaeological perspectives and approaches to study the landscape as it exists today with a view to building a wider, deeper understanding, and doing so with a degree of subjectivity – privileging the most dominant survivals from the past that contribute most to landscape character in the present. This is the principle behind the method of Historic Landscape Characterisation (see Chap. 4).

Why Landscapes Matter

Matthew Johnson (University of Southampton)

Most Sundays, thousands of couples and families across the country take a walk in the countryside. No more than half an hour from any city outside London, one can drive to a rural landscape, and set off across stiles, over hedges and walls, exploring old churches and half-timbered villages, tramping across fields and moors.

A certain tool-kit goes along with this ritual. An Ordnance Survey (OS) map sets out rights of way, indicates places of historic interest, and points out landmarks. The 'county Pevsner' (an architectural historic guidebook authored typically by the renowned architectural historian Nikolaus Pevsner), with concise and often acerbic entries laid out village by village, indicates buildings considered of architectural merit, and even stipulates which should be admired and which castigated by any person of correct cultural taste. A good pair of boots, the muddier the better, and a worn copy of the *Good Pub Guide* completes the assemblage.

Landscapes of the British Isles have been intensively cultivated over thousands of years – even in harsher upland areas the 'natural' vegetation was modified by humans millennia ago. As a result, for anyone who can see the Gothic lettering indicating antiquities on the OS map or who knows a little about enclosure or place-names, every field boundary, every kink or bend in the track, every stone wall or hedge line is full of history. Many visitors walk through the landscape ignorant of the specific historical meanings of what they are looking at, but the sights and sounds of their Sunday walk are resonant nevertheless.

The landscape, though actually owned by very few, is perceived as the heritage of the many. 'England – Fight for it Now!' cried propaganda posters in the 1940s, depicting traditional rural scenes of rolling hills with stone-built farms nestling in their folds. The way the English landscape has come to take on these meanings has been debated endlessly by academics, but the underlying truth is not disputed – the landscape matters.

Landscapes matter because they mean things to people. A sense of place is strongly linked to a sense of who 'we' are. Indigenous peoples such as Native Americans or Australian Aborigines often have deeply held views of the landscape as sacred, in which the landscape merges seamlessly into moral, cultural and spiritual views of the world. The landscape constructed and experienced as 'the countryside' is no different.

Such a view of the landscape remains overwhelmingly White (and, paradoxically, urban: the 'country' is a construction of the city). As such, it raises difficult issues about what exactly one is celebrating with a walk in the countryside, issues which in the last decade have been debated as never before. These are issues I debate every day as I write and teach at an English university – and which I worry about as I scrape the mud off my boots at the end of another Sunday excursion.

Of course, these three approaches overlap and all have their uses today. But a progression can be charted, from the earliest field surveys, to studies of cosmology and phenomenology in the 1970s and 1980s, to landscape characterisation of the mid-1990s and beyond.

Summary

Providing any review of information in an active field of research runs the inevitable risk of being out of date at the time of publication. Even during the course of writing this book we have had to review this chapter several times, and even now, as we complete the text, new discoveries are being made, and new reviews presented. Ten years ago the first edition of *The Archaeology of Britain* was published (Hunter and Ralston, 1999). Now, a decade on and the second edition has appeared. Not only has the overall shape and scope of archaeology changed (there is now a chapter on 'The Modern Age' for example), but so too has the content, and the interpretation of our deeper past. Indeed a comparison of any two chapters on the same period between the two volumes will reveal just how much things have changed in that time. This lack of currency could be seen as a limitation, but it is also of course what makes archaeology so captivating, and such an exciting world to be involved with. We never know when a discovery will be made that either transforms our understanding, or reinforces a point, or causes us to re-examine long-held views and opinions. New finds are made, just as the values we ascribe to particular categories of artefact or place fluctuate. So, in reading this chapter, be aware that it was written, inevitably, at a particular point in time, and that the intervening period may have changed things somewhat. To keep up to date with new discoveries and developments, the Internet is always a good source (as such discoveries are inevitably these days news items – see Chap. 7), as are magazines like *Current Archaeology* and *British Archaeology*. The former is a long-standing subscription based magazine, while the latter can be purchased off the shelf. For readers in higher education, online journals such as *Antiquity* are also quick to produce new results, as are journals such as *Nature*.

Having completed what one of our tutors used to call the 'chronological gallop', we now turn our attention to how these archaeological resources (the places and things, and the information generated through fieldwork) should be managed. This too is a situation constantly in a state of flux, so as with the scope of this chapter, use the Internet to determine what has changed and why.

References and Further Reading

General

Bradley, R. 2007. *The Prehistory of Britain and Ireland*. Cambridge: Cambridge University Press.

Darvill, T. 1996 [1987]. *Prehistoric Britain*. London: Routledge.

Hunter, J. and Ralston, I. (eds) 1999. *The Archaeology of Britain: an introduction from the Upper Palaeolithic to the Industrial Revolution*. London, Routledge.

Hunter, J. and Ralston, I. (eds) 2009. *The Archaeology of Britain: an introduction from earliest times to the twenty-first century* (Second Edition). London: Routledge.

Pollard, J. (ed) 2008. *Prehistoric Britain* (Blackwell Studies in Global Archaeology). Oxford: Wiley-Blackwell.

Palaeolithic

Bahn, Paul G., Pettitt, P. and Ripoll, S. 2004. Discovery of Palaeolithic cave art in Britain. *Antiquity* online: http://antiquity.ac.uk/Ant/077/0227/Ant0770227.pdf (accessed 31 July 2007).
Binford, Lewis R. 1983. *In pursuit of the past: decoding the archaeological record*. London: Thames and Hudson.
Darvill, T. 1996 [1987]. *Prehistoric Britain*. London: Routledge.
Gamble, C.S. 1999. *The Palaeolithic Societies of Europe*. Cambridge: Cambridge University Press.
McNabb, J. 2007. *The British Lower Palaeolithic: Stones in Contention*. London: Routledge.
Parfitt, S. and Stringer, C. 2006. Pakefield: a weekend to remember. *British Archaeology* 86: 18–27.
Wymer, J.J. 1982. *The Palaeolithic Age*. London: Croom Helm.
Wymer, J.J. 1999. *The Lower Palaeolithic Occupation of Britain*. London: Wessex Archaeology and English Heritage.

Mesolithic

Barham, L., Priestley, P. and Targett, A. 1999. *In Search of Cheddar Man*. Stroud: Tempus.
Carter, R.J., 1998. Reassessment of Seasonality at the Early Mesolithic Site of Star Carr, Yorkshire Based on Radiographs of Mandibular Tooth Development in Red Deer (*Cervus elaphus*). *Journal of Archaeological Science* 25, 851–856.
Conneller, C. and Warren, G. (eds) 2006. Mesolithic Britain and Ireland: new approaches. Stroud: Tempus.
Darvill, T. 1996 [1987]. *Prehistoric Britain*. London: Routledge.
Legge, A. and Rowley-Conwy, P. 1988. *Star Carr Revisited*, Birkbeck College, London.
Schulting, R. and M. Wysocki 2005 'Pursuing a rabbit in Burrington Combe': New research on the Early Mesolithic burial cave of Aveline's Hole. *Proceedings of the University of Bristol Spelaeological Society* 23, 171–265. (2005).

Neolithic and Bronze Age

Ashmore, P. 1996. *Neolithic and Bronze Age Scotland*. London, Batsford.
Barclay, G. (ed.) 2008. *Defining a regional Neolithic: the evidence from Britain and Ireland*. Oxford, Oxbow.
Lawson, A. 2007. The nomads of ancient Wessex. *British Archaeology* 93: 28–34.
Malone, C. 2001. *Neolithic Britain and Ireland*. Stroud, Tempus.
Topping, P. (ed) 2000. *Neolithic Landscapes*. Oxford, Oxbow.

Iron Age

Champion, T. & Collis, J. R. (eds) 1996. *The Iron Age in Britain and Ireland : recent trends*. Sheffield, J. Collis.
Cunliffe, B. 1995. *English Heritage Book of Iron Age Britain*. London, Batsford.
Cunliffe, B. 2005. *Iron Age Communities in Britain: an account of England, Scotland and Wales from the seventh century BC until the Roman conquest*. 3rd ed. London, Routledge.

Roman

Jones, R. F. J. 1991. *Britain in the Roman period: recent trends.* Sheffield, J.R. Collis.

Millett, M. 1995. *English Heritage Book of Roman Britain.* London, Batsford.

Salway, P. 1981. *Roman Britain.* Oxford, Clarendon Press.

White, R. 2007. *Britannia Prima: Britain's last Roman Province.* Stroud, Tempus.

Post-Roman

Hills, C. 1999. Early Historic Britain. In Hunter, J. and Ralston, I. (eds) *The Archaeology of Britain: an introduction from the Upper Palaeolithic to the Industrial Revolution.* London, Routledge, 176–193.

Hunter, J. 2003. The Early Norse Period. In Edwards, K.J. and Ralston, I.B.M. (eds) *Scotland after the Ice Age: environment, archaeology and history, 8000 BC – AD 1000.* Edinburgh, Edinburgh University Press, 241–254.

Kerr, M. and Kerr, N. 1983. *Anglo Saxon Architecture.* Aylesbury, Shire Publications.

Ralston, I.B.M. and Armit,. I. 2003. The Early Historic Period: an archaeological perspective. In Edwards, K.J. and Ralston, I.B.M. (eds) *Scotland after the Ice Age: environment, archaeology and history, 8000 BC – AD 1000.* Edinburgh, Edinburgh University Press, 217–240.

Richards, J. D. 1999. The Scandinavian Presence. In Hunter, J. and Ralston, I. (eds) *The Archaeology of Britain: an intrioduction from the Upper Palaeolithic to the Industrial Revolution.* London, Routledge, 194–209.

Wilson, D.M. (ed.) 1976. *The Archaeology of Anglo-Saxon England.* Cambridge, Cambridge University Press.

Medieval

Gilchrist, R. 1999. Landscapes of the Middle Ages: churches, castles and monasteries. In Hunter, J. and Ralston, I. (eds) *The Archaeology of Britain: an introduction from the Upper Palaeolithic to the Industrial Revolution.* London, Routledge, 211–246.

Haslam. J. 1984. *Medieval Pottery.* Aylesbury, Shire Publications.

Schofield, J. 1999. Landscapes of the Middle Ages: towns 1050 to 1500. In Hunter, J. and Ralston, I. (eds) *The Archaeology of Britain: an introduction from the Upper Palaeolithic to the Industrial Revolution.* London, Routledge, 210–227.

Stamper, P. 1999. Landscapes of the Middle Ages: rural settlement and manors. In Hunter, J. and Ralston, I. (eds) *The Archaeology of Britain: an introduction from the Upper Palaeolithic to the Industrial Revolution.* London, Routledge, 247–263.

Yeoman, P. 1995. *Medieval Scotland: an archaeological perspective.* London, Batsford.

Post-Medieval and Industrial

Anon. 1967. Editorial. *Post-Medieval Archaeology 1*, 1–2.

Belford, P., forthcoming. *A Handbook of British Historical Archaeology, c.1500 to the present day.* York: Council for British Archaeology.

Casella, E. & Symonds, J. (eds) 2005. *Industrial Archaeology: future directions.* New York: Springer.

Cossons, N. 1987. *The BP Book of Industrial Archaeology.* Newton Abbott: David & Charles.

Cranstone, D. & Barker, D. (eds) 2004. *The Archaeology of Industrialization.* Society for Post-Medieval Archaeology Monograph 2, Leeds: Maney.

Crossley, D. 1994. *Post-Medieval Archaeology in Britain.* London: Leicester University Press.

Draper, J. 1984. *Post-medieval pottery.* Aylesbury, Shire Publications.

Finch, J. & Giles, K. (eds) 2008. *Estate Landscapes.* Society for Post-Medieval Archaeology Monograph 5, London: Boydell and Brewer.

Gaimster, D. & Stamper, P. (eds) 1997. *The Age of transition : the archaeology of English culture, 1400–1600.* Oxford: Oxbow.

Green, A. & Leech, R. (eds) 2006. *Cities in the World 1500–2000.* Society for Post-Medieval Archaeology Monograph 3, Leeds: Maney.

Gould, S. 1999. Planning, Development and Social Archaeology. In Tarlow, S. and West S. (eds) *The Familiar Past: archaeologies of later historical Britain.* London, Routledge, 140–154.

Horning, A. & Palmer, M. (eds) 2009. *Crossing Paths or Sharing Tracks? Future directions in the archaeological study of post-1550 Britain & Ireland.* Society for Post-Medieval Archaeology Monograph 6, London: Boydell and Brewer.

Hudson, K. 1967. *Handbook for Industrial Archaeologists.* London, John Baker.

Johnson, M.H. 1996. *An Archaeology of Capitalism.* Oxford, Blackwell.

Leone, M. 1995. *A historical archaeology of capitalism.* American Anthropologist 97, 251–68.

Leone, M. & Potter, P.B. (eds) 1999. *An Historical Archaeology of Capitalism.* New York, Kluwer/Plenum.

McAtackney, L., Palus, M. and Piccini, A. (eds), *Contemporary and Historical Archaeology in Theory: Papers from the 2003 and 2004 CHAT conferences.* Oxford: Archaeopress.

Palmer, M. 2004. The archaeology of industrialization: introduction. In Barker, D. and Cranstone, D. (eds) *The Archaeology of Industrialization. Society for Post-Medieval Archaeology 2.* Leeds, Maney, 1–4.

Palmer, M. & Neaverson, P. 1998. *Industrial archaeology: principles and practice.* London: Routledge.

Tarlow, S. & West. S. (eds) 1999. *The Familiar Past? Archaeologies of later historical Britain.* London, Routledge.

West, S. 1999. Introduction. In Tarlow, S. and West, S. (eds) *The Familiar Past: Archaeologies of Later Historic Britain.* London, Routledge, 1–15.

The 20th Century and Beyond

Cocroft, W.D. and Thomas, R.J.C. 2004. *Cold War: Building for nuclear confrontation, 1946–89.* London: English Heritage.

English Heritage 2007. *Conservation Bulletin: Modern Times.* English Heritage. www.english-heritage.org.uk/characterisation.

Graves-Brown, P. 2007. Concrete Islands. In McAtackney, L., Palus, M. and Piccini, A. (eds), *Contemporary and Historical Archaeology in Theory: Papers from the 2003 and 2004 CHAT conferences,* 75–82. Oxford: Archaeopress.

Harrison, R. and Schofield, J. 2010. *After Modernity: Archaeological Approaches to the Contemporary Past.* Oxford: Oxford University Press.

Penrose, S. 2007. *Images of Change: An Archaeology of the Contemporary English Landscape.* London: English Heritage.

www.changeandcreation.org

Maritime Landscapes

Finch, S., Gaffney, V. and Thomson, K. 2007. *Mapping Doggerland: The Mesolithic Landscapes of the Southern North Sea*. Oxford: Archaeopress.
Firth, A. 2006. The management of archaeology underwater. In Hunter, J. and Ralston, I. (eds), *Archaeological Resource Management in the UK: An Introduction*, 85–96. Sutton Publishing Ltd.
Seascapes project: http://www.english-heritage.org.uk/server/show/nav.8684
English Heritage's Maritime Archaeology Team and projects: http://www.english-heritage.org.uk/server/show/nav.1276
The Nautical Archaeology Society: http://www.nasportsmouth.org.uk/

Landscapes

Bowden, M. 1999. *Unravelling the landscape: an inquisitive approach to archaeology*. Stroud: RCHME/Tempus.
English Heritage, 2007. *Understanding the archaeology of landscapes: A guide to good recording practice*. London: English Heritage.
Fairclough, G. 2006. Our place in the landscape? An archaeologist's ideology of landscape perception and management. In Meier, T. (ed), *Landscape Ideologies*. Budapest.
Riley, H. and Wilson-North, R. 2001. *The field archaeology of Exmoor*. Swindon: English Heritage.

Chapter 4
Legal and Administrative Frameworks

An Historical Overview

There is the law; and then there is the lore

(Dennis Denyer, pers. comm., 1972)

This quotation, from the former employer of one of the authors, sums up the need to be aware of two elements in any field where there is a measure of legal regulation: the legislation itself and what it prescribes or proscribes, and the sets of less formal practices and principles that also determine how things should be done. In Britain, since the introduction of ancient monuments legislation in 1882, two systems have operated in parallel, whether enshrined in formal documentation or otherwise: a system of designation of sites worthy of some form of protection under specific laws; and a system whereby archaeologists have gained access to sites for the purposes of investigation.

Until the early twentieth century, all that was required to gain access to a monument or site for the purpose of archaeological investigation was the permission of the landowner. Indeed, most archaeological sites in Britain remain on private land and in private ownership. Artefacts found on a site are also the property of the landowner, with the very important exception of 'treasure' (see box below). In practice (particularly with planning-related fieldwork), an arrangement is nowadays usually made for finds to be transferred to the local museum. Legislation in 1913 created the categories of 'scheduled' and 'guardianship' sites, where responsibility for the management of the site lay with the State. Accordingly, any kind of intervention on these sites – research or otherwise – required express permission from the relevant Government authority. During the 1930s and 1940s, a system of granting permission to development schemes, rather than allowing them to proceed unchecked, also came into effect, placing controls on otherwise unrestricted building work. This system of controls remains largely in place, although the list of types of protected places has grown to encompass historic buildings (churches from 1913, other historic structures from 1944), specific (usually relict) landscapes (from 1949), shipwrecks (from 1973) and military wreck- and crash-sites (from 1979) (see below: 'Legislation Today'; see also Carman 1996, 97–115). In addition, specific arrangements for the management of sites have also altered (see below: 'Who Does What').

J. Schofield et al., *Archaeological Practice in Great Britain: A Heritage Handbook*,
World Archaeological Congress Cultural Heritage Manual Series,
DOI 10.1007/978-0-387-09453-3_4, © Springer Science+Business Media, LLC 2011

With massive government-sponsored rebuilding programmes consequent upon damage caused during, and the need for homes and other facilities following, the Second World War, archaeological teams or units were created to undertake work on specific projects, first in London, and subsequently elsewhere. Such 'Rescue' (or sometimes 'salvage') archaeology grew in importance as development projects became more widespread up to the 1970s and beyond. The responsible government department – until the 1970s, the Office of Works, subsequently the Department of the Environment, and thereafter English Heritage – employed archaeologists specifically to undertake such work, but without any legal requirement for archaeological intervention. This changed in the 1980s, with a move towards commercial developer-funding by private initiatives. After several iterations, legislation to protect archaeological monuments had become complicated and complex. A dispute over who should be responsible for a site in south London, where the remains of Shakespeare's *Rose* theatre had been uncovered then caused a minor crisis. The government refused to schedule the site under the protective legislation despite its recognition as nationally important, at least in part because of the amount of compensation that would then become due to the private developer (Biddle 1989), and the view that scheduling was unnecessary given the desired intent of everyone involved (including the developer) to preserve surviving remains intact beneath the new development. The result was a compromise over the remains, but also an effort to find a new way to protect archaeological remains during the planning and development process. As a consequence of this and other similar cases, and following long-running discussions within the heritage sector, Planning Policy Guidance Note 16 (PPG16) was adopted in 1990. PPG16 made archaeology a material factor to be taken into account in determining planning permission. PPG16 was a significant stage in the emerging practice of archaeological heritage management, transforming the discipline over the next two decades and increasing dramatically the number of contracting units and archaeological consultants who rely on these smaller contracts. Archaeology became more professional in the way it conducted its business, and conditions under which archaeologists work were improved.

PPG16 remained in force for 20 years, being replaced in March 2010 by Planning Policy Statement 5 (PPS5). PPS5 is a high-level strategic document, which is supported by more detailed practice guidance. Its title – 'Planning for the Historic Environment' – reflects the fact that it replaces both PPG16 (archaeology) and PPG15 (historic buildings), and provides a way of managing a wide range of 'heritage assets' as part of the planning process. In many ways, it follows PPG16 in outlining responsibilities for dealing with archaeological and other remains for curators and contractors alike.

Legislation Today

British legislation as it relates to the heritage is not a single codified body of law. Unlike the approach taken in some other countries (Carman in press), different types of object are treated differently under different bodies of law, some of which are summarised in Table 4.1. Here, portable antiquities, human remains, ancient monuments, buildings in use, historic landscapes, church and ecclesiastical buildings and historic and military wrecks all have laws that relate specifically to them. While in general the system of granting permission for development projects is treated as something distinct from actual heritage legislation, it too has a legislative base, and the protection given to historic buildings (so that they cannot be unnecessarily harmed or altered without appropriate permissions) derives from planning law.

The chief mechanisms for protecting the heritage are in the form of various designations, summarised in Table 4.2. Each of these has specific consequences for the object or site it is applied to enforceable by law. In general, the presumption is that the site or building remains undamaged or otherwise interfered with, although this varies with specifics (see 'Treasure Box' below). Guardianship monuments effectively become the property of the guardianship agency – either the State or a local authority – but other protected sites, such as scheduled sites, historic buildings, and landscapes, all remain

Table 4.1 Current British legislation by type of material

Material covered	Legislation/guidance and date
Portable antiquities	Treasure Act 1996
Monuments and archaeological sites	Ancient Monuments and Archaeological Areas Act 1979
	National Heritage Act 1980
	National Heritage Act 1983
	Planning Policy Statement 5: Planning for the Historic Environment 2010
Churches	Inspection of Churches Measure 1955
	Pastoral Measure 1968
	Redundant Churches and Other Religious Buildings Act 1969
	Cathedrals Measure 1990
Wrecks	Protection of Wrecks Act 1973
	National Heritage Act 2002
	Planning Policy Statement 5: Planning for the Historic Environment 2010
Human remains and military aircraft crash sites	Coroners Act 1980
	Protection of Military Remains Act 1986
	Human Tissue Act 2004
	Planning Policy Statement 5: Planning for the Historic Environment 2010
Buildings in Use	Planning (Listed Buildings and Conservation Areas) Act 1990
	Planning Policy Statement 5: Planning for the Historic Environment 2010
Landscapes	National Parks and Access to the Countryside Act 1949
	Countryside Act 1968
	Countryside and Rights of Way Act 2000
	Planning Policy Statement 5: Planning for the Historic Environment 2010

Table 4.2 Main types of designation

Material covered	Designation	Effect of designation
Portable antiquities	Treasure	Ownership by state
Monuments	Scheduling	Introduction of prior consent procedures (scheduled monument consent, or SMC), to control works, and protect sites from unnecessary damage
	Guardianship	State control for public access
Landscapes	National park	(All)
	Heritage coast	Controls (through planning system mainly) to minimise unnecessary or needless change of character
	Registered battlefields	
	Registered parks and gardens	
	Conservation area	
Buildings	Listing	Introduction of consent procedures (listed building consent, or LBC – various dependent on grade), to control works and protect buildings from unnecessary damage/alteration
Churches	Redundant church	Protection from decay, inappropriate change of use
Wrecks, military aircraft crash sites	Protected wreck	(All)
	Controlled site	Protection from unsolicited interference

the property of the private owner who is required not to cause them damage without obtaining prior consent from the Secretary of State (though these powers are currently transferring to English Heritage in England). Wrecks and military aircraft crash sites are given protection from any kind of interference by anyone without appropriate authority.

Treasure

The idea that some artefacts are 'treasure' is a very old one, and it could be said that the law of 'treasure trove' was the first archaeological legislation. Treasure trove was an idea which emerged in the Middle Ages (the word 'trove' is derived from the mediaeval French word meaning 'found'). Under common law, treasure trove was defined as an object (or objects) containing more than 50% gold or silver, and which had been hidden with the intention of later being recovered. Such objects belonged to the state, and had to be declared to the Coroner who would hold an inquiry to determine whether or not they were indeed treasure trove. In theory, if the person who had hidden it (or their descendants) subsequently came to light, they could claim it back. If it was found not to be treasure trove, it was returned to the landowner. Many archaeological finds found their way into the British Museum under this arrangement. However, it was not a perfect system: the famous ship burial at Sutton Hoo (excavated in 1939) was found not to be treasure trove because there was no intention on the part of the owner to later recover the artefacts (although it was subsequently donated to the British Museum). In a well-known case in the 1980s, a metal-detector find of over 7,000 Roman coins was declared not to be treasure trove since the silver content was too low; as a result, the finds were retained by the landowner (Bland 1996).

In 1996, the law for England and Wales was overhauled (although Scotland still retains a system of treasure trove) in the *Treasure Act*. This defines treasure as any prehistoric object of gold or silver, or any later metal object (up to 300 years old) with more than 10% gold or silver content. It also includes groups of objects – such as coins in hoards or votive deposits. It is still the responsibility of the finder to declare such items to the Coroner for a decision to be made. Failure to report the finding of treasure is a crime, but finders who do report it can be rewarded with payment to the equivalent amount they would have received on selling the items. In parallel with the Treasure Act, the Portable Antiquities Scheme (http://www.finds.org.uk/index.php) was set up to encourage metal-detectorists and others to report all finds (not just treasure). This has since proved immensely successful at improving the record of such 'unofficial' discoveries, and many important artefacts have been discovered, catalogued and conserved as a result of the scheme.

A recent example was the 'Staffordshire Hoard' (Fig. 4.1), which was discovered in 2009 by a metal detectorist, and correctly declared by him to the authorities. The site was subsequently excavated under the supervision of English Heritage, and the finder and the farmer on whose land it was found were compensated for the value of the find (over £3 million), which is now in the British Museum.

Fig. 4.1 The Staffordshire hoard was discovered by a metal-detectorist in July 2009, who reported it to the Portable Antiqities Scheme. This important find of Anglo-Saxon objects was subsequently excavated by Birmingham University Field Archaeology Unit and Staffordshire County Council, and conserved at the British Museum. (Photo: courtesy of the Staffordshire Hoard Partnership)

Table 4.2 uses the term 'protection' to describe the effect of designation, but in fact that acts as a short-hand for a more complex arrangement, whereby the state is concerned with preventing unnecessary or inappropriate change. Having a site designated does not necessarily mean it cannot be altered. Rather, the effect is to introduce a set of consent procedures, whereby the owners must apply for prior consent for any changes, consent which may be granted or refused depending on its effects and the merits of the scheme proposed. The idea is to manage change, to ensure that sites and monuments remain in viable use.

Two regulations in particular apply to cultural objects, both created beyond Britain's borders in 1992, although grounded in earlier British law. Where a transfer is made illegally from one member state of the European Union (EU; see above: Chap. 1; and below: 'Great Britain in Europe') to another, an EU Regulation on the return of cultural objects requires its return. Where an object is in the course of transfer outside the EU, a Directive which places limits on the export of cultural property (and any national legislation of the exporting country deriving from it) applies. Since, however, it is the individual member state which has the responsibility for taking action, the possibility arises of the export from the EU of a heritage object valued as such by its country of origin but not by the country in which it presently resides. Only if the item has been transferred illegally from its country of origin will there be any provision for its retention in Britain.

Who Does What?

Archaeology and cultural heritage management in Britain can perhaps be best understood by explaining who does what and why. There is no particular order that makes greater sense of this, but one way is to begin with the planning system where arguably the majority of the work is done, then turn to the state, state heritage officials, and other national bodies and agencies and then deal in turn with the precise nature of the work of: local authority archaeologists (curators), contractors, consultants and clients ('the four Cs'); museums; the higher education (HE) sector; and finally (but definitely not least) amateur archaeologists and enthusiasts. In some cases, text boxes allow others to describe their roles and responsibilities first hand.

The Planning System

How 'the best of the past' is accommodated in planning for the future has been a central feature of the planning system in Britain for some years. The publication of PPG16 in 1990 introduced the 'polluter pays' principle to the historic environment. (see below). Effectively, from this time and for the first time with any teeth, archaeological remains could be protected in ways other than through statutory protection. The general principle that heritage matters was extended in a later PPG (15: The Historic Environment, published in 1994) to the historic environment as a whole. Both the 'polluter pays' principle and the concept of a holistic 'historic environment' have subsequently been enshrined in PPS5 ('Planning for the Historic Environment'), which replaced PPG15 and PPG16 in March 2010.

In short, if remains are considered to be of national importance, then the presumption should be for in situ preservation, whether the remains had statutory protection through scheduling or not. Assets, which are protected (or 'designated'), are given the highest priority for protection: substantial harm to, or loss of, any designated asset should be exceptional, and to those of the highest significance (such as scheduled monuments, protected wreck sites, battlefields, Grade I and II* listed buildings, Grade I and II* parks and gardens and World Heritage Sites) should be 'wholly exceptional' (PPS5 2010, HE9.2).

So how does this work in practice? Simply, if construction or other significant works are proposed, a planning application is submitted for consideration by the local planning authority. If the site has a historic or heritage dimension (archaeology, buildings or other features – known now in some circles as 'heritage assets'), then this is a material consideration in the decision as to whether or not to grant permission. If the location of the planning application coincides with a heritage asset, then the response will partly depend on the designated status of the site. Sites designated by listing or scheduling have a record on the local Historic Environment Record (HER, see 'Curators' below) enabling the local authority archaeologist to provide an appropriate response. If the location is one with known nationally important remains, then as a matter of principle, permission may well be refused, or at least granted with conditions that would minimise damage to archaeological remains on the site. Where there is insufficient information to make an informed decision, an evaluation is likely to be required to establish the extent, character and quality of surviving remains. Some form of mitigation may be required to allow development to proceed in a way that provides some protection for buried remains. The need for such mitigation is decided on the basis of a site's significance, and PPS5 (for England and Wales) notes that 'there are many heritage assets with archaeological interest that are not currently designated…but which are demonstrably of equivalent significance' (PPS5 2010, HE9.6). The definition of significance in PPS5 is quite broad so that the architectural or academic importance of the site is not the only consideration – its significance to the local community or to the wider environment needs also to be taken into account.

If a proposal is submitted for an area where no archaeological remains are known, the historic environment team will draw on their professional judgement, based on experience and knowledge of the area. They might ask, for example, is this a place where we might expect archaeological remains to be found, or are there other grounds for conducting archaeological survey in advance of determining the application? In addition to archaeological remains, some planning applications may affect conservation areas or the fabric or setting of listed buildings. Again in these cases, there is often a presumption against development.

If the loss of all or a significant part of a heritage asset is unavoidable, the polluter pays principle requires the developer to 'record and advance understanding of the significance of the heritage asset before it is lost' (PPS5 2010, HE12.2). This rather broad requirement for 'preservation by understanding' replaced the rather narrow definition in PPG16 for specifically archaeological excavation and post-excavation analysis. This requirement in PPS5 is supported by several pages of guidance in the Planning Practice Guide, which set out the policy principles, scope and mechanisms by which archaeological work can be undertaken – including guidance on quality control and project management.

These procedures represent a reactive response to specific applications that may impact upon the historic environment. The wider strategic planning framework is more proactive: plans are formulated, put out to wider consultation and then enacted by local authorities over a fixed period, often say 10 years. The Planning and Compensation Act 1991 clarified the importance of these 'development plans' by stating a presumption of granting permission for proposals that conform to their policies. Thus, most of these development plans should include a mechanism for ensuring that the historic environment is at least taken account of when considering site-specific issues. It is important to note that a new planning system has recently been introduced in England and Wales, operating at three levels: Nationally, through policies set out by Government in PPGs and PPSs; Regionally through Planning Bodies who prepare Regional Spatial Strategies (RSS) reflecting needs and aspirations for development; and Locally, with local authorities producing Local Development Frameworks which comprise a folder of documents concerning local delivery of the RSS. Unlike in the previous system, this folder must include a Statement of Community Involvement, describing how local communities will be involved in the process of plan- and therefore place-making. This replaces the previous system of Structure and Local Plans. A similar system exists in Scotland, although this is also undergoing change.

The main role of a local authority archaeologist, and the wider conservation team within local authority areas, is finding a balance between curating archaeological resources and the historic environment from the past and allowing and encouraging appropriate change in the future. With the scale and pace of new development, services are often stretched meaning that other key functions, such as public outreach, become difficult to perform. Many historic environment records are now accessible online, however, meaning that individual records at least can be interrogated by researchers and local enthusiasts at an early stage in the process (as we see in Chap. 5).

The State and National Bodies

The State performs a particular and significant role in managing the heritage in Britain, including its archaeological remains, and has done since the later nineteenth century when the first ancient monuments legislation was passed. England,

Scotland and Wales all have robust legislative systems which ensure that selected sites and places have protection in law. These legislative systems are essentially the same and all include provision to 'list' buildings of historic interest, 'schedule' monuments of national importance and – in England and Wales at least – to create registers of battlefields and parks and gardens of historic interest. Wales also has a historic landscapes register. We will now consider listing and scheduling in more detail.

Listing

Listing was introduced immediately after the Second World War, initially to protect war damaged historic buildings from needless demolition, as towns were redesigned and rebuilt. The current system allows listing at one of the several grades: I, II* and II in England and Wales, A, B, B (Group) and C (Statutory) in Scotland. England has over 370,000 entries covering some 500,000 individual listed properties or structures; there are over 47,000 listed buildings in Scotland and 30,000 in Wales (Fig. 4.2). In England, all buildings earlier than 1700 are listed, as well as most dating between 1700 and 1840. After that date, there is greater selection, given that higher proportions of historic buildings survive. There is also provision for listing some later twentieth-century buildings, though given their recent date and the fact that selections are typically based only on architectural merit, these listings are

Fig. 4.2 Listed buildings range from large palaces and castles to smaller and more humble dwellings, such as these 17th to 19th century cottages and former pub. (Photo: Paul Belford)

often controversial. A building has to be over 10 years old to be eligible for listing. Listing in England and Wales is possible under the *Planning (Listed Buildings and Conservation Areas) Act 1990*; in Scotland, the equivalent is the *Planning (Listed Buildings and Conservation Areas) (Scotland) Act 1997*. These Acts are then supplemented by government advice, including in England, *Planning Policy Statement (PPS) 5: Planning for the Historic Environment*; in Wales *Circulars 61/96 and 1/98, Planning and the Historic Environment*; and in Scotland the *Memorandum of Guidance on Listed Buildings and Conservation Areas* and *National Planning Policy Guideline 18: Planning and the Historic Environment*. It is important to stress that listing is mandatory: if a building meets the criteria, the Secretary of State must list it.

Scheduling

Scheduling has its origins in the first ancient monuments legislation in 1882 following efforts by John Lubbock (see Chap. 2). The law has been amended and updated several times since with the most recent iteration being the *Ancient Monuments and Archaeological Areas Act 1979*. 'The Schedule' of ancient monuments is simply a list of scheduled sites, that is sites that have legal protection as monuments by virtue of their national importance. Definition of importance has been formalised since the mid-1980s through assessment according to a series of criteria (see below), but this was previously based more on professional judgement. Currently, there are some 17,500 scheduled monuments in England, 8,000 in Scotland and 4,000 in Wales; the scheduled area may often include more than one 'site' in the conventional sense, so perhaps more than 50,000 individual items are protected in this way.

For an archaeological site to qualify for scheduling, it must first pass three 'tests':

1. That the site is a 'monument' in the terms of the 1979 Ancient Monuments and Archaeological Areas Act.
   The Act defines a monument as 'any building, structure or work ... or the remains thereof'; it can also include 'any site comprising, or comprising the remains of, any vehicle, vessel, aircraft or other moveable structure'. (See Carman 1996 or Breeze 2006 for a full definition and discussion.)
2. The monument must be of national importance.
   The criteria for judging national importance are set out in PPG16 for England (although technically superseded by the publication of PPS5) and Welsh Office Circular 60/96 for Wales while in Scotland the Ancient Monuments Board set out advice and a definition. The criteria refer to survival, archaeological potential, group value, rarity and so on.
3. That scheduling is an appropriate means for protecting the site.
   Unlike listing, scheduling is at the discretion of the Secretary of State and brings with it the implication that the monument remains out of everyday use. Like listing, scheduling is accompanied by stringent consent procedures. Where a nationally important monument would benefit from being brought back into use (a former

barn or airfield building for which conversion seems appropriate) scheduling may not be appropriate. Of course, in the case of a barn it may be listed anyway, depending on its date and significance. It is under these circumstances in particular that a site may be of national importance but not scheduled. It may also be because the site is not a monument, in the case of a flint scatter for example (at least under the present definition). As we have seen, the decision was made not to schedule the Rose Theatre, despite its national importance and its clear status as a monument.

Overlap

The overlap between listing and scheduling can cause confusion, but as we have seen, there are two clear distinctions. First, listing is mandatory and scheduling discretionary. In other words, if a building meets the criteria and is of special architectural or historic interest, the Secretary of State *must* list it; if a monument is of national importance, then the Secretary of State *may* schedule it. Second, listing tends to assume buildings remain in use; scheduling on the other hand tends to be confined to monuments whose future is as monuments in the conventional sense, typically out of everyday use. Key here is the consent procedure that designation brings into play. Where a site or building is designated, the owner must obtain prior consent for any works. At the time of writing, Listed Building Consent is a matter for the local authority for the great majority of listed buildings (Grade II), and by the Secretary of State (advised by the state agency) for Grade II* and I listed buildings (but advised by English Heritage). The degree of acceptable change and alteration depends largely on grade: controls for a Grade I building are far more stringent than for Grade II. Scheduled Monument Consent is always a matter for the state agency and the Secretary of State. As with Listed Building Consent, the owner applies to the Secretary of State who then seeks expert advice, from English Heritage for example. To add to the confusion, some sites are covered by both systems. This is because listing is mandatory and scheduling is discretionary. So, if the management regime afforded by scheduling is deemed more appropriate for an historic (and listed) building, then the site may well have both forms of protection. Because scheduling is the older designation, and because its controls are more robust, this takes precedence over listing.

So What Do Staff in the National Agencies Actually Do?

Many staff within the national heritage agencies work in regional 'casework' teams, where their duties include providing advice to owners and occupiers of listed buildings and scheduled monuments. For English Heritage, these casework teams include ancient monuments and historic building inspectors, historic environment field advisors (previously field monument wardens), conservation architects and historic area advisors. In addition, each regional team has policy advisors and members of the national heritage protection team. The national agencies also provide funding for research and conservation projects, usually determined according to national research frameworks and strategies that determine corporate and sometimes sector-wide priorities. There is also a central policy team that works with government and other agencies on some of the bigger issues, such as renewable energy, sustainable housing, agriculture, urban regeneration, climate change and so on. On 1 April 1999, English Heritage merged with the Royal Commission on the Historic Monuments of England (RCHME), with its survey teams and expertise, aerial photography and National Monuments Record (NMR). In Scotland and Wales, the Royal Commissions still exist as separate bodies. English Heritage maintains England's NMR, a vast archive of archaeological and historic building records, a national excavation archive, aerial photographs and much besides. There are survey teams and aerial photographic interpretation teams, data management and data standards teams and cataloguers who input data onto the Record, an abbreviated version of which can be accessed online at http://www.pastscape.org.uk. English Heritage also administered the recently cancelled Aggregates Levy Sustainability Fund, basically a tax on extractive industries that was available for archaeological research within these particular areas. The Fund had been available since 2002 during which time £24 million was spent on about 100 new projects each year, including surveys, excavations and conservation work. There are over 400 properties that English Heritage manages itself, for which staff act as custodians and researchers.

Much of the same framework applies to the other state agencies, albeit on a smaller scale. In Wales, these duties are undertaken by Cadw, and in Scotland by Historic Scotland. In short, the national heritage agencies have much in common and all share statutory duties to promote enjoyment of the historic environment and its understanding; and to protect those parts of it deemed to have particular significance. Everyone employed by the heritage agencies works to this broad agenda.

What an Inspector Does?

Jon Humble (English Heritage)

As an Inspector of Ancient Monuments, my duties are in the counties of Derbyshire, Leicestershire and Nottinghamshire in the East Midlands. From lowland river valleys to the uplands of the Peak District, the area is very diverse.

Any works to the 816 scheduled monuments in this area require the pemission (scheduled monument consent) of the Department for Culture, Media and Sport – and in discussion with the applicant, it is my job to examine their proposals, draft consent letters, and if consent is forthcoming, to ensure compliance with consent conditions. Another major responsibility is the provision of advice to local authorities on planning matters that affect scheduled monuments and their settings.

Monuments at risk from decay, damage or loss are prioritised for attention and advice to landowners on good conservation management is a key duty. Inspectors and the Historic Environment Field Advisors they manage are experts in heritage conservation and are conversant with the sources of English Heritage and other grant-aid [e.g. Heritage Lottery Fund (HLF)] for undertaking repairs, maintenance, site presentation, and importantly, for incentivising benign land use. Unfortunately, sometimes we have to investigate unauthorised works and activities on scheduled monuments, such as illicit metal-detecting.

Inspectors work closely with local authority archaeologists, contractors, consultants, universities, museums, heritage trusts, the voluntary sector and the many organisations that are involved with land management (e.g. Defra, Natural England) – to ensure that heritage matters are given due consideration alongside other interests, such as nature conservation. Increasingly, we work strategically with other disciplines so that the management of archaeological sites and historic landscapes is tackled thematically – by land use type (e.g. arable cultivation), by geographical area (e.g. the Trent Valley) or by type of site (e.g. the remains of former lead mining).

Good conservation requires good understanding of what makes places special and important, and how they can be affected by change. Archaeological assessment, survey and excavation are fundamental to gaining understanding, and identifying the opportunities for archaeological investigations is another vital component of what we do.

There is always much to do – and much more that could be done. Communicating with people about what, how and why we do it – be it via a published document, the internet or the press, an international conference or a village hall – is essential for promoting enjoyment and appreciation of heritage, and ultimately, for winning a popular and political mandate.

The Decline of State Authority

Recently, a strong case has been argued for the declining influence of state authority in British archaeology. As Roger M Thomas (2008) suggests, people today are less ready to accept the authorised view of the archaeological past, preferring to choose for themselves what sort of past they wish to believe in. We have already seen how heritage decisions are taken by the state, decisions over which the public often have no right to appeal, a system that has existed since the Victorian period.

The extension of market principles into many aspects of British life is key. Generally speaking, consumers now have more choice than before. As recently as 1979, Thomas explains, the public utilities, telecommunications and public transport were almost entirely provided by state monopolies. Now, they are provided by private companies with the notion of consumer choice heavily promoted. Another area of choice has been what people think. There is now a much greater plurality of ideas, interests and belief systems than there was before. And then there is the historic environment. A MORI opinion poll in 2000 (described earlier) showed how different groups of people now wish to create their own histories and heritage rather than simply accept the 'official' one (English Heritage 2000).

The implications of this could be far-reaching – not only in Britain but also globally. The role of the state archaeological or heritage official in the twenty-first century could change, becoming one of guide and facilitator, rather than an authority figure, engaging and building a dialogue with local groups rather than being aloof from them; and helping to empower those groups, giving them tools and guidance to pursue their own explorations of the past.

The National Trust and National Trust for Scotland

The National Trust (and National Trust for Scotland) differs from English Heritage, Cadw and Historic Scotland in being a charity, not a statutory advisor. It protects and opens to the public over 300 historic houses and gardens and about 50 industrial monuments and mills. It also manages and makes accessible vast areas of forest, woodland, fen, beaches and farmland in perpetuity. The National Trust has some 3.5 million members and 43,000 volunteers. More than 12 million people a year visit the National Trust's pay-for-entry properties while an estimated 50 million visit open air properties, such as areas of coastline. Like English Heritage, the National Trust employs archaeologists and historic building experts to advise on the conservation challenges of their estate.

Heritage and the National Trust: A Personal View

Guy Salkeld (National Trust)

The National Trust exists to protect and promote places of historic interest or natural beauty for ever for everyone. It is the largest private owner of archaeological sites, structures and landscapes in Britain: many of these are of national importance, and six sites have World Heritage status. At the time of writing, the National Trust is responsible for 250,000 ha of land, 700 miles of coastline, thousands of buildings and gardens, and approximately 47,000 monuments, of which 1,100 are scheduled. The Trust maintains a small team of regionally based archaeologists to provide expert advice on the management of this extensive resource. Historic and natural landscapes undergo continuing processes of change, and the Trust's definition of 'Conservation' includes the careful management of such change. It is about revealing and sharing the significance of places and ensuring that their special qualities are protected, enhanced, understood and enjoyed by present and future generations.

We understand the significance of our sites by carrying out surveys of all our properties. These include vernacular building, garden, historic landscape, and industrial archaeology surveys which are increasingly undertaken by contracting units to briefs specified by the Trust. Our understanding of the resource is aided by the preparation of a national inventory, the National Trust Sites and Monuments Record. The Trust manages the resource by working with property and regional staff and other advisors to implement any action required. It also promotes access to sites, where appropriate, for the benefit of the public, and promotes the educational value of sites for people of all ages.

It is a privilege to work with the archaeology for its own sake, rather than under the developer-funded imperative of preservation by record. However, the Archaeology Section does not operate in isolation and the advice it gives feeds into a holistic approach to land management and the maintenance of sustainable communities. This philosophy combines other disciplines, such as nature conservation, agriculture and forestry and challenging issues, often arise which mirror those faced by national curatorial agencies. The Trust is exceptionally well placed to respond in innovative ways, such as the reinstatement of habitats removed during renovation of silted ornamental lakes in historic designed parklands.

National Trust archaeologists are primarily curators, but the nature of the Trust means that they also need to be consultants, specialists and community practitioners: for anyone who likes to experience all aspects of archaeology, this is a great place to work. The National Trust is unique, quirky and extraordinary – it carries the message of its Victorian founders down to the present day and its staff are genuinely entitled to claim that they make a difference – I love it!

The Heritage Lottery Fund (HLF)

The HLF was established in 1994 to provide a means of distributing the funds raised by the UK National Lottery to 'heritage' causes. Since then the HLF has awarded over £3.97 billion to more than 26,000 projects across England, Scotland, Wales and Northern Ireland, enabling communities to celebrate, look after and learn more about Britain's heritage. The HLF funds the entire spread of heritage – including buildings, museums, natural heritage and the heritage of cultural traditions and language. Officially, HLF is a 'non-departmental public body', meaning that, although not a government department, the Secretary of State for Culture, Media and Sport issues financial directions and reports to Parliament through the department. However, decisions about individual applications and policies are entirely independent. In its early years, the HLF made substantial grants to existing institutions to repair buildings, improve collections or undertake conservation work.

While this continues, the more recent emphasis has been on encouraging local groups to develop understanding and enjoyment of their own heritage – and improving access for non-traditional audiences of 'heritage'. HLF grants often provide match funding for money from other sources.

HLF is administered by the Trustees of the National Heritage Memorial Fund (NHMF) which allocates around £10 million per year to heritage, acting as a fund of 'last resort'. However, in recent years questions have been asked about how much the 'last resort' might encourage core funding to be cut back; and the use of lottery funds to support the London Olympics in 2012 has impacted on the amount of money available to heritage organisations and projects.

Natural England, Scottish Natural Heritage and the Countryside Council for Wales

In addition to organisations and agencies that deal specifically with cultural heritage, there are those that deal with the landscape more generally, as both a natural and cultural phenomenon. As with English Heritage, Cadw and Historic Scotland, the natural environment is served by statutory bodies which enable conservation, research and access to the wider landscape. Natural England was launched on 2 October 2006 and brought together the environment activities of the Rural Development Service, English Nature and the Countryside Agency's Landscape, Access and Recreation division. Scottish Natural Heritage performs a similar role in Scotland, and the Countryside Council for Wales is the Government's statutory advisor in Wales.

These organisations deliver the Government's programme of financial incentives to farmers and land managers for the protection and enhancement of the natural environment. Environmental Stewardship schemes provide resources for farmers to follow more traditional farming methods that enhance the landscape, encourage wildlife and protect historic features. Natural England includes archaeologists on its staff, and, like its Scottish and Welsh counterparts, will require and commission archaeological and historic environment work where needed as part of broader conservation programmes.

Many areas of Britain are protected in National Parks, Areas of Outstanding Natural Beauty (AONBs), Sites of Special Scientific Interest (SSSIs) and other designated areas, and the condition of the very best wildlife sites is slowly improving as a result. However, many areas of landscape are continuing to lose their ecological richness and their distinctive character. These are all issues Natural England, the Countryside Council for Wales and Scottish Natural Heritage continue to deal with.

National Parks are extensive areas of land, each with their own managing authority to conserve and enhance their natural beauty, wildlife and cultural heritage and to promote opportunities for the understanding and enjoyment of their special qualities. The first National Park in Britain was the Peak District, designated in 1949 under the then new *National Parks and Access to the Countryside Act*.

There are now 14 National Parks in Britain plus the Norfolk and Suffolk Broads, which has equivalent status; the nine National Parks in England account for 8% of its land area. Although receiving 110 million visitors every year, the parks are living and working landscapes with an increasing focus on supporting communities and economic activity. National Parks typically contain a diverse range of archaeological sites which have often been subject to detailed survey. Almost all of the National Parks have at least one archaeologist employed to advise on planning matters, conservation and research; many have a small team which undertakes a wide range of outreach work as well.

SSSIs have statutory protection as wildlife and geological sites. There are over 4,000 SSSIs in England, covering around 7% of the country's land area. They include some of England's most spectacular and beautiful habitats – wetlands teeming with waders and waterfowl, chalkland rivers, gorse and heathlands, flower-rich meadows, shingle beaches and remote moorland and peat bogs. SSSIs support rare plants and animals that now find it difficult to survive in the wider countryside. Marine areas are not normally notified as SSSIs, except in intertidal areas and estuaries. Over half of this SSSI land is also internationally important for its wildlife. Many SSSIs have also been given subsidiary designations, such as:

- *Special Areas of Conservation* (SACs), areas which have been given special protection under the European Union's Habitats Directive. England's SACs include areas which cover marine as well as terrestrial habitats.
- *National Nature Reserves* (NNRs) which have been established to protect and manage features of national and often international importance. As well as being important places for scientific study and research, most NNRs are also open to the public all year round. There are 222 of these reserves, covering over 92,000 ha. At present, there is one Marine Nature Reserve (MNR) in England, at Lundy (Devon). There are also over 1,400 *Local Nature Reserves* (LNRs) which provide living green spaces in towns, cities, villages and countryside important to people, and support a rich variety of wildlife.
- AONBs have been described as the jewels of the English landscape. There are over 35 in all, covering about 15% of England – ranging from the Cotswolds at 2,038 km^2 to the Isles of Scilly at 16 km^2. Areas are designated for their landscape qualities for the purpose of conserving and enhancing their natural beauty, which in many cases includes elements of cultural heritage as well.

England has many popular coastal resorts for those who enjoy the hustle and bustle of seaside towns. Around a third of the coastline of England (1,057 km) and Wales (500 km) is designated as *Heritage Coast*. These special coastlines are managed so that their natural beauty is conserved and, where appropriate, the accessibility for visitors is improved. The first Heritage Coast to be defined was the famous white chalk cliffs of Beachy Head (East Sussex), the latest the Durham Coast. In 2001, the 'Jurassic Coast' of Dorset and East Devon was designated a World Heritage Site by UNESCO, the first natural World Heritage Site in England.

Council for British Archaeology (CBA)

The CBA was founded in 1944 and emerged from the Congress of Archaeological Societies established in 1898 (see Chap. 1). Aware of the enormous task of post-war rebuilding that was imminent, the CBA sought to find ways in which archaeological work could be integrated into the new post-war Britain. Since then the CBA has developed as one of the leading voices in British archaeology, and works as an educational charity throughout the UK involving a wide range of people. Its main aim is to involve people in archaeology and to promote the appreciation and care of the historic environment. The CBA now has over 10,000 members and promotes public enjoyment through corporate and individual membership, regional groups that remain active in the fields of archaeology and conservation, its magazine *British Archaeology*, and the Young Archaeologists Club. The CBA also organises an annual National Archaeology Week, which is a national festival of archaeology that aims to encourage young people and their families to visit sites of archaeological/historical interest or museums, heritage and resource centres, to see archaeology in action and to take part in archaeological activities.

The CBA is also a campaigning body, regularly providing informed comment and critique, for example over proposals to improve visitor facilities and the landscape around Stonehenge. The CBA also gives small grants for research and publishes a series of research reports, as well as producing a series of Handbooks on practical aspects of archaeological method – from building recording to the analysis of human remains. It has also undertaken or facilitated research and fieldwork projects, notably from 1995 to 2002, the Defence of Britain project creating, with funding from the HLF, a national database of Britain's Second World War antiinvasion defences.

The Four C's: Curators, Contractors, Consultants and Clients

As outlined in Chap. 2, archaeology in Britain has moved from a position where the majority of work was undertaken by interested amateurs, whether individually or as part of established groups, to one where most archaeology is now undertaken as part of development control in the planning process. More than 50% of all archaeologists work in the private sector, acting to 'mitigate' the effect of development work on the historic environment. The requirement to undertake this work is based on the 'polluter pays' principle. This is a simple idea derived from environmental principles: those who do damage to or otherwise pollute the environment should pay the costs of repairing the harm they have caused. The same principle is applicable for the factory owners who poison rivers or the air. They are required to clean the water or air they have polluted and compensate those to whom they have done harm and ensure that such harm is not caused again.

Archaeology is part of our common shared heritage. Particular material remains of the past cannot be restored once destroyed. Modern processes of agriculture and of construction inevitably cause destruction to the archaeological heritage that belongs to us all. Accordingly, the developer is required to pay to ensure that any archaeological remains destroyed by their work are at least investigated prior to their total loss. In practice, the costs of archaeological work are a minimal part of the total costs of a major building project and are merely accepted as part of the overall costs of development work. The work to investigate archaeological remains prior to destruction is referred to as 'preservation by record' or 'by understanding', to distinguish it from 'preservation in situ'.

The overall range of scope of such work is specified and monitored by local planning authorities (curators), it might be designed and audited by consultants, it is undertaken by contractors and it is paid for by clients (the developers). These are the four C's of modern British archaeology.

The Rise of Commercial Archaeology

The commercial unit is a product of the 1980s: before that, none existed (although see Everill 2006 for an argument about the long history of the professional 'digger'). Large-scale development required large-scale archaeological teams to investigate and where necessary to mitigate the effect of construction on the archaeological record. At first, the costs were borne by central and local government as part of its remit to protect our cultural heritage, but rising costs and an increasing unwillingness on the part of government to support such work led to a desire to apply free-market principles. A recognition that the costs of mitigating damage to the heritage should be borne by those causing the damage placed the financial burden on developers, who could then legitimately claim the right to choose the contractors who would work on their behalf. An element of competition was introduced whereby rival groups of archaeologists, rather than a single central body, would bid for contracts, in theory overseen by local authorities to ensure proper standards were maintained. Changes in the management of local authority provision, in part driven by the political ideology of the then government, in part by initiatives from Europe, led to local authority units being disbanded or made independent, so they could compete in an open marketplace (Fig. 4.3).

Today, each region has several units that bid to undertake work locally and further afield. Large units can have significant international reputations; smaller units may specialise in particular types of work or operate over a more restricted area where they can offer expertise. After a period of rapid expansion during the 1990s and early 2000s, the market has now matured. There are a handful of very large players – Oxford Archaeology, Wessex Archaeology, Pre-Construct Archaeology (PCA) and Museum of London Archaeology (MOLA) predominant among them. Many of these have regional outposts away from their traditional core of operations: Oxford acquired the former

Fig. 4.3 This is a typical large-scale commercial excavation, undertaken as part of the planning process. This project investigated a post-medieval forge in Wednesbury, in the English west midlands. (Photo: Adam Stanford)

Lancaster University unit in the 1990s, which became 'Oxford North', and more recently took on the Cambridgeshire County Council unit ('Oxford East'). Similarly, Wessex Archaeology now has offices in London, Sheffield and Glasgow. Sometimes, large infrastructure projects are too much even for one of the larger units. Oxford and Wessex have teamed up on several occasions for such work. This began with their work for the British Airports Authority (BAA) at Heathrow Terminal 5, and later Stanstead airport, where they set up a partnership called Framework Archaeology. This joint venture enabled Framework Archaeology to draw on the full resources of both Oxford Archaeology and Wessex Archaeology, including site staff, specialist managers, administrative support and technical facilities. The size and scale of the project enabled Framework Archaeology to develop a particular archaeological philosophy concerned with understanding how people inhabited past landscapes: archaeology as a study of people rather than deposits or objects. Other consortia have included a separate partnership between Oxford and Wessex to deal with the archaeology of the Birmingham North Relief Road (now the M6 Toll) and a multi-agency partnership, including Oxford, Wessex, PCA and MOLA to deal with the archaeology of the Channel Tunnel Rail Link.

The market also supports small specialist teams, as well as consultancies who deal with broader heritage management and planning issues. Despite initial concerns in the 1980s that commercialisation would lower standards, this has generally proved not to be the case. Indeed standards on commercial projects are now much higher than for most university-led research. All of the best commercial archaeological units are Registered Organisations with the IfA, which requires them to adhere to ethical and professional standards. The last two decades have seen the inexorable rise of commercial archaeology, not just as a business, but as the main contributor to archaeological research. Indeed, most new research in British archaeology is undertaken by the private sector, not the public sector – a fact which sometimes surprises people new to British archaeology.

Curators

Not to be confused with museum curators, these are archaeologists and historic environment professionals who mostly work with local and unitary authorities and have responsibility for the cultural heritage of their particular area. Their position is often as 'county archaeologists' who sit within planning or environment sections of the authority for which they work. As we have seen already, they have responsibility both for ensuring that development plans take full account of historic environment matters, as well as maintaining the Historic Environment Record and ensuring consistency and transparency in dealing with planning matters, from the larger spatial planning projects (including major urban regeneration projects, for example) to individual or domestic planning applications. To inform their decision making, local authority archaeologists may take advantage of guidance from the national agencies (often now issued through HELM, Historic Environment – Local Management, see http://www.helm.org.uk) or it may undertake its own research into areas (regional or thematic), where there is a particular local concern or research need.

Since local authorities first had county archaeologists and Sites and Monuments Record Officers in the 1970s, these services have expanded considerably. Many archaeologists had their first real job working for the Sites and Monuments Record as an Assistant Archaeologist, and as we saw earlier, the term Sites and Monuments Record was recently replaced by Historic Environment Record to reflect the broader view of the historic environment, comprising much more than just 'sites' and 'monuments'. The historic environment is holistic and continuous; it is not just a selection of some interesting, significant and historic ruins. So, the way we think about the historic environment has changed as wider acceptance of its cultural value has broadened. That is part of the reason for the expansion of services and interest: a broader cultural view that heritage matters. That view is now enshrined in government advice and guidance. The publication of PPG16 in 1990 which made archaeology a material consideration in the planning process is the main reason why so many more planning archaeologists or curators were needed.

In 2008, there were 628 archaeologists working for national government or agencies (not just national heritage agencies, but other organisations such as Natural England) and 1,151 for local government in Britain (Aitchison and Edwards 2008). Together this represents just over a quarter of all archaeologists in employment.

Contractors

The integration of archaeology into the planning process through PPG16 (1990–2010) and its successor PPS5 (since 2010) also explains why the number of contractors and contracting units has expanded so much over the past two decades. Some contracting units in Britain are now very large organisations while other contractors work alone. Some, of course, are more successful than others. Some work only in their local area, and on particular types of projects – typically, field evaluations undertaken within the context of determining planning applications. Others – generally the larger 'units' – cover a diversity of projects: maritime archaeology for example; desk-top studies; conservation work; large regional field surveys in advance of pipelines or major housing projects; and of course excavations.

Contractors are usually selected by tendering. Where a project is identified, a project 'brief' (an outline of what's needed) is normally issued to several contractors known to operate in that particular area. The contractors then respond to that brief with either a costed project outline or project design. These 'tenders' are then assessed, the contractors perhaps invited for interview, and the contract let based on the quality of the submission, and cost. For small projects, this process may still be undertaken directly, but larger projects are increasingly mediated by consultants (see below). As we have seen, many large infrastructure projects are now too large for a single organisation to handle, and in recent years temporary consortia have been developed.

The larger contracting units are the places where many archaeologists begin their careers, working as field archaeologists on excavations or field evaluation projects.

They may begin as short-term temporary members of staff, and then gradually progress with experience to greater permanence with better pay and greater responsibility. There is a clearer career path now than in the past for these early-career archaeologists. But the amount of work available, and the length of contracts sometimes offered depends both on the success of the unit in delivering results well and on time (satisfying their client in other words), and on the political and economic climate. When the housing market is growing, for example, and more houses are being built or extended, more planning applications inevitably mean that more evaluations or excavations are required. When the housing market slows, perhaps in response to higher inflation or interest rate rises or economic downturn, the demand for archaeologists to undertake these related projects diminishes. It is at times like these that temporary staff are often laid-off, until things pick up, while the permanent staff may switch to other types of work.

Consultants

Archaeological consultants fall into two groups. Traditionally, a 'consultant' was an expert in a particular field who provided specialist advice and support to a larger project or research programme or may have been commissioned directly to undertake a more specialised piece of research. Examples might include specialists in particular ceramic traditions, who are commissioned to study and report on an assemblage, or a buildings specialist who has particular knowledge that does not exist within the contracting unit – such as military or industrial structures.

While these consultants still exist of course, the last decade has seen the emergence of a new breed of consultants, more closely aligned to the consulting model of the architectural or engineering professions. These consultants are usually engaged by a client to manage the archaeological or historic environment aspects of a large project, and the role has developed with the increasing complexity of many infrastructure and development projects – which have to deal with a wide range of planning and other legislation. Such consultancies may be one-person outfits or they may be large firms; of the latter, some are specifically specialists in the historic environment, in other cases an engineering consultancy may have an historic environment section. Usually, their role is to prepare desk-based material and advise on the mitigation strategy that is required; they also procure archaeological services from contractors (see above). Essentially, their role is to act as a mediator between the client and the archaeologist.

In 2008, there were nearly 3,500 archaeologists working in the private sector as consultants and contractors, over 50% of the total of all archaeologists (Aitchison and Edwards 2008).

Clients

Clients, simply, are those for whom the work is undertaken. This can be anyone from a large multinational consortium building a major road, the national heritage agency (often for larger, thematic studies or regional analyses), smaller developers, utility industries and even local authorities. Through liaison with the local planning authority archaeologist, the client determines what is needed, by when and who might be best suited to undertake the work required. Because of the complex structure of many archaeological projects, the archaeologist's immediate client may not be the person paying for the work: a finds specialist, for example, may be subcontracted by a field unit, who may be contracted to an archaeological consultancy, themselves working for a large consultancy or architectural practice, who in turn are working for the actual client.

Museums and the Higher Education Sector

Museums

Sometimes, it might seem that Britain is one big museum, with the number of protected landscapes, places and areas, and it is true that Britain has lots of museums, from the larger 'national' museums to smaller regional, local and more specialised examples. Indeed Julian Barnes' (1998) novel *England, England* explored this idea by creating a world in which the Isle of Wight became Britain's museum, with everything of heritage interest transferred there.

Museums are important places to visit early in any research project, and it is most likely the local museum that will take a project archive. You need to speak to the curator about any project and the types of evidence you expect to recover. They can then help with familiarisation of a local area and those archaeologists that work locally, and they can provide advice on recording standards, storage and curation. With space and funding increasingly hard to find, many museums are changing the way they deal with (and charge for) archaeological storage space.

All museums fall under the umbrella of the Museums, Libraries and Archives Council (MLA), the lead strategic agency for museums, libraries and archives in Britain. The MLA was launched in April 2000 and replaced the Museums and Galleries Commission and the Library and Information Commission, and includes archives within its portfolio. MLA is a non-departmental public body sponsored by the Department for Culture, Media and Sport. Its strategic aims are to: increase and sustain participation; put museums, libraries and archives at the heart of national, regional and local life; establish a world class and sustainable sector and put it on the best footing for the future; and lead sector strategy and policy development.

Higher Education Sector

The HE sector is crucial in developing and shaping the future of the archaeological and heritage profession. HE institutions provide training and education through undergraduate and postgraduate taught courses and research degrees, Continuing

Professional Development (CPD), and increasingly through distance learning. Traditionally, the focus of archaeological research, the HE sector can no longer be said to be leading the field in primary research activity; more than 90% of all archaeological fieldwork is actually undertaken in the commercial sector. Many academics are still not as fully engaged as they might be with the information from commercial projects, as Richard Bradley demonstrated in his re-evaluation of British prehistory using commercially generated information (Bradley 2007). Having said that, the HE sector does play a role in synthesising the mass of data which results from fieldwork projects and to some extent helps to shape the research agenda which determines future research needs. The HE sector employs just over 1,000 archaeologists or about 15% of the total number of archaeologists employed in the UK (Aitchison and Edwards 2008). The universities in Britain offering archaeology and/or heritage degree courses can be easily found online (and see the Appendix). More can be read about the HE sector in Chap. 8.

Professionalism in Archaeology

Since 1982 archaeologists have had a professional institute, and archaeology has been officially labelled 'a profession'. The Institute for Archaeologists (previously the Institute of Field Archaeologists) is the professional organisation for all archaeologists and others involved in protecting and understanding the historic environment. It acts in support of its members, works to improve pay and conditions, represents the interests of archaeology and archaeologists to government, policy makers and industry, keeps members up to date on developments in archaeological practice, sets standards and issues guidelines, promotes and organises training, improves individual career prospects, provides a wide range of membership services, and through its Registered Organisation scheme improves employment practices and raises standards of work. The increasing importance of the IfA in setting and maintaining standards is evident in the fact that the Institute is specifically cited by the latest planning policy statement for England (PPS5: Planning for the Historic Environment), issued in 2010.

The Institute is a democratic organisation run by an elected Council supported by committees responsible for standards, career development and training, working practices, membership validation and appeals, Registered Organisations, conferences and publications. Membership is open to practising archaeologists in all fields, whether professional or amateur. Archaeologists are admitted to corporate membership after rigorous peer review of their experience and qualifications. They may identify themselves as corporate members by using the designation PIfA (Practitioner), AIfA (Associate) and MIfA (Member) depending on membership grade. There are non-corporate membership grades of Student and Affiliate. All members agree to abide by the code of conduct, confirming a duty to adhere to the highest professional and ethical standards.

Why You Should Join the IfA

Kathryn Whittington (Publicity Administrator, IfA)

I completed my MSc in 2002 and as a relative newcomer to the sector the major attraction of the IfA for me was the opportunity to achieve professional recognition. Through joining, however, I also learnt of the Institute's activities and services. Members receive free copies of the Institute's publications, free access to its Jobs Information Service and the Heritage Link e-bulletin, reduced conference fees and free membership of some special interest groups. In addition to this, the Institute acts as a bridge across all areas of the historic environment sector, as membership is not restricted to those who fulfil more traditional archaeological roles (nor to those who earn a living from archaeology). As a result, it serves as a hub for the profession and provides a great opportunity to meet and interact with a wide range of individuals and organisations throughout the profession. The IfA also provides a voice for this diverse community.

At present, the Institute has just over 2,600 individual members and nearly 60 Registered Archaeological Organisations, including many of the largest archaeological employers in the UK. As a result, IfA membership is increasingly sought by historic environment employers. The addition of Student grade membership has opened the Institute up to those who are still studying, offering all membership benefits (bar voting rights) for as little as £15 per year, which represents great value for money. Progressing on to the Corporate grades of membership allows all individuals, regardless of professional role, to play a part in the Institute and the work that it does through joining committees or standing for Council.

Joining the IfA, therefore, gives you access to a range of services and support, as well as presenting you with opportunities to network and educate yourself about the historic environment in its broadest sense. It allows you to play an active part in promoting archaeology and archaeologists through the many opportunities open to all members to engage in the IfA's extensive activities. Above all, however, the IfA gives you recognition as a competent professional archaeologist and the opportunities to help shape your profession.

Non-professional Archaeologists, Enthusiasts and the Public

Archaeology as an activity has always appealed to enthusiasts – and it is something anyone can do. As we have seen, many local societies developed with amateur involvement, and the strongest of these retain a core of committed enthusiasts. Anyone can join one of the excavations that invites public participation (usually advertised through the CBA's calendar of excavations), or join a local group; anyone can do some historic research of their own and then start studying maps or aerial photographs or rummaging in woodland to find old buildings or field boundaries. Very large numbers of people do all of these activities and more, drawn in to large extent by a passion for the past, and enthused by the profusion of television coverage for archaeological fieldwork and historical research in recent years.

Some evidence for the extent of this interest can be seen in memberships. The National Trust has 3.5 million members now, in a country with 60 million people. English Heritage has around a million. Some 3.5 million people typically watch *Time Team* on television (a programme that summarises into an hour of airtime 3-day archaeological investigations). As we have seen, the CBA has 10,000 members. There are an estimated 30,000 metal detector users in England and Wales alone.

One example of a successful public archaeology programme that harnessed this enthusiasm was the Defence of Britain Project, funded by the HLF and coordinated by CBA from 1995 to 2002. This project aimed to mobilise the mass of Second World War archaeology enthusiasts and encourage them to record surviving sites across the country, which they did with great enthusiasm. Over 2,000 volunteers contributed to the project, some regularly and some with only a handful of records. But the result was significant. It was the result of this study that generated the selection of sites in England that English Heritage would later consider for statutory protection, set within a national context that was not previously available.

Nick Merriman (2004) has written about public archaeology and what follows is taken largely from his (2004) publication. He notes how 'public' can mean one of two things: it can be taken to mean association with the state and its institutions, such as public bodies; and it can mean 'the public', a group of people whose reactions inform public opinion. But these definitions imply an obvious contradiction between the state assuming to speak on behalf of the public and acting in the public interest. The other difficulty is that the notion of 'the public' encompasses debate and opinion and can be both unpredictable and contested. The public can criticise or subvert the wishes of the state, for example. These tensions can be positively channelled, but they can have a negative and damaging effect too. At its worst, an unaccountable state apparatus for archaeology could fail to reflect the diversity of views and interests held by the public, and leave the public disenchanted with the archaeology provision of the state. Or, alternatively, state authorities could recognise, respect and work with the great diversity of public attitudes towards the heritage, involving local communities in stewardship and interpretation.

Merriman also considers why we engage with the public and presents two ideas to explain this. The first is what he terms the Deficit Model, which assumes the public is deficient in some way in its understanding, and needs to be informed or educated. In other words, if we engage with the public, then more people will understand what archaeologists are trying to do, and will support them. And there is the Multiple Perspective Model, a benefit of which is the importance of agency. Cornelius Holtorf (2000, 214–5) has said that he sees 'no reason why non-professionals should not be welcomed and indeed be encouraged and supported in their own encounters with archaeology, whether these may closely resemble professional attitudes or not'. No matter how hard archaeologists try, non-archaeologists reappropriate, reinterpret and renegotiate the meanings of archaeological resources to their own personal agendas. It is better to recognise and encourage this, than to try to force people to follow a particular path.

In England, public involvement is on the increase and generally it follows the Multiple Perspectives Model outlined above. It encourages people to tell us what they think. In the East End of London, the Bengali community are telling us which buildings they value in the Brick Lane area, a selection that totally contradicts the official view as represented through those protected by the State as listed buildings (Gard'ner 2004). In the Defence of Britain project, enthusiasts contributed to a national overview – but they visited the sites they wanted to, and made their own records, albeit within the constraints of a prescribed recording system. At landscape scale, local communities are now being encouraged to tell the heritage agencies and local authorities what matters to them. And increasingly there is support for this. The new planning system includes Local Development Frameworks with stated provision for involving local communities throughout the process.

Contexts

Finally in this chapter, there are several contexts within which these legislative and curatorial positions need to be understood. Here, we touch on just two: the position of Britain in Europe, and the wider, holistic view of landscape as exemplified by the practice of historic landscape characterisation (HLC).

Great Britain in Europe

The UK is a member of two organisations that span the European continent. The older of these, which the UK joined on its formation, is the Council of Europe, currently with 47 members. This is an organisation of all the countries of Europe which was created following the Second World War in order to promote cross-border cooperation not only between allies, but also across political divides. Its remit specifically includes cultural matters, including archaeology and heritage. The younger organisation, formed in the 1950s specifically to promote cooperation between France and Germany and thus to prevent further wars in Europe, is the European Union (EU; formerly the European Economic Community), which the UK joined in 1972. Its remit is specifically economic and political, generally excluding cultural matters, aimed at ensuring closer union between its current 26 members by creating a single economic entity out of its diverse and growing membership.

The Council of Europe operates in the cultural sphere especially by promoting cultural exchanges of various kinds. It also promulgates treaties relating to cultural matters to which its members subscribe. These conventions provide a framework within which individual states establish systems for the management of their own national heritage. The main European Conventions that relate to archaeology are the European Cultural Convention of 1954, the European Convention for the Protection of the Architectural Heritage of Europe of 1985, the European Convention for the Protection of the Archaeological Heritage, originally created in 1969 and revised in 1992 and the European Landscape Convention of 2000. These treaties between the member states rely upon the states for compliance, usually by enshrining in their own national systems for heritage management the principles enshrined in the treaties.

The EU, by contrast, can enforce its decisions on member states far more rigorously and so the legislation takes a different form: Directives are instruments requiring member states to legislate in a particular manner on a particular matter, while Regulations have immediate effect upon member states. While the European Commission – effectively the 'civil service' of the EU – oversees the general application of these laws and ensures compliance by member states, the application of the laws to particular cases is the responsibility of the member states themselves. Since the EU is not primarily a cultural organisation, its legislative action in respect of cultural property relates to those items primarily as economic goods. In creating a single market in Europe, the EU must provide for the free movement of all goods within its borders. The transfer of heritage objects is not an issue on which it is qualified to legislate except in terms of freeing the movement of such items. Accordingly, its regulations on controlling the export of cultural property only concern their transfer across the European boundary to a country not a member of the EU: transfers between countries within the EU are not only allowed but – in economic terms at least – encouraged.

The overall consequence of Britain's attachment to these two international bodies – sometimes referred to as Britain being 'in Europe' – is that although the ultimate responsibility for managing the archaeological heritage rests with the national government, that responsibility is exercised with the attention to international obligations to meet certain principles. In practice, it also means an engagement by the relevant heritage agencies (English Heritage, Cadw and Historic Scotland in particular) in pan-European initiatives and close cooperation with partner agencies through bodies, such as the European Association of Archaeologists and the European Archaeological Colloquium.

Understanding Landscape Characterisation

Characterisation is a way of studying the shape of the landscape as it exists today, identifying the historic processes and interventions that have persisted and influenced its present-day character. It is a programme of research that has progressed rapidly in Wales, Scotland and England (as well as elsewhere in Europe) over the past 15 years, influencing the way planners think about future changes, changes that can begin to take account of what happened in the past. Being a national programme, and because it is in such demand by local authorities and government departments involved with agricultural and planning policies, characterisation is necessarily rapid and broad in its approach, glossing over much of the finer detail. It is not surprising, therefore, that characterisation has its critics – those who think detail is necessary for the fuller understanding necessary to meet the requirements of informed conservation. The fact remains though, that with GIS-generated maps that highlight individual character areas, and a database for each area that describes its characteristics, this higher level information is proving most useful for planners.

A national programme of HLC is currently under way in England. There are two strands to this: urban – in the form of intensive urban studies for the 30 or so major cities with a long history of occupation and development (York and Winchester for example), and extensive urban surveys for smaller towns; and rural – HLC. A further dimension is English Heritage's Change and Creation programme, which is examining the late twentieth- and early twenty-first century landscape itself and not just for the traces of earlier landscapes that have persisted within it. All of these initiatives, along with characterisation studies elsewhere, have certain things in common:

- All are generalised not particular. The view of landscape is course- not fine-grained.
- Character is everywhere. This departs from some other approaches to heritage management that designate particular places (scheduled monuments, national parks) in a certain way, and leave all other areas unprotected.
- Character is a statement about the present-day landscape, not that from the Bronze Age or the mediaeval period. In some cases, evidence from the Bronze Age or the mediaeval period may have persisted, in field boundaries for example, so in these cases an area may be described as having Bronze Age character.
- Characterisation does not involve value judgements. There is no such thing as good or bad character.
- It is about shaping the landscape of the future in a way that allows development and change, but in a way that also takes account of past influences.
- Distinctiveness is key. Character areas are defined on the basis that they have characteristics that are distinctive from those of surrounding areas.
- It is also about partnership. In most cases, characterisation projects are commissioned by English Heritage and undertaken by staff in the local authority, who – after all – know their area best. In some cases, local communities have been drawn into this process, a trend that may increase in the future.

HLC is similar in many ways to Landscape Character Assessment (as practiced in Scotland), the key difference being the word 'historic'. The starting point for HLC is recognising the time depth evident in the British landscape. Landscape Character Assessment is more about the character of the landscape as it exists today, but without that historic dimension. Both approaches though are widely used as parts of the heritage sector's contribution to 'sustainable development'. Characterisation might be used, for example, to define briefs for development or designing agri-environment schemes, deciding where to place new areas of forestry; or the best sites for telecommunications infrastructure.

> **What Is Sustainable Development?**
>
> Sustainable development means meeting four objectives at the same time: social progress that recognises the needs of everyone; effective protection of the environment; prudent use of natural resources; and maintenance of high and stable levels of economic growth and employment (Department of the Environment, Transport and Regions 1999).

Summary

The purpose of this chapter has been to summarise some of the main legal and administrative frameworks relevant to undertaking archaeological work in Great Britain. In the summary to the preceding chapter, we explained how the nature of archaeology ensures that the way we understand the past is constantly shifting, with each new discovery, and each interpretation made of it. The same is true here in the way that archaeological resources are managed and curated. Procedures, practices and legal frameworks, ethical codes concerned with how we engage with local communities for example, and with burials, are always shifting. Furthermore, the planning system in England is currently under review, and the new system is more democratic and more prone to public participation than before. The heritage protection systems in Britain are also under review. Heritage protection in England has recently been overhauled to provide a more integrated approach, after much debate and discussion within the heritage sector over the course of the past decade. PPS5 is still bedding down, and its full implications remain untested. So, just as it is hard to present a definitive and up-to-date view of British archaeology, this is equally difficult to achieve for archaeological resource management in Britain. That said, this chapter does provide a key-facts guide to the main legislation and good practice guidelines, as they exist at the time of writing. With that guide to hand, we now proceed to the research phase of any project, first with a chapter (Chap. 5) that considers the preparations for fieldwork, followed by Chap. 6 which examines fieldwork practices and protocols themselves.

References and Further Reading

Aitchison, K. and Edwards, R. 2008. *Archaeology Labour Market Intelligence: Profiling the Profession 2007/8*. Reading: Institute of Field Archaeologists.

Andrews, G.A., Barrett J.C. Lewis J.S.C. 2000. 'Interpretation not record: the practice of archaeology'. *Antiquity* 74, 525–30.

Baker, D. with Smith, K. (with Shepherd, I.) 2006. 'Local authority opportunities'. In Hunter, J. and Ralston, I. (eds), *Archaeological Resource Management in the UK: An Introduction*, 131–146. Sutton Publishing Ltd.

Barnes, J. 1998. *England, England.* London: Jonathan Cape.

Biddle, M. 1989. 'The Rose reviewed: a comedy (?) of errors'. *Antiquity* 63, 753–760

Bland, R. 1996. Treasure trove And the case for reform. *Art, Antiquity and Law* 1(1), 11–26.

Bradley, R. 2007. *The Prehistory of Britain and Ireland.* Cambridge: Cambridge University Press.

Breeze, D. 2006. 'Ancient monuments legislation'. In Hunter, J. & Ralston, I. (eds) *Archaeological Resource Management in the UK: an introduction.* Stroud: Sutton, 57–68.

Carman, J. 1996. *Valuing Ancient Things: archaeology and law.* London, Leicester University Press.

Carman, J. in press. 'Towards an International Comparative History of Heritage Management'. In Skeates, R. McDavid, C. and Carman, J. (eds) *The Oxford Handbook of Public Archaeology.* Oxford Handbooks in Archaeology. Oxford, Oxford University Press.

Darvill, T. 1987. *Ancient Monuments in the Countryside: an archaeological management review.* English Heritage Archaeological Report 5. London, English Heritage.

Department of the Environment, Transport and Regions 1999. *A better quality of life: a strategy for sustainable development in the United Kingdom.* Stationery Office: London.

Everill, P. 2006. *The Invisible Diggers: contemporary commercial archaeology in the UK.* Unpublished PhD thesis, University of Southampton.

Gard'ner, J. 2004. 'Heritage protection and social inclusion: a case study from the Bangladeshi community of East London'. *International Journal of Heritage Studies* 10.1: 75–92.

Hewison, R. 1987. *The Heritage Industry: Britain in a climate of decline.* London, Methuen.

Holtorf, C. 2000. 'Engaging with multiple pasts. Reply to Francis McManamon'. *Public Archaeology* 1(3): 214–5.

McManamon, F. 2000. 'Archaeological Messages and Messengers'. *Public Archaeology* 1(1): 5–20.

Merriman, N. 2004. (ed). *Public Archaeology.* London: Routledge.

Skeates, R. 2000. *Debating the Archaeological Heritage.* Duckworth Debates in Archaeology. London, Duckworth.

Smith, L. 2006. *Uses of Heritage.* London, Routledge.

Thomas, R.M. 2008. 'Archaeology and authority in the twenty-first century'. In Fairclough, G., Harrison, R., Jameson, J.H. Jnr., and Schofield, J. (eds), *The Heritage Reader*, 139–148. London: Routledge.

Wright, P. 1985. *On Living in an Old Country: the national past in contemporary Britain.* London, Verso.

Chapter 5
Acquiring Data, Before Fieldwork

Having now reviewed the types of archaeological evidence that one finds in Britain, and the administrative and legal frameworks through which it is managed and curated, we now turn to address the procedures and practices that precede excavation projects. We then review the procedures of excavation itself in the next chapter, recognising that these procedures can be different from country to country. It is important to recognise also that the methods and techniques described here in the context of preparing for excavation can also stand alone as archaeological methods. It may be, for example, as is often the case, that historical or aerial photographic survey is required or desired as an end in itself, and not merely in preparation for an excavation. Excavation may be the technique most commonly associated with archaeological practice, but it is not the be all and end all. Excavation is a particular method for retrieving and understanding archaeological evidence, alongside numerous other methods, some of which we outline here.

How Archaeological Projects Work

Most archaeological fieldwork in Great Britain today is funded by development (see Chaps. 2 and 4). At one end of the scale are substantial public infrastructure projects, such as airports, railways, roads and energy. These usually consume a great deal of land and have substantial impacts on the environment. As a result, they are carefully regulated by national agencies and archaeological risks are usually factored into the project at an early stage, often as part of an Environmental Impact Assessment (EIA). At the other end are small-scale building works, such as the infilling of urban space in historic settlements, or a private householder building a garage. In between are a full range of small, medium and large-scale private-sector developments – gravel extraction, new industrial estates, offices, housing, building conversions and extensions and so on. Work for such projects is always undertaken by commercial archaeology units or consultancies who usually have to tender for the work by bidding for services in competition with other archaeology units and contractors.

J. Schofield et al., *Archaeological Practice in Great Britain: A Heritage Handbook*, World Archaeological Congress Cultural Heritage Manual Series, DOI 10.1007/978-0-387-09453-3_5, © Springer Science+Business Media, LLC 2011

The remainder of archaeological fieldwork (probably less than 10%) is funded directly from the public purse in one form or another. Such work is usually associated with conservation or research projects. Typical funding agencies are English Heritage (EH), Historic Scotland (HS), Cadw (Wales), the Heritage Lottery Fund (HLF), Natural England (NE) or the various Regional Development agencies (RDAs).

In almost all cases, this publicly funded work is tendered for and undertaken by commercial consultants and contracting units in very similar ways to private-sector projects. Exceptions to this include the work of the various English Heritage specialist teams in landscape survey and building recording, geophysical survey (English Heritage 2008) and excavation. Another exceptional category is that of university research excavations. These form a very small proportion of archaeological fieldwork, and also offer a very different working experience from other types of project – having said that, they are very often most peoples' first experience of field archaeology.

Frameworks for Project Management

Coincident with the introduction of PPG16 was the reissue of English Heritage guidance commonly known as MAP2 – the acronym for 'Management of Archaeological Projects, Second Edition'. This was published in 1991 (the first edition had been issued in 1989), and set out important basic principles of project planning and implementation. One of the key features of this document was the need for a clear 'project design' at the outset, and regular reviews of progress as the work went on. Although originally intended for projects funded or undertaken by English Heritage, the main provisions of MAP2 have been adopted across the archaeological profession. For projects funded or undertaken by English Heritage, MAP2 has been superseded by Management of Research Projects in the Historic Environment (MoRPHE), but this guidance first issued by English Heritage in 2006 does not yet have wider application, for instance in the formulation and development of developer-funded projects.

MAP2 identified five main 'phases through which a large archaeological field project would normally pass' (MAP2, s.3.5). These are:

- Phase 1: Project planning
- Phase 2: Fieldwork
- Phase 3: Assessment of potential for analysis
- Phase 4: Analysis and report preparation
- Phase 5: Dissemination

Within each of these phases, MAP2 outlined a four-stage process of proposal, decision, data-collection and review.

Archaeological Projects in Practice

MAP2 itself noted that its 'system of regular review and follow-up will probably cause some hiatuses in the execution of a project' (MAP2, s.3.9). Indeed, subsequent

Fig. 5.1 On the left a metre-square pit being excavated in Bermuda; on the right an evaluation trench on an urban site in Britain. (Photos: Paul Belford)

practice in commercial archaeology, while acknowledging the need for different assessment and analysis phases, has tended towards compression of these two stages to reduce costs and timescales. As we see, a great deal depends on the rigorousness of individual curatorial archaeologists. The development of the commercial system of archaeology since 1990 has brought about a pragmatic evolution of the principles enshrined in MAP2 and PPG16.

In commercial practice, the 'assessment' and 'analysis' phases have been translated into the two main fieldwork stages of any archaeological project. These are: first, evaluation of the archaeological resource, and the means by which it is best 'preserved', whether in situ or by record; and second, mitigation, achieving a balance between the need for evaluation and a degree of preservation, whether in situ, or by record, or by a combination of both.

In many cases of course, the process of evaluation may conclude that the subsequent stage of mitigation is not required. Nevertheless, each of these two stages may consist of several elements, including historical research, non-intrusive investigation (such as field survey or geophysics) and trial excavation (so-called intrusive investigation). Trial excavation is likely to take place at the evaluation stage, usually in the form of trial trenches or test pits with a view to determining the character of buried remains. Trial trenches may be very large, the tradition of British practice (see below) tending to prefer open-area stratigraphic excavation to the small metre-square test pits often seen in a North American context (Fig. 5.1). Excavation may also continue into the mitigation stage, although the extent of this always depends on the results of evaluation. Mitigation may also take the form of a watching brief on groundworks, or indeed no action may be required at all.

Pre-project Planning

Every archaeological project is (or should be) the result of careful planning and forethought. This is the case both for commercial projects undertaken under the aegis of PPS5 (DCLG 2010), and for research projects which may receive some form of public funding. Pre-project planning inevitably results in archaeologists having to deal not only with 'research'-type questions, such as the nature, extent and state of preservation of the resource, but also with 'management'-type questions, such as costs, timescales, health, safety and so on.

Project Designs, Briefs and Specifications

The 'project design' is identified in MAP2 as being a key document at all stages of the project. Indeed, it 'defines the objectives of the whole project and gives an outline of the overall resources likely to be necessary to achieve these' (MAP2, s.2.4). The phrase 'written scheme of investigation' (WSI) is used in PPS5, and in commercial archaeology the MAP2-style 'project design' has evolved into a more comprehensive document. The purpose of the WSI is to set out the aims, objectives, methodology and intended outcomes of the project. The WSI acts as a benchmark against which the various stages of the project can be measured. It is also a tool for managing the project, and includes timetables and milestones.

The WSI is derived from the project brief, and aims to specify the range of archaeological techniques which are brought to bear on the project. It is, however, a completely different document from either a 'brief' or a 'specification' or even a 'method statement' – although it comes closest to the latter of these and incorporates elements of the first two. Some definitions of these might be helpful at this point.

Brief

In commercial archaeology, this is normally the document issued by the relevant planning authority, represented by the curatorial archaeologist. This accompanies a set of conditions on the planning consent with which the developer is required to comply in order to ensure that he has permission to continue with his project. These include compliance with local authority development plans, building regulations, environmental issues, working practices and other matters – indeed, archaeology is often well down the list of potential liabilities that the developer faces.

The local authority archaeologist's brief sets out the historical background of the site in question and outlines the reasons why archaeological work is required. In so doing, it usually refers to current research frameworks and other previous research. It also sets out the nature and extent of works required.

In many cases, a developer uses this document as the basis to seek tenders for archaeological work. It is then up to the archaeological contractor to develop a WSI which includes a detailed specification of the works as well as the methodology by which this is achieved. Increasingly, however, developers (especially, the larger ones) now tend to employ multidisciplinary consultants to mediate between the requirements of the authorities and their own needs (see Chap. 4). As described in Chap. 4, many of these consultants now have archaeologists on their team, and these consultancy bodies produce a specification against which archaeological contractors can price the work.

Specification

The specification is a document which sits part-way between the local authority brief and the final WSI. It is normally a much more precise and prescriptive document than the brief, and includes details such as the intended timescale and the extent of interventions (for example, the percentage of the site and/or the percentage of features which will be investigated). The purpose of the specification is to try and level the playing field between competing archaeological contractors by eliminating (or at least attempting to reduce) some of the 'unknowns' which are inevitable in designing and costing archaeological projects.

As with briefs, the quality of specifications issued by consultants varies with the site type, its location and the quality of consultancy engaged. The issue of a specification does not remove the obligation on the contracting unit to produce an adequate WSI.

Written Scheme of Investigation

The WSI sets out how the archaeological organisation:

- Understands the site in question.
- Understands the research issues at hand – not only with reference to the local environment, but also looking at regional and national research agenda or frameworks.
- Is suited to undertake the work – setting out not only its capacity in terms of staff and available resources, but also its expertise in the specific themes appropriate to the site, including examples of previous similar work and so on.
- Actually undertakes the work – what phases use which members of staff, what other resources are deployed, how long it takes
- Intends to deploy the array of archaeological methods – very specific information about fieldwork recording methods (see Chap. 6), post-excavation and archiving (see Chap. 7) and publication, if required by the brief (see also Chap. 7).
- Measures project progress against benchmarks.
- Deals with issues, such as health and safety, welfare, insurance, compliance with relevant regulations, confidentiality, copyright, ownership and so on.

The preparation of the WSI is usually undertaken as part of the tendering process, and goes hand-in-hand with working out the costs of the project. Indeed, it is extremely difficult to accurately gauge costs without preparing a WSI, or at least without considering most of the key aspects (see below). Preparation of the WSI does not usually cost as a project item per se. However, the cost of production can usually be factored into the project as part of the overheads or management time involved in later stages, and in some cases the preparation of an archaeological WSI is actually allowed for in the pre-contract costs of the developer.

In developing a WSI, it is essential to bring together the right group of people to undertake the work at the earliest stage in the process. This includes specialists and others who may not be part of the core team but whose role is particularly important. For instance, a project looking at a site with known or suspected metalworking activity needs the input of an archaeometallurgist. Other specialists – such as those concerned with ceramics, palaeoenvironmental evidence, timber and so on – also need to be involved as early as possible. It may also be necessary to involve non-archaeologists, where their expertise can provide useful information. This enables likely potential outcomes to be determined and accurately costed.

Finally, the WSI must consider communication and management structures. It is most important to make sure that everyone in the team (or intended team) understands the aims and objectives of the project, and the relationship between it and other research. Mechanisms for communication between the different people involved should be clearly established – an important point to remember when many of those involved are from different organisations, and may be engaged on several different projects at once.

Quantifying the Work Involved

Accurately costing an archaeological project is an art informed by experience. It is important that project planning ensures that the allocated resources are best spent in meeting the project's aims and objectives, and at the same time allows sufficient flexibility for any changes that inevitably occur.

Some elements are reasonably straightforward to estimate, such as the amount of work involved in a *desk-based assessment* (DBA) (English Heritage 2008). Even here there are variations depending on the size of site, its location (urban, rural or in a conservation area), and the quality and extent of known records.

More complex is planning and costing *field projects*. These might take the form of excavations or building recording, or a combination of both. In all projects, the largest cost is staff time, and the Project Managers' role is to ensure that the optimum resource is specified; that is to say that sufficient staff are deployed to meet the requirements of the brief and specification while keeping to a reasonable budget and timescale. Once the number of staff has been decided upon, it is then necessary to cater for their well-being. The need for on-site accommodation, toilets, generators and so on has to be assessed, bearing in mind the relevant legislation governing matters such as appropriate cooking and heating equipment, area needed per person, drying facilities and so on. Allowances have to be made for fuel, service connection charges and routine maintenance and servicing (such as plant, appliances, toilets and so on). Provision of Personal Protective Equipment (PPE), such as goggles, gloves, face-masks and other items also need to be costed. Wider health and safety aspects, such as the depth of trenches, the location of spoil heaps, the need for shoring, access into and out of excavations, safe manual handling and even sunburn also need to be considered (see also below). Another important factor is the use of machines (excavators, dumpers and the like), which are usually necessary at some stage of the project. These and other aspects are dealt with in more detail in Chap. 6.

Fieldwork is of course only the beginning. Just as important is the design and resourcing of *post-excavation, publication and archiving* (see Chap. 7).

Historical Research

Historical research may not sound like a great archaeological adventure, but in Britain the extensive documentary resource is almost unparalleled in its depth (going back over 1,000 years) its range (personal diaries to documents of state) and in its preservation. In fact, a day in an historical archive can be a wonderful experience, rifling through the dusty pages of often overlooked historical documentation. You will almost invariably find information which will enhance the field project. The continuity of British history is often remarkable to those from the new world, and even if you are looking at a prehistoric site, post-mediaeval documentation will often contain clues in field names, ancient boundaries and antiquarian finds. Historical research should ideally be undertaken at the outset of any project and has two main objectives:

- To understand the historical development of the site
- To assess the significance and likely extent of archaeological remains on the site.

In the context of developer-funded archaeology, historical research usually takes the form of a desk-based assessment (DBA), but may also be included in an EIA or a Conservation Statement or Conservation Plan. Inevitably, the historical record is biased towards the last three centuries, from which leases, maps and other documents are more likely to survive. Nevertheless, it also includes records of finds from earlier periods, and a good DBA should also strive to contain (where possible or relevant) information from previous ground investigations, whether archaeological or geotechnical.

Where to Find Things

Finding information is easy, if you know where to look. There are five principal sources of information appropriate for a DBA or for wider historical research. These are:

The Local Historic Environment Record

This should be the first port of call. Usually, this is maintained by the county council, borough or unitary authority which serves the relevant area. An Historic Environment Record (HER) search gives details of known archaeological sites in the area in question. This may consist of various previous discoveries from nineteenth century find, to place–name evidence, to last year's evaluation on a neighbouring site by an archaeological unit. HERs are typically now tied into other landscape information through a Geographical Information System (GIS). This enables the researcher to place sites within the context of landscape character types (an area characterised by mediaeval enclosure for example, or ancient woodland); it should also reveal any designations which may curtail opportunities in the field, or at least require the client to make formal consent applications prior to starting work. In addition, HERs are now increasingly accessible online, although some information (such as maps) may still necessitate a visit to the HER. An HER search should also provide enough background information and a hand-ful of references to guide the next stage of the DBA. It does not, of itself, provide all of the answers.

Internet

'Googling' (or searching for information by placing keywords into an Internet search engine, such as Google) has almost reached the point of becoming a legiti-mate research method. With some HERs and other data sources placing their cata-logues online (see the National Archive, below) this does have some merit. At the very least, an Internet search might help you track down where your next port of call should be. There are pitfalls, of course, and success does depend on finding the correct combination of keywords for searching, but this technique can produce star-tling results. A tip is to adjust the terms of the search, to persist beyond the first few pages of results, even if things do not look promising, and to search also on images. For general background information, 'Wiki' can be a useful tool, though with all the usual caveats about accuracy and reliability.

National Archives and Repositories

English Heritage maintains a National Monuments Record (NMR) at Swindon, which is a vast resource of the records of archaeological and historical research undertaken over the last 100 years, alongside other relevant documentation, such as aerial photographs (vertical and low level oblique). Although focused on the output of English Heritage and its various predecessors, it also contains records produced by other people organisations. It includes historic photographs, including aerial photography, an excavation index and archive (records and photographs) and buildings records. Much of the NMRs record can be searched online, the records of excavations and surveys through its Pastscape Web site (www.pastscape. co.uk), and photographs through Viewfinder, from which photographs can be ordered and permissions for reproduction sought. There is also the Welsh National Library and Archive, and the Scottish Archives.

The National Archive in Kew (previously the Public Record Office) contains a massive amount of information mainly focused around official, government and legal documents. In most cases (except perhaps in London), the usual level of a DBA does not require a visit to Kew. Similarly, the British Library (also in London, but more conveniently located next to St. Pancras Station) is one of the world's copyright libraries and also has a wide range of maps and other documents. Again, for London projects, this is a very helpful resource, although a visit is not normally justified for DBAs in other parts of the country. That said, while the National Archive itself is not online, the catalogue is, and is supported by a helpful online search facility. This means that relevant catalogues and file numbers can be identified and ordered from home, saving time on arrival.

For archaeological information (i.e. reports of previous archaeological work), the OASIS database is worth consulting. This is a free-to-use national digital online archive of archaeological 'grey literature' and other works that are not readily available elsewhere (such as PhD theses). Submission of 'grey literature' reports to OASIS is not compulsory, but it is increasingly a requirement of many archaeological curators, and it is a useful place to start looking for recent unpublished work on sites in a specific area or of certain types.

Local Archives and Local Studies Libraries

Every county, city and unitary authority has some form of local archive. This either takes the form of a 'local studies library', a 'county archive' or 'county record office' and/or a combination of both. The traditional 'county record office' has seen a number of changes in recent years following the national lead given by the National Archive. The exponential rise in family history research in recent years has led a number of local authorities separating out many of the more popular genealogical resources – such as censuses, registers of baptisms, burials and marriages, local directories, maps and historic photographs. Such 'local studies' centres also house books by local historians and frequently full runs of the local archaeological society proceedings. The 'local studies' institution may be physically part of another building or it may be entirely separate. In most places, it is a part of the county record office (as in Shropshire), but it may be part of the local library (as in Dorset and many London boroughs), or split between both a local library and the local archives (as in Sheffield, South Yorkshire) or indeed it may be in an entirely different facility at another location altogether (as in Worcestershire). It is, therefore, essential to make sure that you visit all of the places which might hold information about your site or project. Again, a comprehensive Internet search before you set out ensures that you have covered all of the ground.

Local archives are usually extremely helpful places, although it is worth bearing in mind that they are usually geared up to provide service to the amateur historian and genealogist and not professional archaeologists. Sometimes, this is beneficial, as the archivist may enjoy dealing with someone who is looking at a wider range of documents than their usual clientele. Archivists usually know their collections intimately, and if you cannot find anything in the catalogue it is worth asking anyway. Occasionally, your visit as an archaeologist might be less welcome, particularly if you are working on a locally sensitive redevelopment or if you are less prepared to accommodate the leisurely ebb and flow of life in the archives. In most archives, the important primary documents are located in a 'strongroom' – a climate controlled area to which only the archivists have access. Usually, visits to the strong room are made by the archivists at certain times of day, and you have to order documents in advance. The number of documents you can have from the archives varies from place to place, so it is best to get there early, plan ahead, and order the most likely sounding documents first. Traditionally, documents could not be photographed or photocopied and so a supply of tracing paper was a prerequisite for visiting the archives; nowadays, most places allow digital photography (sometimes with, sometimes without flash) and photocopy most documents for a fee. Some documents are not photocopiable but can be photographed by the archive – albeit for a fee and a long delay: it is rarely worthwhile doing this for most day-to-day historical research.

Other Libraries and Archives

In many areas, there are substantial local histories and other collections housed in 'private' libraries and archives. These fall into three main categories:

Private archives. Even today, many large landowners hold their own archives on their own property. Increasingly, however, many families have chosen to deposit their documents with the local authority and they may be physically located in the local archives (see above). However, access to these collections may be restricted, and in many cases it is not possible to use or reproduce items from these collections without written authorisation from the estate to which they belonged. While most day-to-day research may not need to examine such archives, in some cases they contain all of the available maps, leases and other documentation for a particular site. Where lodged with the local archives such documents are usually catalogued so you at least get an idea of what is in the archive. Where they are still in a wing of the ancestral mansion, then assessing the value of the documentary resource may be more difficult.

Company archives. As with private archives, many company records are lodged with local archives – although sensitive material is usually weeded out and if the company has closed, then the restrictions on private archives do not usually apply. In urban, industrial and mining areas, company archives are often extremely useful. However, for most day-to-day DBAs it is sufficient to look at the catalogue; in many cases, the archaeologically useful information (such as plans, maps, leases and so on) is duplicated elsewhere.

Society archives. Many counties, districts or unitary authorities have their own long-established local-interest societies, in the form of archaeological, natural history or 'field clubs' (see Chap. 2 above). In many cases, their records are deposited with the county archives, but in some areas these societies have their own repositories – whether supported by the ongoing activities of the Society (as in the prestigious Society of Antiquaries of Newcastle-upon-Tyne, or the Dorset Natural History and Archaeological Society, both with their own Museums and archives), or supported by an endowment from the original founder (as in the Rylands Library in Manchester or the William Salt Library in Stafford). Usually, the local archives or record offices are aware of these sorts of resources in their own area, and point you in the right direction.

Independent Sources

Usually, there is a wide range of local amateur historians and interest groups in any given area. While these are undoubtedly an extremely valuable source of information, the usual commercial DBA eschews contact with such people. However, outside London it is not uncommon for a curatorial archaeologist to specify contact with a particular individual or group as part of their brief for the DBA. Such people and groups may hold valuable information, and be knowledgeable about particular locations or activities. Traditionally, professional archaeology has sought to marginalise these groups, and it is certainly true that in these settings you encounter people with their own 'pet theory' about your site or area of interest. Nevertheless, such groups are often well connected locally and should be treated with great respect; in particular, they may often provide helpful local contacts.

What You Will Find

Maps

The first and easiest source to investigate is historic maps. *Ordnance Survey maps* are a valuable resource which date back to the first half of the nineteenth century. The First Edition *One-Inch* (a scale of 1 in. to the mile or 1:63,360) maps were made from the 1840s. These used shading to show relief, and are not always very detailed. In complete contrast, the following decade saw the creation of the Ordnance Survey *Town Plans*, which were done at the extraordinary scale of '60 in. (5 ft) to the mile' or 1:512 (Fig. 5.2). The towns shown are depicted in great detail with individual houses and garden plots (even the arrangement of individual rooms) shown. The first *Six-Inch* maps (a scale of 6 in. to the mile, or 1:10,560) appeared from the 1870s, and form the bedrock of the Ordnance Survey resource. These were typically revised in the later nineteenth century. Revisions after the First World War were the

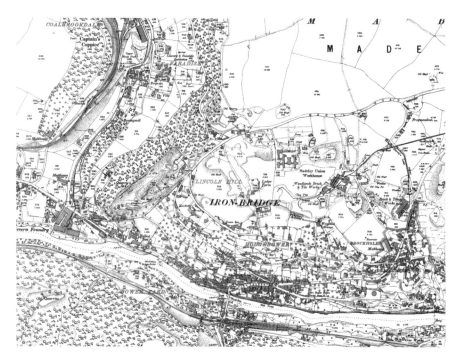

Fig. 5.2 A typical late 19th century Ordnance Survey 'six-inch' map at an original scale of 1:10560

first to include the National Grid – the system of kilometre squares which was laid out as part of the first great triangulation of the 1840s, and which forms the basis for mapping today. Typically, the First Edition maps date from the 1880s and 1890s, the Second Edition from the early 1900s, a Third Edition of the 1920s, and subsequent editions in the 1930s (the first to show contours), 1950s, late 1960s and 1980s. This last was the final great revision before today's continuously updated electronic mapping and the first to use a metric scale – replacing the old 'one-inch' maps with 1:50,000 scale and the 'six-inch' maps with 1:10,000 scale. Today, the 1:10,000 are no longer produced (large-scale maps are supplied as user-scalable electronic GIS 'tiles') and 1:25,000 is the largest printed mapping that is universally available.

Thanks to the unique history of the Ordnance Survey it is possible, through a process of map regression (essentially overlaying Ordnance Survey maps of different periods), to accurately show the locations of buildings and features from the 1850s onwards.

Prior to the 1850s there were two main phases of 'national' large-scale mapping. These took place as the result of legislative changes in land ownership and tenure. The later of these was the readjustment of Tithes in the 1840s, in which payments to the church (anciently a 'tithe' or tenth of the annual value of a plot of land) were regularised. The result of this was a large-scale map of each parish, together with an annexed written document (the 'Apportionment') which listed each plot of land, its owner, the tenant, and its historic name. Although *Tithe Maps* often vary in the quality of surveying,

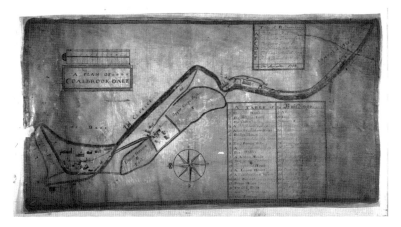

Fig. 5.3 A mid-18th century estate map, in this case showing industrial sites in the Ironbridge Gorge. (Photo: courtesy of the Ironbridge Gorge Museum Trust)

they are usually sufficiently accurate to be related to the First Edition Ordnance Survey of the following generation. They are particularly helpful in tracing land ownership, and, with field names, in linking back to earlier land uses (Fig. 5.3).

The other great 'national' event which produced a large number of good quality maps was the process of Parliamentary Enclosure. This was the enforced rationalisation of the agrarian landscape into privately owned parcels. As with the Tithe awards, property was at stake, so maps were usually quite accurate. Unlike the Tithe awards, the Enclosure Acts were a series of individual actions undertaken over many years, from the 1770s through to the 1820s. Many parts of the country – particularly the lowlands of the Midlands and parts of the West Country – had already been enclosed during the sixteenth and seventeenth centuries and so Parliamentary Enclosure did not occur. Consequently, coverage is patchy. *Enclosure Maps* should be accompanied by a written document (the 'Award') which again lists the individual owners, the size of the fields and their use. There may also be some information concerning the process of enclosure itself, so it can sometimes be possible to reconstruct the pre-enclosure landscape – which in many cases dates back to the 1100s and may also contain elements of the early mediaeval or Roman landscape.

Other useful maps can be found from the late sixteenth century onwards, although in most cases accurate mapping did not begin until the latter part of the seventeenth century. Some of the earliest maps are *Estate Maps*, commissioned by large landowners usually as a precursor to, or as part of, redevelopment schemes. These are often quite crude in terms of scale and execution, but can usually be related to the modern landscape. They are helpful in that they often show the landscape at a moment of transition from its mediaeval to post-mediaeval form. From the mid-eighteenth century onwards, the production and survival of maps is much improved. The purchase and rental of property generated a whole range of *maps relating to leases* and other legal actions. Few places are as lucky as Sheffield with its Fairbanks collection – an archive of exceptionally high-quality large-scale maps of most of the city's properties by three generations of a local surveying dynasty from the 1760s to the 1840s. Nevertheless, most sites have been the subject of some sort of property agreement in the past which generated a map – whether it has survived and is publicly accessible or not is another matter.

Many more maps were produced in the nineteenth century, and for a variety of different reasons. Most sizeable towns were subject to various *private mapping exercises* in the early 1800s, before the universal Ordnance Survey rendered them redundant. While these maps are often not very helpful at individual site level, they do show important information, such as the approximate footprint of the built environment, as well as historic routes of rivers and watercourses and so on. They are usually dated and can therefore sometimes provide useful 'snapshots' when compared with other maps – often labelling features, such as 'quarry', 'brickfields', 'building ground' or 'proposed new street' which can help establish the chronology of urban expansion. Some of the most useful maps are the *Goad Fire Insurance Plans* which date from the 1870s and show industrial premises in extreme detail, with the functions of individual rooms helpfully labelled.

All Ordnance Survey, Tithe and Enclosure maps and associated documents are normally held in the relevant local archives or local studies library. This is usually the source of most other maps too, although some may also be held in the National Archives or in private collections.

Aerial Photographs

Aerial photographs or 'APs' are crucial for the interpretation of archaeological sites and landscape, and have been since the early twentieth century, when it was first realised that archaeological sites not visible on the ground, could be seen from the air. Since that time aerial photographs have been taken and stored, with a massive number being produced around the time of the Second World War, immediately afterwards, and through the period up until the present. At times, aerial photography was undertaken for the whole country, as in 1946 for example. More recently, satellite imagery has also been available, in addition to the targeted archaeological projects and initiatives, such as English Heritage's National Mapping Programme (NMP) which seeks to create a national record (via the NMR) of all archaeological features captured on aerial photography. This national programme has led to the discovery of tens of thousands of previously unrecorded sites.

To consult these records is easy. In the case of England, one can visit the NMR which is publicly accessible and free of charge. In the other home countries national records also exist, as do the Royal Commissions (Royal Commission on the Ancient and Historic Monuments of Scotland and of Wales – RCAHMW and RCAHMS) who conduct aerial reconnaissance and retain an archive. One can also now use Google Mapping (and similar) on the Internet, to get an impression of the lie of the land, the terrain, topography and so on, and also in some cases resolution is high enough to identify archaeological sites.

Secondary Documents

For any given area, there is usually a plethora of local histories written from a variety of perspectives and using a wide range of evidence (some of which may not be easily verifiable). Perhaps the most valuable outline of the history of any given area is found in the Victoria County History (VCH). Dedicated to Queen Victoria, this vast project was inaugurated in 1899, seeking to provide an overview of the history of each county. Since 1933 it has been based at the Institute for Historical Research in the University of London. The ambitiousness of this project is evident in the fact that many County Histories are still unfinished. However, for those areas that are covered, the VCH is an invaluable first stop – it not only provides a broad overview of most antiquarian and historical discoveries, but also provides (in the form of extensive footnotes and references) clues to the most suitable primary and secondary sources for further research.

Apart from the VCH, in most areas the secondary documentation consists of local history studies. Of these, the oldest is preserved in restricted-access areas (such as strongrooms) while the more recent – although more readily available – may need to be treated with caution as sources of hard data.

Where details of architectural history are concerned, the local 'Pevsner' is the main source. A hugely respected scholar and a fabulously detailed and informed set of books, one for each county or city, this source is invaluable with (often copious) details of every building of interest.

Primary Documents

Usually for a preliminary DBA, it is not necessary to consult primary documents. These are often referred to in sufficient detail by the available secondary sources, such as the VCH (see above). However, there are occasions – when the secondary source is unclear, where 'new' documents have come to light, or where more site-specific information is likely to be found – when a consultation of the primary documentation is essential.

One category of primary documentation which is readily available for the post-1800 period is *local directories*. These were prepared by private firms, such as Kelly's, and list businesses and individuals by street, trade and alphabetically. They usually contain a short potted history of the area and a small-scale map. Using such directories requires some caution, however, since people had to pay to be featured in them. They may be checked against *census records*, almost universally available on microfilm reels – a reading machine usually needs to be booked in advance for this. Censuses (taken every 10 years from 1801, but with the detailed returns only being kept after 1851) are a valuable record of individual streets and homes in the nineteenth century. Census returns are only available after 100 years; at the time of writing, the 1901 census is the most recent in the public domain, in 2011 the 1911 census will become available.

Other primary sources include a wide range of *legal documents* (such as leases and partnerships, disputes and rentals), company and personal *accounts, letters,* diaries and so on. In such cases, it is important to be aware of the reasons why these documents were created; in all cases, there was never the intention of informing future archaeologists about land use and property boundaries – which is of course one of the main motives why we consult them. Also, their survival is often fragmentary and is often bundled together in archives as 'Miscellaneous Documents'. While the information they contain might be very valuable, the amount of time needed to trawl through often mundane reports of tangential interest needs to be balanced against the likely significance of any evidence found within them.

The average non-specialist with English as their mother tongue is likely to be able to read most documents from the early nineteenth century onwards. Non-native English speakers are likely to struggle – not so much in deciphering individual words, but in dealing with the often tortuous legal language in which many documents are written. It is not untypical for a basic description of the date, names of the parties and the origins and the nature of the document itself to run to several paragraphs. Handwriting before the nineteenth century, and especially from before the eighteenth century, is extremely specialised and difficult to read without extensive practice. Before the seventeenth century, the use of Latin was common; however, this is not the classical Latin with which most people are familiar, but a parochial late-mediaeval Latin interspersed with English, French and a wide range of abbreviations peculiar to the individual author. There are guides to early handwriting, but in practice a project which requires extensive consultation of early primary sources is better off engaging a specialist.

Photographs

Photographic collections are held in most local archives and local studies centres, as well as the collections of aerial photographs noted above. An initial search of the photograph catalogue for references to a particular site or area is always helpful. Usually, you will not have more than a dozen images to deal with. Most photography is not earlier than the 1870s and usually consists of street scenes or photographs of notable historic buildings. Such photographs were usually taken speculatively for the postcard market (Fig. 5.4). By the early twentieth century, photographers were also being employed for specific recording which may have archaeological value. For example, many industrial firms commissioned studies of their workers and factories. Photographic surveys of many districts were made during the slum clearances of the 1920s and 1930s – although intended to emphasise poverty and degradation for propaganda purposes, they frequently depict vernacular buildings of some antiquity which may be related to historic mapping. In the later twentieth century, photographic coverage is much improved, and further modernisation of the urban fabric in the 1950s and 1960s (the demolition of older houses, construction of new roads and so on) inspired official and amateur recording of many areas.

Fig 5.4 Old postcards can prove a useful source of historical, architectural, social and topographic information. (Photo: courtesy of Ironbridge Gorge Museum Trust)

The English Heritage NMR contains millions of photographs, including aerial, social historical, archaeological and architectural, some of which can be searched online, and others would require a visit. It is worth mentioning also that the NMR is host to a number of very specific collections, such as the British Rail archive, which unsurprisingly contains thousands of photographs of British railway stations, many of which were closed down in the 1960s.

Oral History

Oral history has been the subject of a boom in the last 30 years, and many local archives contain recordings of individuals concerned with particular local events or industries. These are unlikely to be consulted directly in the first stage of historical research; however, it is worth noting whether or not they exist. Some oral histories are more useful than others. Recollections of life in a particular neighbourhood are more likely to help you get a general feel for the area within the last hundred years; occasionally, a particular building or feature which is central to your project might be mentioned. Oral histories of factory workers might be more helpful if working on an industrial site as memories of how processes worked or where individual machines were located might well assist in the post-excavation interpretation.

Previous Ground Investigations

For archaeologists compiling a DBA with a view to informing future stages of intrusive fieldwork, it is essential to find out what previous work has been done on or near the site. This helps in understanding the basic make-up of the ground on site. Some of this previous work may have been done by archaeologists (such as an earlier evaluation or site investigation), in which case record of it should be held in the HER. It is more likely that various geotechnical surveys have been undertaken for non-archaeological reasons. These records might be held by the current client, or may be on file in the Local Authority archives. Although they may not be easy to find, they are worth seeking out if possible. The records of such work tend to identify geological strata very well, but are very likely to have lumped together all of the archaeology as 'fill' or 'made ground' containing 'bricks, stone, slate, charcoal, wood fragments'. However, even where detail is limited, it is possible to estimate the likely total depth of archaeological deposits, the nature of the underlying 'natural' and even to some extent the sort of material which might be encountered during excavation.

Summary

These then are some of the procedures and suggestions for sourcing information that typically precede fieldwork. Projects do need to be planned, and it is necessary nowadays to understand professional and other obligations to the client, the landowner, and to the public, the local community in the area where work is to take place. These days communities are interested and knowledgeable, and archaeologists should engage with that enthusiasm, not ignore it, however tight the schedule. The chapter has also provided a rapid overview of information gathering at this, the so-called DBA stage. To provide a comprehensive guide to sources in all of the home countries would be impossible, not least as these are constantly evolving, usually with more information being made freely available online. But the basics are there: national and local records offices; the local HER, normally housed with the local authority's Planning Department, the national monument records of the home countries, and the Internet, where anything is possible. We now proceed to describe the field techniques and recording procedures typically used on fieldwork projects in Britain today.

References and Further Reading

Department for Communities and Local Government. 2010. *Planning Policy Statement 5: Planning for the Historic Environment*. London, TPO.

Department of the Environment. 1990. *Planning Policy Guideline Note 16: archaeology and planning*. London, HMSO.

English Heritage. 1991. *The Management of Archaeological Projects (MAP2)*. London: English Heritage. www.english-heritage.org.uk.

English Heritage 2006. *Management of Research Projects in the Historic Environment: The MoRPHE Project Managers Guide (MoRPHE)*. London: English Heritage. http://www.english-heritage. org.uk/upload/pdf/MoRPHE-Project-Managers-Guide.pdf.

English Heritage. 2008. *Geophysical Survey in Archaeological Field Evaluation*. Swindon: English Heritage.

Institute for Archaeologists. 2008. *Standard and Guidance for Archaeological Desk-based assessment*.

Chapter 6
Acquiring Data During Excavation and Survey

In the previous chapter, we described some of the desk-based research methods that can precede fieldwork. We looked at mapping, archives and aerial photographs, and the ways in which these sources can be combined to respond to the desk-based assessment typically stipulated in a project 'brief'. Here, we take it one step further. Of course, all of the methods associated with desk-based assessment can stand alone as a study in their own right, without any intention of following this up with fieldwork. But in the commercial sector, fieldwork is a typical next stage. Here, we not only look at excavation, but also some non-intrusive methods, such as surveying earthwork sites and buildings, and the various standards that any work in these areas should achieve.

Types of Excavation

Field excavation is the classic technique of archaeology, and the techniques of excavation have evolved over the last 150 years into a sophisticated and nuanced set of methodologies for extracting information about past human activity from the ground. Indeed, the story of British archaeology is largely also one of its 'great excavations', the sites and the people who dug them which now comprise much of the social history and 'archaeography' of our profession (Schofield 2011). The outline of much of this story has already been told in Chap. 2. Here, we briefly consider some of the techniques of archaeological excavation used in Great Britain today. The rest of this first part of the chapter looks briefly at some of the main principles of excavation, concerning how to dig and how to record what has been dug up.

All interventions involving the removal of soil for an archaeological purpose are by definition excavations, and the actual techniques of excavation and recording are more or less the same on all archaeological excavations in Britain. However, there are some regional variations in detail, and the speed and thoroughness of investigation does vary depending on the type of excavation and its circumstances. Broadly speaking, there are three different types of excavation project with which you might find yourself involved.

J. Schofield et al., *Archaeological Practice in Great Britain: A Heritage Handbook*,
World Archaeological Congress Cultural Heritage Manual Series,
DOI 10.1007/978-0-387-09453-3_6, © Springer Science+Business Media, LLC 2011

Evaluations

Evaluations take the form of trial trenches and/or test pits. Evaluation trenches can sometimes be quite large and often take the form of mini-excavations such is their size. Evaluations may take place in a research-led context (see below), but they are most often used in commercial archaeology – and indeed most commercial archaeological excavation work consists of evaluations. The primary purpose of an evaluation is to determine the extent and survival of archaeological remains – in other words, to characterise the resource – rather than to provide a complete narrative. This is important to remember. Because of this, an evaluation is typically regarded as a sampling exercise. In commercial archaeology, the amount of trial trenching is usually specified in the brief (typically between 5 and 10% of any given site area, although this may vary), and the locations of individual trenches is normally decided during the initial tendering process through discussion by the archaeological contractor and the curatorial archaeologist. Trench locations are decided by a combination of factors. Sometimes, the trial trenches follow the alignment of proposed foundations in a development; at other times, they may be called upon to investigate or attempt to locate known or supposed features identified through historical research. Because evaluation is a sampling exercise, it may not be possible or desirable to completely dissect the whole stratigraphic sequence from topsoil to 'natural'. Sometimes, it is sufficient to reveal the presence of substantial structures or features, and to partly investigate them to get an idea of their potential for specialist analysis, such as pollen, insects or other palaeoenvironmental sampling (see below). Evaluations are typically short in duration: sometimes, lasting only a few days. Time is, therefore, at a premium, and archaeologists are expected to work quickly.

Commercial Excavations

Large-scale excavations usually take place as part of the mitigation strategy (see Chap. 4) and may therefore aim for total excavation of the entire site. In practice, this is rarely achievable. This may be due to the presence of intrusive structures, such as piles, drains, tanks and concrete (which of course could themselves be part of the site), and it is usually not necessary to excavate each and every feature to its fullest extent. Therefore pits, wells and ditches may only be partly excavated. Inevitably, later features are entirely removed once recorded to get to earlier features below them. The whole process is often referred to as 'preservation by record' or 'preservation by understanding'. Such excavations are normally informed by the results of prior evaluation. This theoretically means that they are then appropriately resourced – there is a reasonable understanding as to the nature and extent of surviving archaeological remains, which should be reflected in the costs and timescales that have been allocated to the project. Having said that, it is a general rule that some of the most impressive findings are made as the excavation is about to end and, as a result, post-excavation budgets can often be underestimated (see Chap. 7). For various reasons (not normally archaeological ones, they are usually to do with land ownership, changes to the development and planning law), it is possible that full-scale excavation does not take place until several years after the initial evaluation. Historically, the same archaeological contractor was usually deployed to undertake all stages of fieldwork, although this is increasingly no longer the case. As with all aspects of commercial fieldwork, time is critical. Depending on how the contract has been arranged, the archaeological unit may even be subject to financial penalties if they overrun.

Research-Led Excavations

While all archaeological fieldwork is by definition 'research', the location, extent and thoroughness of commercial fieldwork is usually decided by non-archaeological factors. So, although the results of such excavations are considered in the light of broader research questions, the motive for excavating in the first place may not have been to enhance research per se. However, outside the commercial sphere, there are numerous projects whose *raison d'être* is not impending destruction through development. Such research-led excavations are undertaken by universities, local societies, community groups and others. Such projects usually have several aims, and pure research may not always be the most important. Research-led excavations frequently provide an opportunity for training, especially undergraduate and post-graduate students, although local volunteers and adult education groups may also be involved. These types of excavations increasingly have a community aspect. They may not be community-led (see Chap. 4), but they certainly try to engage with interested amateurs and 'the public'. The pace of work on research-led excavations is usually much slower than in commercial archaeology. It is also the case that recording systems may be more variable, and the personality of the project director also plays a part in this. There is also considerable leeway for discussion and engagement with the excavated material, and it is on these sorts of projects that some of the more ambitious attempts to develop post-processual 'reflexive' approaches have begun. The experience offered on many research-led projects can be very different from the world of commercial archaeology, and it has been suggested that not all of the skills learnt are immediately transferable to the 'real world'. Having said that, most people in British archaeology have started out on these sorts of excavations and have survived to tell the tale.

...and Finally

Whether you are working on a rapid city-centre commercial evaluation in a trench measuring only a few metres wide or on a long-term large-scale research excavation in the countryside, it is important to remember that the process of excavation is a destructive one. Philip Barker wrote more than 30 years ago:

> To dig holes, however well recorded, in an ancient site is like cutting pieces out of a hitherto unexamined manuscript, transcribing the fragments, and then destroying them (Barker 1977, 41–2).

Excavation can also be very frustrating because the most interesting features tend to disappear outside the boundaries of any trial trench or excavation area; or later intrusions such as cellars, piles and below-ground storage tanks have sterilised that very area where all the different phases of the site came together.

Processes of Excavation

Archaeological excavation is one of the few jobs which is still predominantly manual, a situation that presents its own risks to the practitioners. Modern understanding of occupational health is much greater than it was even 10 years ago, and by adopting sensible working practices (see Manual Handling, below), you will minimise the back, joint and tendon injuries prevalent among an earlier generation of archaeologists. Having said that, there is still a relict 'macho' culture on many sites which is best avoided – although this is much diminished since official health and safety guidance (see below) now frowns on shovelling and barrowing competitions.

Opening Up the Site

Traditionally, the entire process of archaeological excavation was undertaken by hand, and in some areas – such as parks and historic gardens – the back-breaking task of deturfing by hand is still unavoidable. This may also be insisted upon by the curator where buried remains are believed to be either sensitive or close to the surface.

Yet nowadays, the majority of archaeological excavations are opened up by hydraulic excavating machine ('digger'). The type of machine used depends upon the nature of the site; but there are two basic types. The smallest, and most frequently used for evaluations and other operations, is the 'JCB' – a tractor with a front shovel and 'back-actor' with bucket. The term 'JCB' is actually the trade name of an English manufacturer of site plant, and is used in Britain almost universally to describe such small machines – just as 'Hoover' might be used to refer to a vacuum cleaner. Of course, the JCB concern manufactures other plant, while similar smaller excavators are made by other manufacturers. Larger machines are usually tracked, and can swivel through 360 degrees – so here you deal with a 'tracked 360 excavator'. These range in size from 12 to over 70 tonnes. The larger machines are best employed on urban sites, where overburden may include concrete and rubble made ground. Sometimes, these machines are used in conjunction with 'dumpers'. Dumpers again range in size from 3 tonnes upwards.

Both 'JCB' and '360' excavators can attach a 'breaker' (sometimes called colloquially a 'pecker') to their hydraulic systems which is useful for breaking through concrete slabs and removing other intrusive structures. It is worth noting that the smaller excavators with tyres are road-legal and can be driven to site; the larger tracked excavators need to be transported by low-loader and this can add considerably to the excavation costs.

Plant hire firms usually supply experienced operators with plant; usual rates are quoted per hour, but a minimum 8 h day is often specified. Self-driven machines may charge an extra hour for travel; tracked machines charge for delivery and collection. Traditionally, fuel was included in the cost, but rising oil prices have encouraged a charge for diesel as a separate item. Note also that both types of excavator have inter-changeable buckets. Normal construction practice is to use a toothed bucket, but this wreaks havoc with archaeological remains so it is best to use a 'ditching bucket' which has a smooth face. Bucket sizes are stubbornly non-metric, so ask for a 'six-foot bucket' (1.8 m wide), a 'four-foot bucket' (1.2 m wide) or a 'three-foot bucket' (0.9 m wide) depending on the size of the area you need excavating.

A good digger driver is worth his (or her) weight in gold. An experienced operator is very sensitive to their controls, detecting walls and other features through minute vibrations in the cab. They can peel back layers as little as 1 cm deep and are usually very interested in the archaeological project which represents a break with the usual routine. An inexperienced or careless operator, on the other hand, is a liability. Good rapport with the digger driver is essential during evaluations and excavations.

Excavation of Layers

Machine removal of the upper layers is always supervised by an experienced archaeologist. Machining will stop once archaeological features are encountered, and it is the archaeologist's job to determine when that is. On urban sites, this usually means locating a wall or similarly solid evidence of archaeological remains, while on rural sites it may be immediately after the removal of the turf layer. From then on, excavation is a more arduous and meticulous process.

In Britain, the normal excavation tool is the trowel. The most favoured of these is a 'WHS' 4-in. pointing trowel. 'WHS' is a brand name of Neill Tools of Sheffield. Their trowels are expensive (usually around £15), but the key feature is that they are 'solid-forged', that is to say the tang and blade are a single forging. Cheaper trowels tend to have the tang welded onto the blade and are prone to breakage. The 'WHS' is a very stiff trowel, quite different from the springy 'Marshalltown' favoured by North American archaeologists. While the 'Marshalltown' might be excellent in sandy or loamy deposits with few intrusions, the 'WHS' is sufficiently robust to be able to prise out rocks and bricks, clean back masonry structures and scrape away endless layers of clay. The 4-in. blade was once used in the building trade, but no longer. Now, it is the staple of archaeo-logical excavation in Britain, preferred to larger ones because it can work into smaller areas. Novices turning up with the more commonly available 6-in. pointing trowel find themselves the butt of jokes. As trowels are used they become more worn, and the expe-rienced archaeologist prides himself on their stubby implement worn by years of hard graft and often with a blade no more than 1-in. long (Fig. 6.1).

As mentioned above, British archaeology is geared to stratigraphic excavation, and the use of arbitrary layers (or 'spits') is generally frowned upon. Stratigraphic excavation requires the complete removal of individual contexts in reverse order to

Fig. 6.1 WHS trowels: the trowel is an iconic badge of archaeological experience – the more worn the better; these trowels have been arranged to represent the various levels of membership of the IfA. Photograph by Peter Hinton, Chief Executive of the IfA

the sequence in which they were deposited. Thus, the trowel-wielding excavator is expected to identify such contexts as they go along, by paying careful attention to the different colours and textures of different layers.

Sieving is not common practice, so you are expected to use your trowel to extract everything from the context on which you are working. To do this effectively the trowelling operation is best performed from the elbow, with the lower arm more or less rigid. If you use the wrist, you will find that you suffer very badly after a few days. The blade of the trowel is usually held at around 45°, enabling artefacts to be flicked up as you go and placed into the finds tray or finds bag. Needless to say, a single tray or bag should only be used for finds from each context, although the details of how this system works vary from site to site.

The trowelling action should take you backwards across the surface, scraping up the loose soil (generally just referred to as 'loose') using a hand-shovel into a bucket. Periodically, the bucket is emptied into a wheelbarrow, which, once full, is taken to the spoil heap. Usually, the labour of trowelling, shovelling and barrowing is equally divided within the small teams working on different parts of the site.

Trowelling is sometimes discarded in favour of more rapid excavation methods, particularly if the layer is devoid of artefacts or is considered to be less significant or less sensitive. In such cases, the most common and preferred tool is the mattock.

Virtually, unknown outside Great Britain (and greeted with horror by many North American archaeologists) the mattock is a ubiquitous and revered tool on British excavations. Essentially, a pick-axe with one flattened blade, the mattock originated as a trenching tool for the British army. It can be used brutally – to prise rocks from stubborn layers – or with great subtlety, almost as a trowel, to 'shave' away a layer in successive horizons. It can be difficult to acquire the skills of mattocking. However, once you have done so you will wonder why you had not used such a versatile tool before. The key is to use the weight of the mattock to do the work for you.

Spades and shovels are quite different implements. A spade is a cutting tool, used for cleaning sections (see below) and for digging out small features. It is also used for de-turfing (see above). The shovel is a load-carrying tool and is used to transfer the spoil from excavations to the bucket, wheelbarrow or spoil heap. Long-handled shovels used in mainland Europe, North America and Australia are still rare in Britain and are regarded with suspicion despite their greater leverage.

Excavation of Features

Cut features are usually evident in plan (Fig. 6.2). In Britain, unlike the Republic of Ireland, cut features are rarely 100% excavated. Instead, a sample is taken. In the case of circular features (such as pits, post-holes and wells), it is common practice to do a 'half-section' – that is, a 50% sample; larger features may be 'quarter-sectioned' in a manner reminiscent of Mortimer Wheeler's baulks. Linear features (such as ditches) are usually sampled at intervals along their length. In both cases, this sampling strategy enables the recording of the 'section' (see below) as well as the 'shape in plan' (see below) of the feature.

Positive features are those which are formed on top of the underlying layers. In stratigraphic terms, these are 'upstanding layers'. Positive features take various forms – classic examples include banks or mounds, such as Neolithic henges, Bronze Age barrows, Iron Age hill forts, mediaeval motte-and-bailey castles, post-mediaeval field boundaries and so on. Positive features also include buildings (or the remains of buildings). These are usually referred to on site as 'structures'. Stratigraphically, there is no difference between a mound and a wall; both are 'upstanding layers' and relate to their surroundings in similar ways. However, the details of their form are inevitably very different, and so the ways in which they are excavated and recorded (see also below) varies. Thus, it is still common practice to excavate a section through earthwork features to determine the composition of the section. Structures are rarely sectioned, as they are usually deconstructed stratigraphically in reverse order to the sequence of construction. Since it is recognised that structures are part of the overall stratigraphic sequence, you will not be expected (or asked) in British archaeology to leave bits of walls or structures on pillars of underlying soil, as is sometimes the case in other parts of the world.

Fig. 6.2 Archaeological excavation in progress, with cut features being excavated. Near the trowelling figure are several small pits which have already been excavated; in the foreground is a clay-filled feature which has yet to be excavated. Photograph by Paul Belford

Other Excavation Tips

It is important that you manage your spoil, or 'loose', and refrain from making great piles of it – more than a few bucket-loads and you will be in trouble. Tea breaks and lunches are announced with the traditional cry of 'clear up your loose', and you will be expected to do just that before you stop working. In the variable British climate, this is a sensible approach. It is quite possible for a sudden shower to descend on a bright sunny day, and that pile of clean dry soil left at the side of your trench will turn into a slimy muddy film which will run back down into and across whatever you were doing.

It is important also that you remain aware of what is going on around you. In archaeological terms, this means seeing what your neighbouring colleagues are up to, and discussing interpretation of each other's features and finds. While excessive time spent in discussion is frowned upon, a good site director encourages this sort of informal dialogue which can usually take place while shovelling or while passing each other with buckets and barrows. Good managers also try and brief people about what is going on. One common approach is a short tour on Friday afternoon in which everyone tells everyone else what they have been doing. A more general awareness is also important on site, especially from a safety point of view. Deep excavations can be dangerous, machinery is often used and needs to be given a wide berth, and colleagues may call on you to assist them in difficult jobs.

Always ask for help if you are uncertain. On most sites there are one or two (or maybe more) people with specialist knowledge of the area or site type, and most colleagues welcome questions. It is usually better to ask questions of individual supervisors or site directors as you go along, usually when they visit your particular area of excavation. Do not be afraid to ask seemingly simple questions. Everyone has been a novice, and sometimes the simpler and more obvious questions are actually those that best help the process of interpretation. Beware the jaded and cynical attitudes of many of your more experienced colleagues – they have a very good understanding of the field evidence, but may not always have the most positive approach to their employer or to the profession in general. Beware also the robust British sense of humour – there is always the temptation to lead 'newbies' slightly astray by inventing tasks or situations to tease them: 'Could you go and fetch the water table?' for example.

Recording Methods for Excavation

Archaeological Recording on Site

There is no nationally applied standard for archaeological recording on site and every archaeological unit has slightly different ways of doing things. Having said that, most recording systems are broadly similar in principle. What does vary is the layout of the various recording forms and some of the terminology used.

The Written Record

The widespread adoption of recording by 'units of stratification' led to the development in 1975 of the 'context sheet' – a pro forma recording form on which various attributes of each stratigraphic unit could be described by the person excavating the context in question. The context sheets of the Museum of London's Department of Urban Archaeology (now 'Museum of London Archaeology' or 'MOLA' for short), together with the now-classic excavation manual (see below), have formed the template for those used by most units – and have of course continued to develop over the years (Fig. 6.3).

Different types of archaeological remains require different aspects to be recorded – the cut for a post-hole is a very different item to a wall. Therefore, several different types of context sheet are usually used for layers (deposits), cut features, structures, timber, and so on. Also, since understanding of the archaeological deposits improve as excavation proceeds, the sheets are designed to be added to as you go along. All context sheets normally consist of six main 'zones'. The details of the site come first. Next is the description of the context itself. This description is just that: colour, texture, thickness, extent, depth, bonding (if a wall), shape (of cut features) and construction (of timber). Finds (from layers) are also described. The third zone describes the stratigraphic relationship of the present layer to those around it while

CONTEXT RECORD

PROJECT CODE	TRENCH / AREA	CO-ORDINATES	CONTEXT NO
LENGTH	WIDTH	DIAMETER	HEIGHT/DEPTH

CONTEXT CATEGORY (fill/cut/layer/structure):

DESCRIPTION (definition/colour/texture/consistence/components/finds/shape/sides/base/excavation method/fabric/size/bonding/bond):

(PTO for sketches)

FINDS:

PART OF GROUP: Context Nos.:

STRATIGRAPHIC RELATIONSHIPS	STRATIGRAPHIC MATRIX
Below:	▢ ▢ ▢ ▢ ▢ ▢
Same as:	THIS CONTEXT: ▢
Above:	▢ ▢ ▢ ▢ ▢ ▢

INTERPRETATION (Date of Deposit/Construction/Formation Processes/Function):

SMALL FIND NO:	SAMPLE NO:
PLAN NO:	SECTION NO:

PHOTOGRAPH NOS:

RECORDED BY:	DATE:	CHECKED BY:	DATE:

Fig. 6.3 A typical 'context sheet' universally used in British archaeology and derived from the MOLA sheet of the 1970s. Courtesy of Nexus Heritage

the fourth area ties in this record with all the other records – drawing and photograph numbers, levels and so on. There is then space to sketch a plan, profile or section (or all three). Finally, the context sheet includes an area for interpretation. This may initially be left blank or filled in simply as 'wall' or 'ditch'. As excavation proceeds to gather evidence, more sophisticated interpretations might be considered: 'east wall of rectilinear structure' or 'recut of drainage ditch'. Almost always these interim interpretations are revised by site managers and again at the post-excavation stage, the 'east wall' is now becoming a 'late thirteenth century east wall of church' or 'Phase 3 recut of northern drainage ditch', for example.

The details of how to describe these things in a consistent way include certain standards for the description of sediments and terminology. Most units follow the comprehensive guidance in the MOLA 'Archaeological Site Manual' (Spence 1990) or have their own variation on it. This is a useful and widely available publication which is worth investing in if you are committed to serious fieldwork.

As well as context sheets, the written record also includes lists. These include: lists of contexts, drawings, levels taken, 'small finds' (see below) and so on. It also includes the site matrix.

The Drawn Record

The majority of field drawings are undertaken by hand on waterproof drawing film (sometimes known by the proprietary name 'Permatrace') using a hard pencil (5H or 6H is best). Most field units use pre-printed sheets at A3 size, with a cartouche for details of drawing number, orientation, relation to other records and so on. The weather-proof quality and cheapness of this system has ensured its survival, although it is being replaced or supplemented on some large projects with electronic data capture. Typically, drawings are made of sections and features. A site plan, and detailed plans of particular areas of the site, is also made in the field during the normal course of the excavation.

The Photographic Record

Despite the rapid development of digital photography in the last 10 years, conventional film-based photography is still preferred. This is for two main reasons. Firstly, film has a known archival permanence. Traditional silver-based black-and-white negative film (and the resulting prints) can last well over 100 years, and even good quality colour slide film can survive for at least 50 years if properly archived. Sadly, the much loved Kodachrome has now been discontinued after a 74-year production run. In contrast, the rapidly changing nature of digital storage (not to mention the compression algorithms used in some formats, such as JPEGs) means that digital photographs taken today may be unreadable in 20 years' time. Secondly, however mega your pixels, the resolution of a good quality low-speed medium format film is always better. An ISO 50 6×4 negative has the equivalent of 60 or 70 megapixel resolution.

Taking good photographs requires a good knowledge of the camera and of light conditions. Film cameras come in two basic forms – viewfinder and 'single-lens reflex' (SLR) types. The SLR is best because you see exactly what the camera sees through the lens, and you can change lenses for different conditions. The most common is the 35 mm camera, which uses cassettes of film on which each negative measures 36 mm×28 mm. Film normally comes in 24 or 36 exposure rolls.

For detail, publishable photographs and architectural recording, a medium format camera is used. This uses 120 roll film, which needs to be carefully loaded. Different manufacturers use different formats, so a '6×4.5' allows 15 shots on a roll of film, whereas a '6×7' only allows 12. As well as superior resolution, medium format cameras also have features, such as 'perspective lenses' which allow correction of the converging vertical lines when taking photographs of tall buildings, for example.

Digital cameras are increasingly sophisticated, some affordable SLRs now being available with 15 megapixel resolution, which is approaching the quality of some 35 mm images. The advantage of digital photography is that you can see what you have taken instantly, delete unwanted images, and store many more photographs on a memory card than can be accommodated on a roll of film. They can then be instantly downloaded, and are generally of an acceptable quality for most reports, working shots and lecture presentations. They are also useful as a tool for photogrammetry (see standing building recording, below). However, the archival permanence of this medium is still a significant concern (see Chap. 7).

Photographs taken on site fall into two categories – working shots and record shots. Working shots show people undertaking various tasks, such as excavating or drawing. They are useful as illustrative material (for websites, lectures and some publications) because as they feature people doing things, they are usually more interesting. They are also useful as a record of how the site was actually excavated, and therefore do form an important part of the site archive. There is also a social historical quality to them. Record shots are more formal, and show features at certain stages of excavation, or 'fully excavated'. Record photographs require meticulous cleaning of the area to be photographed – every surface must be trowelled, not brushed, and care taken not to leave foot- or hand-prints: the camera shows every imperfection. Section edges must be neat, clean and vertical. All trench-side debris (such as random finds, gloves, hats, recording forms, tools, wheelbarrows, etc.) must be taken well out of shot. A metric scale rod is always used, ranging from 1 to 4 m in length depending on the size of area being photographed. For sections, it is always preferable to photograph the north-facing section of any trench, as it is always in shadow. In fact, all record photography is best done under a bright but diffuse light; direct sunlight makes for dramatic pictures (especially of structures) but may overpower some of the subtleties of different soil horizons.

Non-Intrusive Fieldwork

Despite the popular association of archaeology with excavation, Britain has a long tradition of non-intrusive archaeological work. Usually applied in rural or semi-rural locations, non-intrusive techniques have the advantage of being able to cover large areas relatively quickly, and to pinpoint particular places where further work may be required. As with historical research, non-intrusive survey might be used as part of the evaluation stages of a project.

Survey

Since the seventeenth century, a strong tradition has built up which is more or less unique to the British Isles. Survey in the British tradition usually refers specifically to a measured survey of earthworks and other features; as distinct from fieldwalking or a walkover survey.

Survey is not purely the art of taking measurements, but rather it concerns 'providing information about the monument's form, construction, function, condition and on how it has been affected by subsequent developments and later use' (RCHME 1999). While the traditional plane table is still in use, in more recent decades instruments, such as Electronic Data Measurement (EDM) and Geographical Positioning Systems (GPSs) have become widely used, and in skilled hands can delivery accurate and quick results.

A survey project might involve four main stages:

Historical research

Reconnaissance (see Chap. 5)

The purpose of the reconnaissance is twofold – firstly to get an idea of the landscape itself, and secondly (perhaps more importantly) to consider the practical aspects of the survey stage which follows. Such questions might include:

- Site ownership and access issues, health and safety, legal constraints, such as SAMs, SSSI, etc., land use (any grazing animals, amount and height of vegetation)
- Identifying how the purpose of the survey might affect the ways in which it is undertaken – also considering the survival and significance of the features involved
- The size of the survey area and the amount of surviving archaeological remains visible: a small area with a density of archaeological remains on the site may take longer than a large area with few visible archaeological remains
- How does the site tie in with its surrounding area: do any large linear features, such as field boundaries, leats, or railways, run across the site?
- What is the most appropriate technique and equipment to use on the study site? For example, GPS is not suitable for a site in woodland
- What scale will the survey be done at? Scale is usually defined by the purpose of the survey. If fine detail of earthworks and structures are required, then the smallest scale practical is 1:500 or 1:250. If the purpose of the survey is to illustrate the location of sites over a wide coverage, then large-scale mapping at 1:2,500 or 1:1,250 would be more appropriate
- Staffing and timescale: this depends on the experience of the surveyors, the type of equipment used and health and safety concerns. Although survey can be conducted by an individual or a team, most surveys are usually best done with two people. In remote areas, this provides a margin of safety; it also allows for discussion of the survey results as the work proceeds

Survey

The survey itself consists of measuring the tops and bottoms of earthwork features and plotting them. Modern survey equipment means that this is done very quickly and some GPS and EDM equipment actually draw up the survey (as a series of lines) as work proceeds.

The survey is contained within a 'grid' of control points – either a regular or an irregular grid depending on field conditions. The Ordnance Survey National Grid is one example of a regular grid created without reference to existing landscape features.

Once the control framework has been established, a detailed survey of the archaeological features can be undertaken. Small to medium scale surveys (1:10,000–1:2,500) can be conducted by adding features to existing maps by tapes, optical squares, compasses or hand-held GPS. Surveys of almost all sizes can be conducted with EDM/theodolites, GPS, plane-tables and tape measures. Small to medium sized areas can be completed with plane tables, optical squares and tapes. Compasses or hand-held GPS can be used for small scale surveys. Detailed analytical earthwork survey uses the measuring process to examine slopes, ditches and other features, their forms and patterns, and examines the relationships between them. Measurements can be taken off the control points. The process of measurement and drawing of each earthwork ensures an accurate plan and facilitates critical observation.

Drawing Up

The field survey output usually takes the form of lines plotted along the tops, bottoms, edges and corners of features observed. The traditional method of drawing up involves hachures, which are lines drawn down the slope to indicate its length and gradient. Although various alternative methods, such as hill shading, contours and multi-coloured lines have been attempted, the hachure plan still remains the clearest way of depicting features. A hachure plan can be read at a glance; the relative size and shape of different features is immediately apparent. Hachure plans fit within the existing tradition of earthwork survey, meaning that a plan done in 2010 can be readily compared with one done many decades before.

Traditionally, as in other forms of archaeology, all the drawing up was done by hand. However, most earthwork surveys are now completed using proprietary software, such as AutoCAD, Adobe Illustrator or CorelDraw. Nevertheless, the same conventions apply.

Geophysical Survey

Geophysics is normally deployed as part of a wider project, as opposed to being used in isolation. It is important that the correct type of geophysical technique is adopted for the site in question, and some sites may require more than one technique to be deployed.

The most commonly applied geophysical survey techniques in British archaeology are magnetometry, resistivity (electrical resistance), electromagnetic conductivity (EM) and ground-penetrating radar (GPR). Magnetic susceptibility was widely used in the late twentieth century but has been largely replaced by wide-area magnetometry surveys.

Magnetometry

There are two basic types of magnetometer in use on archaeological projects in Britain. Traditionally, British archaeologists have preferred the 'gradiometer' (often called a 'fluxgate gradiometer') which is a hand-held vertically oriented device which measures the relative magnetism between two sensors – one near the bottom of the instrument (typically about 0.3–0.5 m above the ground) and one near the top (typically between 0.5 and 1 m above the lower sensor). In recent years, British archaeology has also begun to employ 'alkali-vapour' magnetometers (also known as 'caesium magnetometers') which use a single sensor to measure the total magnetic field strength. There is little to choose between the two, although alkali-vapour machines are ultimately more sensitive.

Resistivity

Resistivity measures the electrical resistance in the ground between two or four probes. These are inserted into the ground along a grid, conventionally by using a hand-held frame (a 'zimmerframe'); this is connected to control probes located in a 'neutral' area some distance away from the survey.

Ground-Penetrating Radar

GPR was initially developed for geological survey, and is still relatively rare in British archaeology. GPR can often be more expensive and is relatively slow compared with other geophysical survey methods, but unlike other methods, can effectively provide a 'cross-section' of the buried landscape with information about depth. In some circumstances, GPR can effectively present a three dimensional (3D) image of archaeological features. It is also helpfully deployed in urban areas and other sites where solid overburden (such as concrete slabs) mean that more traditional methods would be ruled out.

Aerial Survey

The use of aerial photography has a long history in British archaeology, beginning in the early 1900s with photographs taken from balloons. Aerial photography has more recently been supplemented by Light Detection and Ranging (LiDAR), another application originally used for military purposes but now widely in use for archaeology.

Aerial Photography

Most peoples' involvement with aerial survey involves browsing the existing resource of aerial photographs rather than actually flying. Many of these photographs were not taken for archaeological purposes – such as the fairly comprehensive coverage of urban and industrial centres by the Royal Air Force and German Luftwaffe in the 1940s, or large-scale national surveys by the Royal Air Force and others in the 1950s and 1960s. Private companies – such as Aerofilms – also captured a wide range of images during the mid-twentieth century, and their collection is now held by the National Monuments Record. Specifically, archaeological surveys were undertaken in the post-war period, notably by the Cambridge University Committee for Aerial Photography which has undertaken annual surveys since 1947 and now has more than 500,000 images on file. Relatively high resolution high-level satellite images are now freely accessible online, and can be used for less detailed work, such as the mapping of sites as present/absent or basic management information. English Heritage's National Mapping Programme has for more than 20 years been recording aerial photographic transcriptions and placing that information on the National Monuments Record.

Light Detection and Ranging

Probably, the most widely used archaeological application of LiDAR to date has been in the mapping of features in woodland. By appropriate manipulation of the software, it is possible to 'remove' the data points collected from the tree canopy and thus 'see' the ground. However, this is not an entirely foolproof method – confusion can be caused by areas of dense vegetation (such as holly), fallen trees and steep slopes – and the LiDAR results need to be 'ground truthed' by a physical inspection of the landscape. It is also possible to create high-resolution digital elevation models of archaeological sites which can reveal micro-topography that is not detectable on the ground.

Surface Collection

Fieldwalking is a method of sample-prospecting rural sites. Usually, it is limited to recently ploughed fields. A grid is set up and archaeologists traverse across the field at various intervals (between 1 and 5 m depending on the size of the site and the objectives of the fieldwork) collecting artefacts and other objects (such as metalworking debris) as they go along. The grid is, of course, tied into control points (see 'Earthwork Survey' above). Finds from each grid square are bagged separately so that the type and density of finds and variations in artefact distribution can be plotted. This technique has been applied most frequently for those periods characterised by the survival of significant quantities of artefacts, notably the Neolithic (flint tools and waste flakes) and the Roman and post-mediaeval periods (pottery).

Geotechnical Investigations

Geotechnical investigations usually involve a core (or a borehole) being taken either by hand or using a powered machine. They generally fall into two categories – those undertaken by archaeologists and those undertaken by others.

Archaeological coring is primarily undertaken by environmental archaeologists as a means of looking at palaeoenvironments. Peat bogs and alluvial sites are particularly favourable for the preservation of pollen, seeds, insects and other items which can shed light on past environments and human activities within them. The traditional method is to use a hand-auger. Probably, the most common is a screw-auger, which consists of a large-diameter screw attached to a bar with a T-handle. The thread is twisted into the ground (usually very hard work); extra rods can be added as the hole goes deeper – depths of up to 20 m can be reached. The resulting sample (usually about 5 cm in diameter) is taken from the auger as coring proceeds and bagged according to depth. A gouge-auger is similar in operation, but instead of a screw thread it has a pointed tube with a slot in one side. This is pushed vertically into the ground, twisted to capture the sample, and then withdrawn providing a core which can be taken away for analysis intact. The related Russian auger is used for peaty deposits. Some powered augers are also used – notably the 'post-hole auger' which is a percussive coring tool usually powered from a vehicle.

Larger plant is used by geotechnical specialists who are usually employed to look at the underlying geology. As such, they are therefore not interested in the overburden – usually characterised in their reports as 'fill'. However, since this 'fill' often extends (at least in urban areas) up to 5 m in depth and as it often contains intriguing items, such as slag, brick, charcoal and wood, it can be worth archaeologically monitoring such operations. At the very least, the use of non-archaeological geotechnical survey results can provide information about the overall depth of deposits. With luck and close observation in the field, it may also be possible to distinguish between different layers and activities.

Historic Building Recording

The archaeological approach to building recording has a different rationale from that employed by architects or engineers. The way in which an engineer understands a building relates more to the ways in which it manages the various loads imposed on it, how various services operate and how these aspects may be improved in the future. An engineer is only interested in the historic development of a structure inasmuch as it can inform his knowledge about these other interests. An architect is usually more concerned with the social and logistical functions of a building. An archaeological understanding of the building is more concerned with interpreting how the building was constructed, used and modified in the past. Blocked openings, walled-up fireplaces and structural ironwork may all have their future engineering or architectural uses, but the archaeologist's role is to record how these things were built, inserted, abandoned and changed – and then to try and provide a coherent narrative of the building's development, from its initial construction to the present. An archaeologist visually unravels the layers evident within the fabric of a building in much the same way as peeling back the stratigraphic layers on a buried site.

Of course engineering, architectural and archaeological approaches are (or should be) complementary. As with other forms of archaeology, if the historic building recording is undertaken at an appropriately early stage, then the results of this can be used to inform engineering assessments and architectural designs.

Recording Methods

As with excavation, the maturation of historic building analysis has seen the broad acceptance of fairly universal archaeological recording methods. These relate to the recording systems used in archaeology, but only recently has the 'context'-based system of recording been adopted more widely in dealing with historic buildings. In England, at least there is an accepted convention of four different levels of recording (see below), all of which require written, drawn and photographic accounts to be made of the building.

The Written Record

As with below-ground archaeology, the written record consists both of site observations and historical information. Most surviving standing buildings are either of relatively recent date (i.e. within the last few hundred years) or, if earlier, are of sufficient status to have found a place in the documentary record. Use the tips in the previous chapter when looking up a building's history – census returns are useful when exploring who lived there and when, and if it is an urban building then historic mapping and photographs might give a good idea of the development of the building since the mid-nineteenth century. Urban characterisation of the town or city (usually available through the local HER) provides a view of the wider context and how the surrounding area has evolved over time. There may also have been previous surveys, or photographs or drawings of the building showing features now lost or hidden.

Exploring the building also generates a written record. A single-context recording system can be adopted for this, useful especially when dealing with smaller structures or those which have seen complex alteration over the years. On buildings with only one or two phases (such as many later industrial buildings, for instance), this level of detail may not be required. However, certain features need to be identified, so some form of unambiguous numbering system is needed so that the written record can be related to the drawn and photographic record. At the very least, you need a master plan (or plans) showing the location of your numbered features and the locations of the photographs which you have taken.

Having investigated the building, the next stage is to prepare some form of written analysis. This can range from a basic overview to a detailed interrogation of the various rooms, fixtures, fittings and changing uses of space. Your narrative should be constructed according to the different phases of the building, but the precise scope varies depending on the level of recording that has been chosen (see below). Trying to tie in the archaeological evidence from the building with historical documentary evidence is extremely useful.

The Drawn Record

The purpose of the drawn record is to try to investigate the original form of the building, its function, the ways people moved through it, and the alterations that have been made to it over the years.

The drawn record should at the very least consist of a sketch plan and elevations, and perhaps detailed drawings of different parts of the building (Fig. 6.4). Usually, a measured sketch is a more acceptable minimum, but in many cases you need to produce measured scaled drawings of plans, elevations and (sometimes) cross-sections. The level of detail shown on these varies.

Measuring buildings has traditionally been done using tape measures, and a hand tape is still a quicker way of measuring small features (such as architraves or fireplaces). However, modern hand-held lasers are much quicker (and require only one person) – but be aware of what precisely the device is measuring. For more complex buildings, you can use a total station EDM. Some units deploy a sophisticated laser scanning device which can plot entire elevations and rooms to a very high level of accuracy within minutes, thus saving time (and money) on site.

For many years now, photogrammetry has been used, which involves taking a series of photographs at regular intervals and spacings (tied into a grid) which are then spliced together and used as the basis for a drawing. This process has been made much more widely available with digital photography and its associated processing software. Photogrammetry is only possible with a slightly larger lens (between 70 and 90 mm focal length on a 35 mm SLR is ideal), since the distortion from a wider angle lens makes stitching the individual views together much more difficult. To some extent this can be overcome in the post-fieldwork stages by digital manipulation using proprietary software, such as Adobe Photoshop. As with other methods of digital recording, photogrammetry does save time on site, although the main advantage is that it allows inaccessible parts of the building or structure to be recorded, and it also permits recording of fragile or easily damaged structures.

Fig. 6.4 Historic building recording in action, using electronic distance measuring equipment on a site in Staffordshire. Photograph by Sophie Watson, Clwyd-Powys Archaeological Trust

EDM and laser-scanned drawings are usually downloaded directly into AutoCAD. With AutoCAD, sophisticated drawings can be produced from the basic outline; although it is still the case that detailed features are often hand-drawn. AutoCAD software is the medium of choice for architects and engineers, and so drawings made in this medium are easily transmitted to-and-fro during the course of a project – to the benefit of all. However, beware of architectural CAD drawings. They may be used as the basis for an archaeological record, but experience suggests that they tend to contain inaccuracies, such as inventing right-angles where they do not exist.

The field drawings are conventionally worked up into plans, sections and elevations. Traditionally, building plans and elevations are executed at 1:50, but larger or smaller scales may be deployed depending on the size of the building. From these, it is possible to produce phase plans and 3D reconstructions. Traditionally, reconstructions were rarely produced for most projects, since they were time-consuming and required considerable expertise. However, the latest advances in digital recording mean that CAD software can produce 3D renderings quite easily, as well as walk- and fly-through models.

The Photographic Record

In general, and leaving aside photogrammetry (see above), the same comments apply to building photography as they do to work on an excavation (see above). However, it is still the case that medium format photography is used specifically for building work not only because of the higher resolution, but also because of the fact that medium-format cameras can accommodate a perspective control lens. Normally, when photographing a building from ground level, the camera has to be pointed upwards to some extent; this results in distortion of the vertical lines, which all appear to be converging upwards. This effect is reduced or eliminated by the perspective control lens. Photography can be used to document phases evident within the fabric of the building, as well as features (e.g. fireplaces) and wall art.

For most purposes, a conventional 35 mm SLR camera using black-and-white film is acceptable. Aside from its archival quality, black and white film has a greater tolerance of different light levels. Supplementary photographs can be taken using a high-resolution (10 megapixel or larger) digital SLR. Buildings are impossible to photograph without a good wide-angle lens. For a conventional 35 mm SLR, this means a 28 mm lens as a minimum, although in practice a 20 or 24 mm lens is often preferable for tight spots inside a building. Of course, such lenses also produce a great deal of distortion.

Standards and Guidance

Following the experience of the Royal Commission on the Historic Monuments of England (RCHME), a set of guidelines were drawn up for archaeological recording of historic structures. These rank the levels of recording at different levels. More information is available in the 'Understanding Historic Buildings' guidance available from the HELM Web site: http://www.helm.org.uk/. This English Heritage guidance was last updated in 2006, and is essentially a revision of the RCHME guidance first issued in 1989.

Level 1

This is a very basic record – as the guidelines suggest this is 'not normally an end in itself but contributing to a wider aim'. In other words, the specific building you encounter may be part of a wider landscape or range of buildings. Therefore, you need to include basic information, such as location, type, date and so on, but do not need to include much historical information. A sketch drawing and an exterior photograph is usually sufficient.

Level 2

A Level 2 record is more detailed than that for Level 1, and may include more detailed drawings, as well as interior photography and some basic historical research. It should include measured plans, sections and elevations, as well as fairly comprehensive photographic coverage (at least one shot of each room for instance). A Level 2 record is essentially descriptive rather than analytical – and although it might come to some conclusions about the broad phasing or development of a site, it does not necessarily discuss these aspects in much detail.

Level 3

This is much more detailed and analytical. As well as all of the components of a Level 2 record it may also include cross-sections and detail drawings, detailed photography and a robust but not exhaustive programme of historical research. Samples (for instance of mortar, masonry or timber) might also be taken. As the guidelines suggest, most of the information in a Level 3 record 'will have been obtained from the building itself' rather than documentary sources. The purpose of a Level 3 record is to provide a record of the building rather than to contribute to a wider understanding of the building type or the locale.

Level 4

A Level 4 survey is, according to the guidelines, 'a comprehensive analytical record…for buildings of special importance'. Building on the Level 3 record, there is additional survey work, such as cross-sections, detail drawings and analytical phase plans. There is a lot of detail recording, sampling of the historic fabric and an extensive photographic record. There is also a comprehensive historical study – looking not just at maps and secondary sources, but also investigating primary sources and other documentation – which seeks to place the building in its local, regional, national and even international contexts.

Practical Considerations

Health, Safety and Welfare

Derelict historic buildings can be extremely dangerous places (see also 'Keeping Safe', Chap. 8). Two key things to watch out for with historic buildings are asbestos and pigeons.

Asbestos was widely used as an insulator and general building material until the late 1980s, and is likely to be found in any abandoned building – especially, but not exclusively, industrial structures. It can be used as a heat shield behind radiators, as panelling in walls, as insulation for pipes and as a roofing material. When in the form of intact and painted sheets, it is relatively benign – but as soon as any of those sheets are even slightly frayed, or if it has been used as pipe lagging – then asbestos fibres are in the atmosphere and are extremely dangerous. Inhalation can prove fatal, and not now, but after a long and painful illness. Therefore be extremely wary of asbestos! Protection is (in the extreme) by full suit and specially fitted face mask which needs to be disposed of after use. Specialist training in handling asbestos can be time-consuming (a week-long course is common) and should be included in the project specification at the outset. If you are in any doubt about asbestos, seek advice from your supervisor.

Pigeons are perhaps not life-threatening, but they roost in quite large numbers in derelict buildings. You are likely to encounter guano that is thickly matted over the floors, as well as dead birds in various states of decay. Pigeons (as with all birds) can carry various diseases. Again protective clothing might be necessary.

In short, make sure that you (or whoever is sending you) wear a hard hat and safety boots with suitable soles if there is the risk of chemicals, and that you have done a comprehensive risk assessment and acted on its recommendations. Insist on seeing the risk assessment before you enter the building and if it has identified an issue, such as asbestos, then make sure that the appropriate steps have been taken to ensure your safety. When inside the building take particular care on floors and other surfaces. It may be worth being quite noisy at first, to frighten off any animals or people who may be there.

Logistics and Other Management Issues

As well as the need for protective clothing and other equipment, you are also very likely to need supplementary lighting. Many historic structures, particularly abandoned ones, have usually been boarded up to prevent access by teenagers and pigeons, even though the act of boarding-up merely seems to challenge people and animals to find another way in. Free-standing halogen lights powered by a generator can be hired, usually in clusters – a plant supplier can advise you. In extreme cases, an automated rising platform (referred to as a 'cherry-picker' for its use in the fruit industry) may be needed to reach the upper elevations or even some parts of the building, especially if access routes have fallen apart or been removed.

Never work alone in a derelict building, and always carry a mobile phone and ensure that it has a signal. Also, tell someone where you will be and at what time, and then agree to call at a certain time to confirm that the visit is complete. Make sure that you have a first aid kit with you actually in the building (it is no use in a site hut in the yard if you are on the third floor and cut yourself on a shard of glass).

Finally – enjoy it! There is much fun to be had wondering around derelict buildings.

Summary

This chapter has provided an outline of how archaeologists collect information through various forms of fieldwork, whether it is non-intrusive geophysical or aerial photographic techniques, the survey of earthworks, buildings or on excavation. The information presented here simplifies things hugely; some of the more specialised areas of archaeology (such as underwater or battlefield investigations) have been entirely excluded; and there is a great deal to debate and discuss under every one of the headings and subheadings listed above. But this is a summary of the situation as it exists today in Britain. For further information on techniques, there are numerous books and guidance notes which provide further detail. Most of these are referred to in the text and some of the main sources are listed in the bibliography. We now turn our attention to what happens once the fieldwork is completed. What happens when the archaeologist goes back indoors?

References and Further Reading

Andrews, D., Blake, B., Clowes, M. and Wilson, K. 1995. *The Survey and Recording of Historic Buildings*. Association of Archaeological Illustrators and Surveyors Technical Paper No.12.

Barker, P. 1977. *Techniques of Archaeological Excavation*, London: Batsford.

Bettess, F. 1992. *Surveying for Archaeologists*. Durham: University of Durham.

Brickley, M. and McKinley, J. 2004. *Guidelines to the Standards for Recording Human Remains*, IfA Technical Paper No.7.

Dorrell, P.G. 1994. *Photography in Archaeology and Conservation*. Cambridge University Press.

English Heritage. 2001. *Archaeometallurgy*. Centre for Archaeology Guidelines, Portsmouth: English Heritage.

English Heritage. 2002. *Environmental Archaeology: a guide to the theory and practice of methods, from sampling and recovery to post-excavation*. Swindon: English Heritage.

English Heritage. 2002. *With Alidade and Tape: graphical and plane table survey of archaeological earthworks*. Swindon: English Heritage.

English Heritage. 2004. *Dendrochronology: Guidelines on producing and interpreting dendrochronological dates*. Swindon: English Heritage.

English Heritage. 2005. *Guidance for best practice for treatment of human remains excavated from Christian burial grounds in England*. Swindon: English Heritage.

English Heritage. 2006. *Archaeomagnetic Dating: guidelines on producing and interpreting archaeomagnetic dates*. Swindon: English Heritage.

English Heritage. 2006. *Understanding Historic Buildings: a guide to good recording practice*, Swindon: English Heritage.

English Heritage. 2007. *Geoarchaeology: using earth sciences to understand the archaeological record*. Swindon: English Heritage.

English Heritage. 2007. *Understanding the Archaeology of Landscapes: a guide to good recording practice*. Swindon: English Heritage.

English Heritage. 2008. *Luminescence dating: guidelines on using luminescence dating in archaeology*. Swindon: English Heritage.

Gaffney, C., Gater, J. and Ovendon, S. 2002. *The use of geophysical techniques in archaeological evaluations*, IfA Technical Paper No.6.

Harris, E.C. 1989. *Principles of Archaeological Stratigraphy*. London: Academic Press.

Howard, P. 2007. *Archaeological Surveying and Mapping*. London: Routledge.

Institute for Archaeologists. 2008. *Standard and Guidance for archaeological field evaluation*.

Institute for Archaeologists. 2008. *Standard and Guidance for archaeological watching brief*.

Institute for Archaeologists. 2008. *Standard and Guidance for archaeological excavation*.

Institute for Archaeologists. 2008. *Standard and Guidance for archaeological investigation and recording of buildings or structures*.

Major, J. K. 1975. *Fieldwork in Industrial Archaeology*. London: Batsford.

McKinley, J. and Roberts, C. 1993. *Excavation and Post-excavation treatment of cremated and inhumed human remains*. IfA Technical Paper No.13.

Palmer, M. and Neaverson, P. 1998. *Industrial Archaeology: Principles and Practice*. London: Routledge.

Royal Commission on Historical Monuments for England (RCHME). 1999. *Recording Archaeological Field Monuments: a descriptive specification*. London: Royal Commission on the Historical Monuments of England.

Spence, C. (ed.) 1990. *Archaeological site manual*. 2nd ed. London : Department of Urban Archaeology, Museum of London.

Schofield, J. (ed.) 2011. *Great Excavations: shaping the archaeological profession*. Oxford: Oxbow.

Taylor, C. 1974. *Fieldwork in Medieval Archaeology*. London: Batsford.

Chapter 7
Achieving Results: Analysis, Application, Publication and Dissemination

Fieldwork is only part of a programme of archaeological research. For many archaeologists, it is the most interesting bit, but just as important (and for some just as much, if not more fun) are the 'post-excavation' stages – sorting out what you have found and making sense of it, and then telling your story to the rest of the world.

Essentially the fieldwork process produces data or information which, like any information, needs to be analysed or decoded to be fully understood. For non-intrusive fieldwork, these data usually come in the form of measured surveys or geophysical plots; for excavation the data will include plans and sections, carefully drawn, but also notes, photographs and of course artefacts and 'ecofacts' recovered from the soil. Sometimes the sheer quantity of data recovered can seem overwhelming, but it can be broken down into various categories, for each of which there are dedicated specialists.

Finds

Basic Finds Processing

Cleaning of most finds (fired ceramics, glass, slags, bone, shell and non-ferrous metal) is done in plain water using a toothbrush. On larger excavations, finds processing may be undertaken on site, but in most cases this is done after the fieldwork stage. Once cleaned, finds are dried on newspaper (some facilities will have special drying racks) and then marked (Fig. 7.1).

Finds are marked with a number, usually down to the level of the context in which they were found rather than the individual find itself, although some specific small finds might have a unique identifier. In most cases, the number is decided by the institution (usually a museum) which will ultimately look after the finds in the long term. Thus for most commercial excavations, the local museum will supply an accession number; this may be included in the brief or specification, or it may be

J. Schofield et al., *Archaeological Practice in Great Britain: A Heritage Handbook*,   161
World Archaeological Congress Cultural Heritage Manual Series,
DOI 10.1007/978-0-387-09453-3_7, © Springer Science+Business Media, LLC 2011

Fig. 7.1 The often cold, wet and tedious task of washing the finds recovered from site is an essential part of the archaeological process. Here staff are cleaning mediaeval pottery sherds from a kiln site, before they are sent for specialist analysis.
Photograph by Paul Belford

supplied by the curatorial archaeologist. Otherwise the number is a combination of the project or site code and the context number. The number is written on the artefact using India ink and a nib, then sealed with protective varnish.

Once marked, the finds can be catalogued. For most projects, cataloguing is a two-stage process, corresponding roughly to the 'assessment' and 'analysis' stages outlined in MAP2 (see Chap. 5). Even basic cataloguing requires some knowledge of the period and site type, as well as a broad idea of pottery types and animal bone. A basic catalogue might look as shown in Table 7.1.

Such catalogues are essentially working documents. They are helpful in the early stages of post-excavation, serving three main purposes. Firstly, it is a record of what exists in the excavation archive (and where to find it). Secondly, it is helpful in writing up the stratigraphic report (see below). Finally, the main purpose of a catalogue is to quantify the material so that the amount of detailed post-excavation analysis can be decided upon, and the necessary specialists engaged.

Specialists in all areas are quite thin on the ground. Each region usually has no more than a handful of specialists in any particular field (post-mediaeval pottery of the West Midlands, for example). In the past, many larger organisations had an in-house team of specialists, and some still do (larger units such as MOLA, Wessex Archaeology or Oxford Archaeology, as well as some university departments).

Table 7.1 Finds catalogue

Context	Type	Description	No.	Remarks
1014	Pottery	Green-glazed red earthenware (C14)	3	1 rim sherd
1014	Clay pipe	Stem fragments	2	–
1014	Bone	Large animal femur (part)	1	Cut marks
1015	Pottery	Unglazed grey tempered earthenware	4	–
1015	Pottery	Creamware (C18)	2	–
1015	Cu alloy	Coin – possibly C18 or C19 penny	1	Corroded
1015	Flint	Retouched flake	1	–
1016	Fe object	Nails, hand-forged, 10–12 mm long	4	–

However, the last decade (and in particular the last few years) has seen cutbacks in this area, with the result that most specialists are self-employed and frequently overwhelmed by their workload. Thus it pays to contact specialists in all fields at the earliest opportunity. Ceramic specialists are the most numerous, and experts in metallurgy extremely rare. Usually the local curatorial archaeologist will have a list of post-excavation specialists in different areas and can provide contact information. Otherwise, a useful first port of call is the national body. English Heritage has a Regional Science Advisor (RSA) in each of their regions who can suggest possible specialist support. Historic Scotland's Inspectorate can provide a similar service, and in Wales the four archaeological trusts will also be able to assist.

Although finds washing, marking and cataloguing is labour-intensive and sometimes tedious, it is actually an extremely valuable learning experience. It does provide an opportunity to familiarise oneself with the artefacts of a particular type, area or period – skills once learnt (often by endless repetition in a cold shed) are not easily forgotten.

Different Types of Finds and What to Do with Them

Inorganic Artefacts

Stone. Prehistoric tools were made by knapping (or working) flint and other stones, and this activity leaves clear evidence on the finished article or on the byproducts of the process. Flint is an extremely durable material and was widely transported even in prehistory. Other prehistoric stone items might include fire-cracked pebbles (alluvial cobbles heated in the fire and then used to boil water in earthen pots). Roman, mediaeval and later sites are likely to contain a wide range of building stones. The British Isles contain an abundance of stones of all types with various properties. Unless severely eroded or degraded, all stone is suitable for cleaning in the usual way; flint artefacts (but not usually the waste flakes) and carved masonry fragments are often selected for drawing.

Pottery. Pottery is probably the most abundant type of artefact in most situations and is extremely helpful for dating. Ceramic items usually survive well, and do not normally have particular storage or handling requirements. Unglazed pottery is generally fragile, particularly some types of untempered prehistoric coarseware. Rough post-mediaeval pottery can also be easily abraded. Glazed pottery is usually more robust; however, certain glazes (such as early post-mediaeval 'tin-glaze' or 'delftware') can be fragile and will easily come away from the main fabric. A vast amount of information exists for almost all periods of pottery manufacture, and specialists are usually able to closely date material. In choosing pottery for specialist analysis, care should be taken to include 'diagnostic' items – that is to say sherds which can be readily identified as belonging to a particular form or type of pottery. These might include rims, bases, and handles (or fragments of them). Diagnostic items may also be chosen for illustration or for photography (see below).

Clay Pipes. Clay pipes were introduced for smoking tobacco (and other substances) in the late sixteenth century and their use gradually declined during the early twentieth century with the introduction of cigarettes. Clay pipe stems are frequent finds, but are not, contrary to popular belief, diagnostic by the measurement of the bore of the pipe (except in certain very particular circumstances where the sequence is dated by other evidence). Bowls (the bit at the end where the smoker put their tobacco) are, however, extremely valuable as dating evidence – both in a general sense (older bowls are smaller), and sometimes very specifically if they have a particular design or bear the stamp of an individual maker. Clay pipe stem fragments are fairly tough but the bowls can be fragile. Intact bowls with decoration are excellent diagnostic items and will be looked at by specialists and usually drawn.

Glass. Glass objects occur in Roman, mediaeval and post-mediaeval deposits. Roman glass is of particularly fine quality and often coloured. Mediaeval glass was manufactured in wood-fired kilns in small quantities, a tradition that continued into the seventeenth century. From c. 1600 to c. 1700 glassmaking technology changed rapidly (becoming coal-fired) and the quality and quantity of glass greatly increased. The most common finds will be bottle glass (various shades of green, brown or clear glass in nineteenth and twentieth-century levels; darker green glass in eighteenth-century and earlier horizons). Window glass is very rare from before the eighteenth-century and may be painted. All glass is prone to oxidation and decay, and after more than a hundred years or so in the ground the outer surface will have been eroded through chemical attack – leaving an opaque and sometimes rough surface. There is no rule about the speed of this process – a great deal depends on the conditions of the layer in which it was found. Most recent glass can be treated in the same way as pottery, but older glass will need to be kept separate from other finds. Cleaning of badly corroded items should be done dry, using a paintbrush. If in any doubt consult a specialist.

Bricks and Tiles. Ceramic building materials are commonly found everywhere, although they have quite specific distributions. There was very little brick building in Scotland, Wales and north-west England before the nineteenth century. In southern England, bricks were used in the Roman period (and were often re-used later). Large-scale brickmaking returned from the thirteenth century in the eastern parts of

England; but in the west of the country, bricks were not widely used until the eighteenth century. Individual brick sherds are not particularly interesting of themselves. However, their presence or absence may indicate the approximate date range of a layer. Whole bricks can actually be dated with varying degrees of accuracy. As a general rule bricks became thicker and shorter from the seventeenth to the nineteenth centuries – thus a seventeenth century brick may be $5 \times 11 \times 26$ cm, whereas a late nineteenth-century brick may measure $7 \times 11 \times 22$ cm. However, brick dating is not an exact science, and as with many such things, local knowledge (and looking at local buildings of known date) is critical. Brickmaking was a fairly localised activity until well into the twentieth century (with some exceptions such as ubiquitous and virtually indestructible Accrington Reds which seem to appear in all late nineteenth-century contexts), and many brick- and tilemakers stamped their name on their product – so it is possible to refine dating by looking through the local trade directories. This is also an area where enthusiastic non-professionals may be able to offer considerable expertise.

Metal Objects. These range in scale from fine copper pins to large steel water turbines. Iron does corrode relatively quickly and the original form of the artefact may be obscured by the accumulation of corrosion products. Do not try and remove this by cleaning in water or by scratching and scraping at the object. Severely corroded ironwork should be X-radiographed (see below: 'Photography') (see Fig. 7.2). Other metals may survive better. Nevertheless, cleaning should be done only with care and dry where possible. Avoid using home-made remedies (although Coca Cola is particularly effective at removing corrosion from metal, for example) as their effect on ancient materials might be catastrophic. Copper is probably the next

Fig. 7.2 Laboratory analysis of metallurgical samples at the English Heritage Centre for Archaeology in Portsmouth. Laboratory analysis of a wide range of material is a key part of archaeological work, and can make a significant contribution to understanding. Photograph by David Dungworth, English Heritage

most-common metal after iron and is usually found as an alloy with tin (bronze) or zinc (brass). Copper and its alloys tend to develop a corrosion product which protects the artefact – the characteristic blue-green hue may leach onto adjacent bone, fabric or other materials. Other non-ferrous metals which survive well include silver, gold and lead. Pewter (an alloy of lead and tin) was commonly used for various domestic items and usually survives well.

Organic Artefacts

The best environment for the survival of organic artefacts is an anaerobic one – that is to say an environment without oxygen. Waterlogged deposits are normally anaerobic. Some anaerobic environments preserve organics such as leather but destroy other items – for example in the case of the famous 'bog bodies' where the tannin in the peat had effectively preserved the skin and hair, but the acidity of the bog had destroyed the bone.

Wooden Objects. Wood is frequently encountered, and may survive well even in apparently hostile environments. Any timber recovered from a site must be considered to have potential for radiocarbon or dendrochronological dating. Timbers suitable for 'dendro' need to include a good cross-section of the timber, including more than 50 rings together with heartwood (the core of the tree). A very precise date may be obtained if sapwood (the last few years of growth before the tree was felled) also survives. Coffins can survive quite well. The survival of smaller wooden objects is far less predictable and sometimes depends on the macro-environment of their immediate surroundings. The presence of oak, for example, can help in the preservation of other organic materials by the release of tannic acids. Wooden objects need to be recorded immediately on excavation (see Chap. 5), as they then need to be kept wet. Specialist long-term conservation techniques may be applied to wooden objects, and choice of these needs to be made by specialists. Some timbers may have been treated with preservatives (such as pitch, tar or oils) in antiquity, which will have a bearing on how they might react to modern conservation treatment. Probably, the most widely used method for large items (such as boats) is the injection of a variety of molecular weights of polyethylene glycol (PEG) into timbers to replace the water molecules. PEG treatments are reversible, but it has more recently been realised that the PEG treatment can decay over time. Perhaps the best-known example of this in British archaeology is the sixteenth-century warship Mary Rose, which has been under a continuous programme of 'wet' conservation since she was raised from the Solent in 1982. For smaller items freeze drying is a common approach.

Leather. Leather usually survives well in waterlogged anaerobic conditions (as well as marine environments), but is very easily damaged by being allowed to dry out too rapidly or being over-handled. Leather items should be recorded as soon as possible after excavation, as shrinkage may occur during processing and conservation. The easiest way to do this is to draw round the leather object onto a piece of waterproof drawing film. Once off site, leather can be gently cleaned in water – and this is often a good time to inspect the artefact closely for details of its form and construction. Longer-term conservation is – like timber – done by replacing the water with PEG solution. Conservation requirements for waterlogged leather are usually in direct opposition to those for metals, so if a leather artefact contains metal fittings (such as iron eyelets or a brass buckle), a quick and difficult decision will have to be made!

Textiles. Textiles are encountered either in very dry or very wet conditions. Most common are survivals from waterlogged and anaerobic conditions, such as from peat bogs and the lower levels of urban sites. Textiles derived from animals (such as wool and hair) tend to survive better than those from plants (such as flax and linen). In some cases, an impression of textiles survives due to the leaching of minerals from the decay of adjacent metals such as iron and lead. When found, most textiles appear colourless, but information about the original dyes can be recovered by submitting them for examination by chromatography and spectroscopy. Wet cleaning of textiles is best avoided until specialist advice has been sought.

Plant and Animal Remains (or 'Ecofacts')

Palaeobotany. Palaeobotany (or archaeobotany) has a long history in British archaeology, and research has tended to concentrate its efforts on prehistoric environments. Early successes included the identification of the Neolithic 'elm decline' which resulted from woodland clearance and the role of grazing in the development of Bronze Age landscapes. More recently, attention has been turned to mediaeval and post-mediaeval deposits, for example identifying indicators of pollution during the eighteenth and nineteenth centuries. Palaeobotanical samples are usually taken en masse in the field (see Chap. 5), and then the technique of 'flotation' is used to separate seeds and other material from the soil. Plant fibres, seeds, pollen and insect remains can all be recovered and analysed. Usually, paleoenvironmental samples are taken on site by the specialists and rarely need post-excavation treatment.

Osteology. Osteology is the study of bones, and detailed analysis is generally undertaken by specialists. Usually animal bone is cleaned along with other general artefacts – it is generally fairly robust. However, very small bones might be picked out through the flotation process described above – particularly so in the case of marine creatures. Basic animal bone identification is fairly straightforward: the principal bones of horse, cow, sheep/goat and pig are easily differentiated from one another with a bit of practice. Domestic animals such as dogs and cats are also commonly represented. Quite often the animal remains will be fragmentary, and cuts of meat can be identified, along with cut- or saw-marks where the bones have been butchered. Human bones are treated in much the same way, although they will come off site separately bagged and will not be washed with ordinary finds. Human osteology is a specialist subject usually requiring masters-level study. However, the non-specialist can learn how to distinguish male from female and the broad age of a person by looking at the shape and structure of the pelvis and skull and the degree to which certain bones (for instance shoulders) have fused.

Industrial Residues

Slag. This general term is used to describe all manner of materials which stem from the excavation of industrial sites. However, slags proper are the by-product of metallurgical activity in which metals are refined – either through smelting or alloying or forging of metal. They usually contain some quantity of the metal itself, together with the gangue or dross from the ore or unrefined metal which was removed during the process. Such materials need to be treated very carefully. Some slags, such as iron blast-furnace slag or lead-smelting slag, are glassy and hard and can be washed in the normal way. Other materials – such as those which result from the smithing process and are extremely friable – should not be washed. In such cases specialist advice will be needed.

Refractories. High temperature processes require materials resistant to high temperatures, and such refractory materials can be found on industrial and other sites. These will range from small crucibles for precious metal refining to large firebricks used in the linings of furnaces. They might also include 'kiln furniture' used in pottery manufacture. Large 'saggars' contained the wares to be fired and were stacked in the kiln. Inside the saggar wares were kept separate by various small pieces of pipe clay. Once used, such materials are usually very friable and conventional cleaning methods might cause a lot of damage. Dry brushing is usually best for fragments of crucible and other materials such as kiln furniture. For metalliferous refractories, analysis by scanning electron microscope (SEM) can give an idea of the sorts of processing being undertaken. The structural fabric of kilns and furnaces will be more robust, and again SEM analysis can reveal a great deal about materials, processes and fuels.

These then are the main categories of finds that result from excavations in Britain, recognising that increasingly more familiar modern artefacts are also being recorded and collected, as archaeology of the contemporary past. We now discuss the reporting of excavations and survey projects, including the technical report, archive and publications.

Reporting

Reports are amongst the most important products of archaeological endeavour. Indeed, as Historic Scotland points out on its website: 'excavation without reporting is simply the destruction of a site for no benefit'. All field projects should result in a technical report, and, regardless of the type of work undertaken, this will include sections on:

- The background to the project – why it was undertaken, who paid for it, who did the work, where the site is and the nature of the geology
- The historical and archaeological background of the site – known history of the site, current land use, previous land use, any other archaeological work
- The aims of the fieldwork – what were you trying to find out?

- The methodologies used – the details of methods and equipment, the recording strategy and system and the timescale of works
- The results – the detailed outcome: this may be an interpreted survey drawing or a complex stratigraphic report
- A discussion of the results and their relationship to other sites of the same period or in the same area
- A conclusion.

There will also be appendices containing technical material such as the original specification and project design, lists of data (contexts, finds catalogues, etc.) and specialist reports. Any report must include information on the site's location, and the ultimate location and nature of the archive (see below). It is also good practice to include a non-technical summary.

In most archaeological field projects, this sort of technical report is the principal source of information. This is usually termed 'grey literature', and although publicly available at the local HER, it is not usually aimed at a wide readership. Wider publication may range from a short summary report to a full-scale monograph.

Preparing to Write: Dealing with Field Records

As we have seen in the previous chapter, records of fieldwork projects normally consist of some combination of notes (the written record), drawings (the drawn record) and photographs (the photographic record). Some specialised fieldwork also generates an 'electronic record' – such as CAD drawings, GPS-based landscape survey or geophysical survey.

The typical site record will consist of folders of context sheets and other records, together with the drawings. The context sheets form the primary record, and the first task is to try and collate the data from them. It is quite likely that some of the cross-referencing between sheets, and between different records (noting which contexts appear on which drawings, for example) might not have been completed in the field, so this needs to be done straight away.

The most important tool in working out the sequence of events on a site is the Harris Matrix. The Matrix is essentially a diagram which shows the relationships of different parts of the site to one another (Harris 1989).

Writing the Technical (Stratigraphic) Report

The basic contents of the report can be broken down into four main areas – the 'book-end' elements (project and historical background, aims, methods and archiving, dissemination), the main stratigraphic report (results), the discussion and conclusions, and finally any appendices. Each of these requires a slightly different approach.

The *'bookend' elements* are essentially factual and tend to follow certain conventions. Most organisations have a template into which much of the text is actually written. 'The project was commissioned by [insert name of client] and undertaken between [date] and [date] [year]…' Methodologies are usually fairly standard, and in most cases will be those as described in the Project Design or WSI. However, it is worth remembering at this stage that the WSI is a benchmark against which the performance of the project is measured – so any variations in methodology (including staffing, timescale and areas actually investigated) need to be described and accounted for. The sections at the end on archiving, copyright and dissemination also need to be completed. Check carefully when cutting and pasting from other similar documents that the correct site, client, local authority and museum are mentioned!

The *main body of the report* comprises the description of the stratigraphic sequence. For an evaluation consisting of one or more trenches, this description is usually arranged by trench and each trench is treated as a discrete site. For an open-area excavation, it is customary to group the results in terms of the period and phasing for the site as a whole. However, on very complex sites, it may be more convenient to divide the narrative into thematic sections (the church, cemetery, main house, outbuildings, water-power system, furnace, etc.) and then subdivide this by periods or phases.

Chronologically the report is written in stratigraphic order; in other words the reverse order to the excavation. This is where the 'interpretation' section of the context sheet needs to be carefully examined, since interpretation on site is likely to be at variance with the final understanding of what happened. The stratigraphic report will need to refer to each and every context, and a description of most of them will need to be provided – although, of course, a more detailed list will be included in the appendices. Try and avoid, however, providing a simple list in the text, and describe features in the way in which they were created. This requires something of a shift in mind-set from that adopted in the field. The following two descriptions of the same set of features explains:

> After the removal of eighteenth century rubble layer 1033, a linear feature was noted running N–S. This consisted of fill 1045 in a cut 1046. The fill 1045 was a mid-grey-brown sandy silt with numerous sandstone inclusions, which contained seventeenth century slipware; this was 0.30 m in depth and overlay 1048, a slightly darker and sandier version of 1045 with fewer inclusions and 0.45 m in depth. Below 1048 was 1067, a dark red-brown silt 0.23 m deep, with no inclusions and containing a rim-sherd of black-glazed earthenware of probable sixteenth century date. This overlay the primary ditch fill 1069, a black humic silt 0.15 m in depth containing charcoal flecks. The cut 1046 was U-shaped in profile, and measured 0.80±0.10 m in width and 0.50±0.10 m in depth; it had been cut through the natural clay 1133. This was probably the original boundary ditch for Plot 12.

and

> A linear feature had been cut into the underlying natural clay 1133 (cut 1046). This ran N–S and probably represented the original boundary ditch for Plot 12. The ditch was U-shaped in profile, and measured 0.80±0.10 m in width and 0.50±0.10 m in depth. When still in use it had silted up slightly, as represented by 1069, a black humic silt 0.15 m in depth containing charcoal flecks. Some dumping subsequently took place, as evinced by 1067, a dark red-brown silt some 0.23 m in depth containing sixteenth century black-glazed earthenware. Deliberate infilling followed in two stages. The first was represented by 1048, a dark grey-brown sandy silt 0.45 m deep with sandstone inclusions; this was followed by 1045, a mid-grey-brown silty sand

containing seventeenth century slipware. The former ditch was completely obliterated in the eighteenth century by the deposition of the rubble fill 1033.

Neither of these paragraphs is going to win the Nobel Prize for literature, but the second example has turned the evidence around to provide a narrative of events. The *discussion and conclusions* allow more room for creative thought. The purpose of the discussion is twofold. Firstly, it should aim to break down the detailed data presented in the results section into key phases in the site development. On a large site, the chronology may well be divided into periods and phases, while on a smaller site it may only be necessary to summarise the broad narrative. Secondly, the discussion should seek to place the site-specific results into the wider archaeological context. Reference should be made to other archaeological research in the immediate locality and the wider region; and broader national or international studies relevant to the period(s) in question will also need to be considered.

A good place to start is with the regional (or national) research framework (see Chap. 4). In England, these have been produced under the guidance of English Heritage over the last 10 years and comprise a 'resource assessment' (what do we know – the 'known knowns' as Donald Rumsfeld put it) and a 'research agenda' (what do we need to know – Rumsfeld's 'known unknowns'). Most regions now have some form of Framework, and in some cases the original ones are now being revised. A criticism often levelled at these research frameworks is that they do not provide much scope for researching outside of these boundaries – there is little scope for research into the 'unknown unknowns', for example!

Editing, Assembling and Publishing the Report

Most technical (stratigraphic) reports are bound together with the illustrations, so these will normally be produced in A4 or A3 format – although occasionally larger sizes may be used and appended as separate folded drawings. Traditionally, these are included at the end of the report, although this is not always the case. Photographs used to be bundled together as 'plates' at the end of the report, but nowadays are inserted into the text where appropriate. Photographs and drawings need to be saved at an appropriate resolution and file size for the finished product, otherwise the resulting electronic file will be too large and unwieldy. Each archaeological organisation will have its own house style and a template for producing reports.

Editing the text is usually done by a Project Manager or equivalent. Large or complex reports may be edited several times, but the final edit is always best done with all the supporting drawings and photographs in their proper places. Report editing is a difficult task, in which a balance needs to be struck between maintaining house style and consistency and allowing the character of the individual project and its team to prevail. It is advisable to spell-check and double-spell check your report before submitting it for editing; likewise get a colleague to read through for grammatical errors. The editing Project Manager will be irritated by basic errors (or a failure to conform to house conventions for references or technical data) – he or she is reading the report from the point of view of the client and is looking for narrative cohesion, consistent use of evidence to support arguments and weaknesses of interpretation.

Once edited, the report is prepared for dispatch to the client and the curatorial archaeologist. Even at this stage further corrections may be required by either party, so the first offering may be presented as a 'draught' and is often sent electronically.

The final report is then prepared both as an electronic and a hard copy. The client may specify a certain number of hard copies (bound or unbound), and there will also need to be copies made for the HER, for the final archive (see below) and for the organisation's own archive. Copyright of the technical report is usually with the archaeological organisation rather than the individual author or the client who commissioned the work, but the precise arrangement for intellectual property will vary according to the circumstances of the project.

Once accepted by the HER (sometimes subject to a time restriction), the report is effectively in the public domain and can be said to have been 'published'. However, greater access is possible through internet publication. Some units have a policy of putting their technical reports on the web either on their own websites or through third-party sites.

Writing Archaeological Reports for Publication

The technical report is rarely publishable in its unaltered form, but it usually forms the basis for any subsequent publication. The specific requirements for formal publication are discussed at greater length below. However, some general points are worth considering:

- The writing style will be less technical and more discursive
- The details of each and every context will not be included – rather, reference will be made to features and sequences within them, and to broader phasing
- Less information will need to be given about the project background and methodology (unless the methods used are particularly unusual), but...
- Rather more information will need to be given about the historical background and the broader archaeological research framework within which the project has been undertaken
- More detailed reference may need to be made to other local, regional and even national studies, and to prevailing academic and theoretical thinking
- Further reading and/or documentary research will almost always be necessary
- The conclusion will be much more about the impact of the project on archaeological thought rather than the consequences for the site specifically.

Illustration

Although the techniques of archaeological illustration have changed remarkably in the past two decades, the overriding principles behind them remain much the same as before. Advances in computer hardware and software have revolutionised

Illustration   173

the practicalities of post-fieldwork illustration, even if field drawings are still hand-drawn in the traditional way (see Chap. 5).

General Principles and Conventions

Until the late 1990s, all archaeological field drawings were 'inked up' in the drawing office using technology that had changed little since Mortimer Wheeler's day. Using purpose-made drawing pens (usually the Rotring Rapidograph) filled with India ink, field drawings were painstakingly traced over to produce final illustrations. Corrections were made by scratching out the mistake with a scalpel – but carefully so as not to destroy the smooth face of the drawing film – and redrawing. Scaling had to be carefully considered at the outset, so as to get the most detail in the most convenient drawing size. Various line thicknesses were used: 0.13 for very fine work (rarely used in practice), 0.18 for fine detail such as wood grain, 0.25 for context interfaces and masonry, 0.35 for significant interfaces or section edges, 0.50 for major boundaries or the edge of the excavation, and so on. Perhaps the most tedious task was stippling large areas – many older archaeologists remember hours hunched over a large drawing board drawing dots to represent water, mortar and the like.

This whole tradition was largely swept away by the advent of increasingly powerful computers capable of storing many high-resolution images, together with user-friendly drawing software. Surprisingly, despite being well-used in the architectural and engineering professions, AutoCAD was not at first readily adopted by archaeologists. Instead software such as CorelDraw and Adobe Illustrator was preferred; and indeed Illustrator is probably the most widespread software currently in use. Subsequent versions of AutoCAD have been better-suited to archaeological applications, particularly for survey work. Modern practice is to scan in the field drawing and then 'ink in' using proprietary software. It is much easier to stitch together a series of images digitally than – as formerly – creating ingenious assemblages held together with the ubiquitous 'magic tape'.

Despite the advances in computer technology, certain drawing conventions (including the hierarchy of line widths, and the type of lines used to denote certain things) have survived. There is insufficient space to go into detail here, but Fig. 7.3 shows some of the most commonly used conventions for excavated sites.

Field survey and building recording illustrations have their own conventions – again developed in the pre-digital age and adapted. The best guide to conventions for these areas is to be found in English Heritage guidelines for Historic Building Recording and for Earthwork Survey, both of which can be found on the HELM website (http://www.helm.org.uk).

Colour for all types of archaeological illustration has been traditionally frowned upon in British practice (unlike in parts of continental Europe). There was originally a good reason for this: the prohibitive cost of colour illustrations in printed publications meant that any colour applied at field- or drawing-board stage would have to be later rendered in black and white. However, this is no longer universally the case, and colour drawings are often used in reports and publications for some artefacts (see below), phase plans and plans of structures.

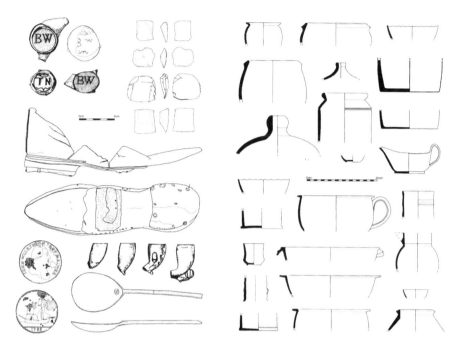

Fig. 7.3 Finds drawings. Pottery, leather, metal objects, clay pipes and coins are all objects which are typically represented by drawing rather than photography. Drawing is an interpretive act which enables some features to be emphasised. Drawings by Keith Hinton and Sophie Watson for the Ironbridge Gorge Museum Trust

The increasing use of colour has been one of the results of adopting new technology, and with a digital drawing the use of colour is of course optional depending on the requirements of the finished product. The other advantage of digital illustration is that several versions of the same drawing (needed for instance when producing interpretive drawings, phase plans and the like) can be easily produced, whereas previously they all had to be drawn separately from scratch.

Archaeological illustration is a specialist field within archaeology, and those with a particular aptitude are often attracted towards it. Most units have their own drawing teams for providing basic illustrations, although there are also freelance archaeological illustrators who specialise in specific types of drawings such as finds drawings and reconstructions.

Finds Drawings

As with other forms of archaeological illustration, the drawing of finds follows certain long-established conventions. The purpose of such conventions is to enable artefacts to be depicted to a common standard so that inter-site comparisons can be made. Traditionally, a monochrome line drawing, an illustration of an artefact is an

Illustration 175

interpretive exercise, enabling certain features (such as decoration, wear or working surfaces) to be clearly shown where they might not be so obviously apparent on a photograph. The classic finds drawing provides four principal views – front, back, side-on and a section. For many pottery drawings, this convention is abbreviated to show the front, back and a section, and sometimes the form of the rest of the pot is extrapolated. Artefact drawings are always to scale, the choice of scale being decided by the size of the original artefact and the intended size of reproduction. It is best practice to use one scale for each drawing, although it is not always possible to do this. Examples of finds drawings are provided in Fig. 7.3.

For some finds, the traditional hand drawing methods are still unavoidable. Timber, for instance, is frequently recovered in a waterlogged state and is best drawn on site before it becomes distorted. Metalwork is also usually best illustrated with a conventional monochrome drawing, as is worked stone. Certain types of ceramic decoration (such as moulded designs on clay pipes) are best represented by a line drawing. Having said that the use of colour is now quite commonplace for items such as decorated polychrome ceramics.

Reconstruction Drawings

A reconstruction drawing is essentially an artist's impression of a site or area at a particular point in its development. Such drawings are rarely undertaken except on larger (and better funded) projects and are usually the last thing to be done either as part of a publication (see below) or as part of on-site or museum-based interpretation. The preparation of reconstruction drawings was always a particular specialism, since it required a more comprehensive set of artistic skills (the ability to draw people and animals, for example) than conventional line-drawings of finds or features. To some extent, this is still the case, and many fine reconstructions are still done by hand. Preparing a reconstruction drawing also requires a detailed knowledge of the site layout (from excavation drawings) and of the period being represented – structures, buildings, fashions, weaponry and domestic artefacts.

Selecting What Needs to Be Drawn

The range of drawings that needs to be included in an archaeological report will depend on the purpose of that report. For the detailed technical (stratigraphic) report, it will be necessary to include the following:

- A location map or maps showing not only where the site is but also how it relates to the surrounding landscape
- A pre-excavation plan showing the topography or any features extant on site
- An overall plan showing the extent of excavations – this might be one area or a series of trenches

- Other plans to show other interventions such as boreholes or the extent of subsequent watching briefs
- Detailed plans of each trench (in the case of an evaluation) or
- Detailed plans of particular parts of the site (all of which must relate to the narrative structure of the report)
- Sections of individual trenches and features such as ditches
- Phase plans showing the development of the site (or parts of it) over time
- Other interpretation plans or diagrams (for instance showing how timber structures were put together).

The first four items in the list above should be related to the Ordnance Survey National Grid. The site grid (see Chap. 5) should be shown on more detailed drawings, and if for some reason the site grid is not orientated with the Ordnance Survey grid, then the relationship between the two needs to be shown on at least one of the drawings. Depending on the results of the fieldwork, it may also be necessary to include finds drawings as an appendix with the specialist report. Historic mapping should also be included, where available, although this will rarely need to be redrawn.

Whilst the technical report will not necessarily include an 'inked-up' version of every field drawing, it will include a lot of detail. For the stratigraphic report, it is good practice to make sure that every context is shown on at least one plan and/or section, where possible. The precise requirements may vary depending on the brief set by the curatorial archaeologist – if in doubt follow *Standards and Guidance* issued by the IfA, and refer to Guidance produced by the Association of Archaeological Illustrators and Surveyors (AAIAS).

The drawing requirements for publications are somewhat different. Happily the use of digital technology means that the drawings prepared for the technical report can be easily modified, whereas before they would have to be done from scratch. For a monograph or journal paper, illustrations should include:

- A location map or maps
- Historic mapping (either originals or redrawn as map regression)
- An overall plan of the excavations
- Detail plans and sections of particular parts of the site, depending on the structure of the narrative
- Phase and period plans
- Interpretive drawings
- Finds drawings
- Reconstruction drawings if appropriate.

Here the nature and style of the drawings will need to be more closely specified depending on the final page size and allowance of colour pages in the finished product. Many monographs have A4-sized pages and can use a great deal of colour, and a good example is the impressively illustrated series of monographs produced by MOLA and Wessex Archaeology. However, journals still tend to be printed in a smaller format (a typical page size is 200×140 mm^2) and are largely colour-free, although in some cases colour illustrations can be supplied for inclusion on the journal's web pages.

Photography

Photography in the field has already been dealt with in some detail in Chap. 5. This section will look at photography of artefacts and the selection of photographs for reports.

Ordinary Photography of Artefacts

For most purposes, artefact photography can be undertaken using the same equipment as in the field. Generally speaking the photography of artefacts is not a record-making exercise, therefore some of the considerations regarding archiving can be relaxed. Good quality digital photography (i.e. using a digital SLR) is generally acceptable for most artefact photography. The exceptions to this are when the artefacts need to be recorded because they will deteriorate prior to or during storage (organic items such as leather, wood and paper), or when the resolution or other aspects of the technical ability of digital photography is insufficient. This may include the photography of particularly small or particularly large items.

Selecting Which Photographs to Use

As with illustration, the choice of photographs depends on the nature of the report for which they are intended. For the technical (stratigraphic) report, it will be necessary to show not only the results of the fieldwork but also to give some idea of the methodologies deployed. It is good practice to include at least one photograph of each trench or substantial feature – even where the results were 'negative' (i.e. there were no archaeological finds or deposits). In general, the following photographs should be included:

- The site before excavation
- At least one photograph of each trench (in an evaluation) or area (in an open-area excavation), sometimes several photographs if the stratigraphy was particularly complex
- Detail photographs of the sections of each trench (in an evaluation) or of key sections (in an open-area excavation)
- Detail photographs of every feature encountered, sometimes several photographs (for instance a pit may be illustrated by a photograph showing it in plan before excavation, during excavation [half-section] and after excavation)
- Working shots showing, for instance, machine stripping, excavation in progress and recording in progress
- The site (or trench) as a whole when cleaned at various stages of excavation
- Photographs of artefacts.

Clearly a degree of flexibility is required. On a site where a building is represented by 20 identical postholes, for example, then include a shot of the building outline as a whole, plus one or two photographs of representative examples of post-holes. Similarly with a linear cut feature this may be best illustrated with an overall shot plus a handful of photographs taken at key locations showing the profile, sections and relationships with other features. Conversely some features may need more than one photograph.

The selection of photographs for publication will typically include more working shots and overall shots and fewer detail photographs of less significant features. Remember that you will also need to include archive photographs (where possible), while aerial or satellite images make a lively supplement to drawings showing the site in its broader landscape context.

Publication

Once the technical (stratigraphic) report is completed, then attention needs to turn to publication proper. In British archaeology, there are five basic levels of publication, ranging from short summaries of a few hundred words to substantive monographs running to several volumes.

Summary Reports

For commercial archaeology projects, it is usually a requirement of the curatorial brief that some sort of summary is published. For all projects – regardless of formal require-ments – it is good practice to do so anyway. A summary publication means that the basic findings of the project are available to a wider audience. The usual outlets for this are:

- A regional round-up of archaeological work – in some areas produced by the relevant regional branch of the Council for British Archaeology (CBA), else-where compiled by the local authority, and usually published annually
- A round-up of archaeological work by period, usually a feature of the journals of most period societies – such as the Society for Mediaeval Archaeology
- A local gazetteer of archaeological work, sometimes to be found in the local society journal
- A newsletter of one of the learned societies.

In many cases, the non-technical summary of the stratigraphic report is a good starting point for this kind of publication. Most summaries will be not more than 500 words (in some cases much less) and there may be the opportunity to include a single illustration. The writing style should be approachable but do not shy away from widely understood technical terms as the audience is archaeologically literate. Note that these summaries are usually about 12 months in arrears. It is always worth making contact with the editor of the relevant publication well in advance of intended submission.

Papers in Local or Regional Journals

Many projects produce more exciting results which are worth conveying in a more substantial report. Again submission to a local or regional journal can be a requirement of the curatorial brief, although it should be considered with any project. Usually local journals are produced by a local archaeological society. On the whole, such organisations are financially poor but rich in enthusiasm. Typically, a local society is governed by a Council or Committee consisting of a mixture of amateur enthusiasts and local professionals and academics. The editor of the journal may be drawn from any of these groups. The remit of individual societies varies considerably – many have their origins in the nineteenth century when scientific investigation was more interdisciplinary – such as the Thoroton Society of Nottinghamshire, or the Dorset Natural History and Archaeological Society. Others are distinctively and impressively archaeological and have a much wider membership than their geographical coverage would suggest – such as the Society of Antiquaries of Newcastle-upon-Tyne or the Oxfordshire Archaeological Society with its highly regarded journal *Oxoniensia*.

It is always best to approach the relevant society in the early stages of the project to see if publication in their journal is appropriate. Commercial projects will need to make sure that they have budgeted for some sort of subvention to the society for publication. There is likely to be a long lead-in time. Requirements for style and format for submission of illustrations will vary considerably. It is wise to have a look at recent previous volumes or consult the style-guide which is generally available online.

When writing for a local or regional journal it is worth noting that the readership will be acutely aware of local historical events, but generally (although not always) less familiar with the latest developments in archaeological theory. Therefore, a more empirical approach to discussing the results is preferred.

Papers in National Period or Specialist Journals

If the project has involved work on a large site or has delivered results of national importance, then consideration should be given to publication in one of the national period or specialist journals. As with local journals, these are usually the organ of a particular society with certain interests. Some of these deal with all types of archaeological work in a particular time-frame, for example:

- Proceedings of the Prehistoric Society (http://www.le.ac.uk/has/ps/pps/pps.html)
- Britannia (http://www.romansociety.org/publications/journals/britannia.html)
- 'Mediaeval Archaeology', the journal of the Society for Mediaeval Archaeology (http://www.medievalarchaeology.org/)
- 'Post-Mediaeval Archaeology', the journal of the Society for Post-Mediaeval Archaeology (http://www.spma.org.uk/journal.php)
- 'Industrial Archaeology Review', the journal of the Association for Industrial Archaeology (http://www.maney.co.uk/index.php/journals/iar/).

Others deal with specific types of site or artefact, such as:

- 'Archaeometry', a journal of archaeological science (http://www.arch.ox.ac.uk/rlaha.html)
- 'Environmental Archaeology', the journal of human palaeoecology (http://www.envarch.net/publications/envarch/index.html)
- 'Historical Metallurgy', the journal of the Historical Metallurgy Society (http://hist-met.org/)
- 'The International Journal of Nautical Archaeology' (http://www.nasportsmouth.org.uk/).

Papers in Other National Journals

There are a handful of societies whose remit is to look at nationally and internationally significant work in all periods and geographical areas. Their journals are prestigious publications and papers are usually either significant projects with international implications for the study of a particular period or site type or are synthetic analyses of the current state of play in a particular area of archaeology. These include:

- The Archaeological Journal (http://www.royalarchaeolinst.org/)
- The Journal of the British Archaeological Association (http://maney.co.uk/index.php/journals/jba/)
- Antiquaries Journal (http://www.sal.org.uk/books/theantiquariesjournal/)
- Antiquity (http://antiquity.ac.uk/).

Monographs

A monograph is conventionally a publication on a single site or project. However, the term is no longer so strictly defined, and 'monographs' have appeared in recent years which have included proceedings of conferences, multi-authored thematic works and other subjects.

Monographs can be very time consuming and expensive to produce, and rarely reach a wide readership. Most monographs sell a few hundred copies at most, and in terms of information circulation, it may be preferable to publish a site report as an article in one of the appropriate journals. However, monographs can often include much more detailed information (notably from specialist reports) than a journal article, as well as more detailed work on the wider context. Monographs are usually collaborative undertakings, normally with a limited number of leading authors but with a large number of specialist contributors. In some cases, the publication of a monograph is a required outcome of developer-funded projects.

There are several vehicles for monograph publication. The cheapest and easiest is to produce a British Archaeological Report. These A4-sized paperbacks with blue covers (for British reports) and red covers (for International reports) have graced the shelves of many archaeological libraries since the 1970s and are nowadays produced by Archaeopress. They have a quick turn around (typically 6–8 weeks). Traditionally a vehicle for the publication of PhDs, they are also a convenient way of publishing synthetic work as well as individual site reports. Their advantage is in their rapidity and relative cheapness, and although widely read they can be looked down upon by some scholars.

Other publishers also produce monographs – probably the largest publisher of archaeological work is Oxbow Books. They have produced a wide range of books over many years and have an international distribution. With Oxbow and other publishers, the work of typesetting, layout and design is all done by the publishers, but at a cost – so you need to weigh up the balance between the value of your time and the quality of the final product, which will always be higher with conventional publishing. Typical turnaround for a conventional published monograph will be between 9 and 18 months, with costs of around £5,000 or more.

Probably the most highly regarded monographs are those produced by, or on behalf of, the various learned societies. The Society of Antiquaries of London, British Archaeological Association and the Royal Archaeological Institute all have publication series, as do the individual period or regional societies.

Archiving

Archaeological excavation is destructive; therefore, the records derived from the excavation need to be archived permanently and accessibly. Archaeological archives are an essential component of the archaeological resource, and it should theoretically be possible to re-interrogate and reinterpret raw data from fieldwork which is held in archives. Thus, archaeological archives provide the raw material for further research, they inform public interpretation, and provide material for teaching. An archaeological archive essentially consists of two components:

• The documentary archive, which consists of all records made during an archaeological project – in hard copy and digital form – including written records, drawings and photographs (negatives, prints, transparencies and X-radiographs), reports, publication draughts, published work and publication drawings and photographs. Digital material consists of all material that was originally produced in a digital format (including text, data, drawings, 3D models, photographs and video) as well as files generated from digitised material.
• The material archive, which comprises all objects – artefacts, building materials or environmental remains (and/or associated samples) – of contextual materials or objects.

Existing points of access to archaeological archives include the HER – which provides information on the extent of the archaeological work carried out in a particular area – and archive repositories which facilitate access to records and objects. These include accredited museums, local record offices and the NMR.

Every archaeological project must aim to produce a stable, ordered and accessible archive that can be assimilated easily into the collections of recognised repositories. All aspects of the archaeological process affect the quality of the resulting archive. If recording during the project is not consistent or up to standard the archive will not be ordered or accessible and therefore is of limited value. Standards can be maintained by establishing systems for managing documentation and collecting material, and by using appropriate materials, applying consistent terminology, documenting all activities, creating copies of documentation and preserving draught versions of key reports and report components.

The archive must be a record of every part of an archaeological project: the aims and methods, information and artefacts collected, results and interpretations and the final publication. As with other aspects of a project, standards for the creation, management and preparation of the archive must be understood and agreed at the outset. The project has not been completed until the archive had been transferred successfully. It may be appropriate to deposit an archive before the project has been published. Archaeological repositories must be suitable for providing long-term care and public access.

A museum disposition standard might list the types of material to be used in packing particular objects, explain how drawings are to be labelled and packed or stipulate a particular box size for bulk finds. There are national and international standards for the management of various archive elements, e.g. long-term preservation of documents and objects and also national standards for individual disciplines.

Summary of Standards for Archives

The Documentary Archive

Paper. All types of record must use a consistent terminology and format, both within a project and ideally across all projects – although as noted above there are variations across the British Isles. Permanent or high-quality paper and writing materials must be used. Copies of reports, draughts (where appropriate) and associated illustrative material, as well as correspondence and other items, must be included in the archives, and all of these documents must be marked with the project identifier (e.g. site code) and the museum accession number. Use non-metal fastenings and packaging and binding materials that ensure longevity of documents (guidelines for this are usually provided by the receiving institution). All paper-based material must be stored in conditions that minimise the risk of damage or deterioration. Ideal temperature is a fixed point in the range of 13–19°C, while humidity should be a fixed point between 45 and 60%.

Drawings. Polyester-based film must be used for field drawings, and ideally 'inked up' versions should also be produced on a similarly permanent medium (electronic copies should also be stored – see below). As with written material, all drawings must be marked with the project identifier (e.g. site code) and the museum accession number. They must identify the subject and location and include a scale and a north arrow. All original drawings should be included in the archive and stored flat in dark, dust-free containers. Ideal temperature is a fixed point in the range of 5–10°C, while humidity, as above, should be a fixed point between 45 and 60%.

Photographs. Photographs must be stored in conditions that minimise the risk of damage or deterioration. The original media should be used to record photographs. Processed black and white film is ideal for archiving and is suitable for long-term storage. Video must not be used as a primary record; instead it should be transferred to DVD. Again all photographs must be marked with the project identifier (e.g. site code) and the museum accession number. They must identify the subject, location, scale and show a north arrow. Prints should be stored in archival boxes at a fixed point between 13 and 19°C and a relative humidity of 40–60%. Negatives should be stored in dust-proof cabinets. Colour film should be stored in a temperature range of 1 ± 1°C; black-and-white film is inherently more robust so can cope with a wider storage range, but the temperature should be fixed at no more than 18°C. Relative humidity for all film types should be between 30 and 40%.

Reports and Publications. Reports and publications should also be included in the archive, and these must be produced on materials of comparable quality to other paper records. It is also worth including an index or guide to the archive itself, which should also include a short summary report explaining the background to the project.

Digital Material. The digital archive consists of all digital data such as CAD files, databases, excavation archive, survey data, GIS files, images, satellite imagery, spreadsheets and so on. Short-term storage media includes CD-ROMs, data-sticks or flash dries, DVDs, floppy discs, and hard discs. These should only be used to submit digital material for permanent archiving. Long-term storage must be on permanent servers that are regularly backed up, such as those of the Archaeological Data Service (ADS) hosted by the University of York. Creation of the digital archive must be fully documented with information such as software used, operating systems, types of hardware, dates, personnel, field descriptions and the meaning of any codes.

Data must be created with consistent, standard terminology, content and formatting. They should conform to existing standards and guidelines on how data should be structured, preserved and accessed. The files must be regularly backed up throughout the course of a project. A digital archive must be compiled and deposited in digital form, with copies of archives stored in a secure digital, anti-magnetic archiving facility; needless to say all media files must be free of viruses!

The Material Archive

All finds must be cleaned, marked and labelled (with project and context identifiers and individual identifier if applicable in permanent ink), treated carefully and kept secure. They must be recorded and classified to a consistent format and accepted terminologies. All metal objects retained with the archive must be recorded by

X-radiograph (with some exceptions, including gold or lead). Of course, not all finds are retained during archaeological projects. Unstratified material may have little archaeological significance and some types of finds like fragmented slate roofing material can be recorded on-site or in post-excavation and does not need to be retained in the final archive. However, the finds selection should be carried out with the aims of the project and the requirements of the archive repository in mind. This selection strategy must be put in place at the outset of the project.

All finds must be packed in appropriate materials to ensure risk-free, long-term storage and stored in conditions conducive to the long-term survival of each object.

The material archive is composed of four elements: bulk finds (which occur in quantity and do not require special treatment – animal bone, building material, slag), sensitive finds (small-finds or registered finds – glass, leather, textile, wood), human remains and materials recovered from scientific sampling. All finds must be stored in the dark and in conditions that are not susceptible to wide fluctuations in temperature or relative humidity – bulk finds around 15°C and humidity between 35 and 70%; metals between 15 and 24°C and below 35% relative humidity; organic finds must be dried and stored at between 18 and 22°C and a relative humidity of between 45 and 55%.

Archive Transfer, Copyright and Title

Archive repositories should have ownership of any archive deposited with them and ideally should have copyright, sole or shared. This must be in line with existing legislation such as the *Copyright, Designs and Patent Act* 1988, the *Treasure Act* 1996 and the *Burials Act* 1857. If the copyright holder wishes to retain certain rights to the material, then the archive repository could agree an appropriate copyright licence. The licence must also represent the interest of third parties such as the NMR and ADS.

At present, landowners retain all rights of ownership to archaeological materials found on their land, with the exception of items classified as 'treasure' (see Chap. 4). It is desirable that the landowner transfers title to all archaeological objects to the appropriate archive. The archaeologist undertaking fieldwork is responsible for obtaining the written consent of the landowner to transfer ownership to the identified archive.

The seabed in British waters is owned by the Crown and all seabed finds must be reported to the Receiver of Wreck. If the wreck is not claimed for ownership within 1 year of being reported to the Receiver of the Wreck, then ownership is decided by the Receiver of the Wreck.

Engaging with the World

There is more to 'publication' than an academic paper. Indeed even in the relatively cloistered world of academia, increasing attention is being placed on 'impact' in the wider world as well as publication in the more conventional sense. Regardless of the way in which archaeology is funded, it is still essentially a 'public' activity.

One of the most basic, but also one of the most immediate, ways of engaging with the public is through site tours and site visits. Increasingly in the modern health-and-safety-dominated world, opportunities for site visits are fairly formal and restricted; however, there is usually considerable local interest about sites being excavated – especially in urban areas. Very quickly the archaeologist will learn to brush aside the usual less than witty remarks of visitors – such as 'found any gold yet?', 'I dropped a sixpence there in 1965, if you find it its mine', 'are those skeletons real?' – and begin to engage with those who are genuinely interested in the past. Most people will have a generic interest, and more recently this has been enhanced with TV programmes, notably *Time Team*, which has improved public understanding of what archaeologists actually do.

Dealing with the Media

It is also during or shortly after excavation that you may be required to deal with the media. In Britain, there is a fairly vibrant network of local newspapers and BBC local radio stations which are always looking for good human interest stories – including archaeology. It is important that any engagement with the media takes place with the approval of both the client (or funder of the work if non-commercial) and the local authority archaeologist (curator). The first thing to do is to prepare a press release. If your organisation has a press officer or marketing department they will usually prepare the final version, but you will still need to supply the basic facts – what have you found, why are you doing the work, what will happen next… and, most importantly, why should anyone be interested? Whilst admirable in academic circles, the usual archaeological circumspection does not lend itself to eye-catching press releases. Things that are 'previously unknown' or that 'change the way we think about the past' are more likely to get noticed than 'we dug a hole and found some pot' – all the more so if you can include some universal themes such as death and violence. Association of a site with a local or national personality, or some significant historical event, will also help.

Local newspapers are usually after a large picture and a small number of words, and will typically try to produce a feature that goes somewhere in the middle of the paper. If you are lucky a reporter will be sent, but more commonly a photographer will arrive with a half-read crumpled copy of the press release in his or her pocket. The photographer will usually prefer to use young female subjects in his photograph, ideally holding the star find whilst crouching down in a muddy hole. Local radio (the BBC operates a network of local radio stations that are usually county- or city-based) may also respond to your press release. Again a single reporter will be sent with a remarkably small digital recorder. Occasionally you might be invited to the studio for a fuller interview. Typically the visit of local newspaper or radio might take half an hour of your time. A well-organised press event can cram all of the disruption into a single 1–2 h slot.

Television is an entirely different prospect. Even local TV programmes require a crew of at least two people, and more commonly a team of three or four will be sent.

Traditionally, the TV crew will include a producer, camera operator, sound recordist and the presenter. The producer is usually well-informed, articulate and interested in what you are doing, and will do his best to try and showcase the story you want to tell. However, they are limited by the time slot available and by the convention of the presenter, who will always have the first and last word. For archaeologists, filming can be an extremely boring process, not least because each question and answer will often need to be filmed several times. There will need to be a long-distance shot, showing the presenter and interviewee in the broader setting of the site; a shot of both talking to each other; 'head shots' of the interviewer asking the questions, and of the interviewee answering them; and finally some 'walking' shots where lots of frantic gesticulation is usually required. Aeroplanes, sunlight, motorbikes and other distractions will also require repeated attempts to film the same scene; there may be technical problems as well. As a rough guide, experience suggests that it takes about 2 h to film a typical short (2 or 3 min) piece for local television involving three or four shots.

Always ask to see the list of proposed questions as soon as the film crew (or radio reporter) arrives, to give yourself the best chance of thinking up short and coherent answers. If a particular question looks as though it might be difficult to answer effectively, then do not be afraid to suggest an alternative. Remember that dealing with the media is not like having a conversation – it is important to realise that, unlike an ordinary conversation, you have no control over how it is ultimately presented. Whatever you say can work against you! Because of the way in which film and tape can be manipulated, you cannot rely on the gradual build-up of context as you would in a normal lecture or conversation – instead every statement stands on its own. Therefore, you have to make sure that what you say is clear, unambiguous and continually makes reference to key points that you want to get across. It was once suggested that if you say something you might regret, then a string of completely unbroadcastable expletives immediately afterwards will ensure it is never shown!

Talks and Presentations

After the dust has settled on the excavation, or even during the project, you may be invited or wish to give presentations to various audiences. These really fall into three main categories. The first is an academic presentation to a national conference – usually for one of the learned societies that deal with the period or subject which your site represents. Secondly, requiring some academic grounding but generally much more popular in tone are the various regional 'archaeology days' which are usually organised under the aegis of the CBA and/or by local authority curators. These are usually annual events which try and showcase recent projects in the area, and usually attract a good audience of inquisitive and interested people of all ages. They are in fact a good forum for archaeologists and may represent their first public presentation. The third category consists of evening talks to local groups – they may be local history societies or groups such as the Women's Institute (WI).

Whilst the audiences are different for each of these categories, and the content and delivery will also vary, there are certain important aspects of presentation preparation which are common to all.

Text. Unless you are extremely confident in your knowledge of the site or project, and are naturally well-organised and well-structured in your approach to presenting information, then it is usually best to prepare a text. Having said that there is nothing worse than someone reading through a text in a monotone and not looking up (see below), so you might be better served by having notes. As a general rule, a page of text in 12 point Aerial, double spaced, will take about 3 min to read. Typically talks for academic conferences are about 20 or 25 min in length (i.e. around 7 pages), whilst those for local groups can be as long as an hour (i.e. up to 20 pages). Practice reading through the script or notes in advance, and remember that a read-through in the privacy of your own office or bedroom will always be a couple of minutes shorter than the real thing. Much better to use less time than your slot, enabling questions or digressions, and earning you the praise of the chairman and the audience.

Slides. Powerpoint is now universally accepted, even amongst formerly die-hard slide enthusiasts. A good rule of thumb is to allow one Powerpoint 'slide' per minute of talk. If you are talking for 20 min and have 150 slides, then you are either not going to make it or your audience will get dizzy. Powerpoint has lots of very tempting features, but spinning letters and colour changes are extremely distracting. Try to avoid reading the words embedded in your presentation. There is nothing worse than a slide show which consists of a set of bullet points which the speaker then reads to the audience – the audience's reading speed will always be much faster than the speaker can get through them. Instead, use the best features of Powerpoint – the ability to put dots on maps, highlight areas, label features and so on – and use them sparingly. Text should be at 24 point or larger, and try and avoid distracting backgrounds or too much fussy clutter.

Talking. The way in which the talk is delivered will depend upon the audience and the formality of the occasion. At all times speak clearly and try and project to the person sitting at the back. Be aware that not everyone's hearing will be as sharp as yours. As you get more used to dealing with different situations you are likely to be able to gauge in advance the likely atmosphere. A joke about phenomenology might go down well in an academic context, but may fall completely flat when talking to the Lower Brockhampton Local History Group. Having said that on no account attempt to patronise your local group! You never know who will be in the audience, and chances are they know things that you do not. In fact the local group can be more intimidating than a national conference… when talking to the Society for Mediaeval Archaeology a mispronounced name or a slightly wrong date is unlikely to be noticed, but members of the Local History Group in whose parish your excavation took place will certainly notice such things! A 1-h evening slot in the church hall is usually quite relaxed. You will almost always be given tea and biscuits, and there will be genuine interest and enthusiasm. You will be nervous if it is your first time. But be assured: an audience can be very forgiving , and chances are your confidence will grow as your talk progresses.

Summary

With this chapter, the process of project management comes to a close. We have planned our project, thought it through, consulted, done the desk-based assessment, the survey and excavation, the post-excavation analysis and archiving, and we have written the report, published a paper or two and spoken about it at conferences. It is about time to begin another project, and the whole management cycle begins again. But there will be one difference next time. You are now more experienced than you were before. Skills have been learnt or fine-tuned. You may be more confident now, in your own ability or those around you. You may also be starting to question a long-held belief that archaeology was quite simply good fun. Some cynical older archaeologists sometimes seem to forget this, and you may be starting to understand why this transition happens. There is a lot of management and administration that goes with every archaeology project, but that is inevitable. It is also universal. So, whatever you may think of your chosen career, and there will definitely be down-times, when you question your choice, remind yourself just how much fun archaeology can be.

In the final chapter, we return to the early stages of the process and provide an introduction to the various entry points into archaeology, through career opportunities and education, and ending with a section on keeping safe, authored for us by people who know best.

References and Further Reading

Adkins, L. and Adkins, R.A. 1989. *Archaeological Illustration*. Cambridge: Cambridge University Press.

Aitchison, K. 2004. *Disaster management planning for archaeological archives*. IfA Technical Paper No.8.

Brown, D. H. 2007. *Archaeological Archives: A guide to best practice in creation, compilation, transfer and curation*. Archaeological Archives Forum/Institute for Archaeologists.

Collett, L. 1996. *Introduction to Drawing Archaeological Pottery*. Association of Archaeological Illustrators and Surveyors, Occasional Papers No.1.

English Heritage. 2001. *The Presentation of Historic Building Survey in CAD*. Swindon: English Heritage.

English Heritage. 2004. *Human Bones from Archaeological Sites: Guidelines for producing assessment documents and analytical reports*. Swindon: English Heritage.

English Heritage. 2006. *Guidelines on the X-radiography of archaeological metalwork*. Swindon: English Heritage.

English Heritage. 2006. *Science for Historic Industries: guidelines for the investigation of 17th- to 19th-century industries*. Swindon: English Heritage.

Ferguson, L.M and Murray, D.M. 1997. *Archaeological Documentary Archives*. IfA Technical Paper No.1.

Harris, E.C. 1989. *Principles of Archaeological Stratigraphy*. London: Academic Press.

Institute for Archaeologists. 2008. *Standard and Guidance for the collection, documentation, conservation and research of archaeological materials*.

Hodgson, J. 2001. *Archaeological reconstruction: illustrating the past*. IfA Technical Paper No.5.

Philo, C. and Swann, A. 1992. *Preparation of Artwork for Publication*. IfA Technical Paper No.10.

Chapter 8
Opportunities, Funding and Keeping Safe

Having now followed the various processes involving archaeologists and heritage practitioners in Britain, from the desk-based assessment to post-excavation analysis and publication, this chapter outlines some of the opportunities that exist for working in the heritage sector in Britain. The chapter is as complete and comprehensive as space allows, and covers most types of opportunity, whether one is seeking full-time employment, part-time, seasonal or voluntary work, or exploring possibilities for further education. It will examine, first, what opportunities exist where and how to find out about them; second, how to obtain funding for research, and finally the conditions of employment, health and safety and other practical considerations. Inevitably this overview cannot be comprehensive as the numbers and types of vacancies will vary according to political and economic circumstances. We also indicate websites and publications where more information is available.

Finding Work

Career Opportunities

Following earlier studies (Aitchison 1999; Aitchison and Edwards 2003), *Discovering the Archaeologists of Europe – Archaeology Labour Market Intelligence: Profiling the Profession 2007/2008* provides a comprehensive survey and assessment of employment within professional archaeology in the UK (Aitchison and Edwards 2008). As well as aiding business planning and improving organisational performance and competitiveness, it assists individuals to identify their own position within the profession and inform personal career decisions. Here, we present a few key facts from the report, although with the proviso that – as one of the report's original authors recently pointed out – the report was undertaken at the 'high water mark' of British archaeological employment, 1 month before the collapse of Lehman Brothers and the global financial crisis.

In August 2008, it was estimated that 6,865 paid archaeologists were working in the UK, an increase of 20% on the previous survey 5 years earlier and a 55% increase over 10 years on the results of the 1997–1998 survey. In addition, there were some 866 dedicated support staff working with these archaeologists. Therefore, over 7,700 people in the UK rely on professional archaeology for their livelihoods. Further, an estimated 510 people work as unpaid volunteer archaeologists alongside the professionals, and 16 people contribute as unpaid volunteer support staff within professional archaeological organisations. It can no longer be said that there are no jobs in British archaeology, though that will be no consolation to those currently looking for work.

How often jobs become available will depend on staff turnover, career progression and job creation. One consideration here is the profession's age profile. The average age of professional archaeologists in the UK is 38 years. In all, 84% of archaeologists are between 20 and 50 years old, so archaeology has a relatively young age profile compared with UK statistics, which have 34% of employees aged 45–64. 41% of professional archaeologists are female and 59% male, 99% are white, and 1.6% disabled as defined as being work-limited disabled by the terms of the *Disability Discrimination Act* 1995.

It is worth summarising some of the study's other key findings, as these also have a bearing on current and future opportunities. Of the 6,865 archaeologists working in the UK, 3,888 (57%) work for organisations that provide field investigation and research services (largely 'contractors' and contracting units), 1,831 (27%) work for organisations providing historic environment advice (largely 'curators' and also 'consultants'), 310 (4%) work for museum services and 836 (12%) for those providing educational and academic research services. If we recast this slightly, and present it as a table, we have Table 8.1.

More archaeologists work in London and the south-east of England than elsewhere, although this merely reflects national patterns of economic activity and employment.

It is often said that archaeologists are poorly paid. In 2007/2008, the average salary for archaeologists was £23,310. This falls short of the overall national average in all occupations of £29,999. Since the previous survey in 2002/2003, the average salary for archaeologists has remained consistently behind the national average, from being 78% of the national average in 2002/2003 to 77% in 2007–2008. By comparison, in 1997–1998, archaeologists earned 89% of the national average. The highest

Table 8.1 Archaeological employers

Type of employer	Numbers employed	%
Central government	666	10
Local government	1,151	17
Universities	1,009	15
Private sector	3,504	51
Other	535	8

Source: Aitchison and Edwards 2008

Table 8.2 Lengths of contract

Length of contract	Number of people	%
Up to 3 months	119	5
3–6 months	113	4
6–12 months	213	8
12–24	89	3
>24	87	3
Permanent	1,859	73
Other	69	3

paid post-profile was academic staff, with an average salary of £31,131. The lowest profile was excavator or site assistant, at £12,140. It is worth considering the all-round 'package' as well as salary – public sector jobs (universities, national and local bodies) usually have quite generous pension provision, whereas private sector jobs very rarely do. One of the authors has earned a total of 2½ years pension entitlements after 20 years continuous employment in archaeology!

Many senior jobs are now fairly permanent, although even apparently secure jobs have been seen to be extremely vulnerable in the recent downturn. In the 2007/2008, survey the following results were returned on length of contract (Table 8.2).

Many full-time vacancies arise each year. The trouble is that, with several hundred archaeology graduates emerging from British universities each year, there is considerable competition, even for the most junior posts. What follows is, first, an overview of some of the vacancies that typically arise, and second, some suggestions of how to be better equipped, ensuring first that one gets short-listed and second that one gives a good account of oneself at interview.

Vacancies

How does a prospective archaeologist or heritage professional find out about relevant jobs in Britain? For a long time, the best advice was 'the Wednesday *Guardian*'. Now most vacancies are listed in the IfA's Jobs Information Service (JIS), a regular newsletter emailed to members on a weekly basis, and then often widely distributed within organisations where a staff member is also a member of the IfA. Non-members can also subscribe to the newsletter for a fee, though it is better to join the IfA and receive it for nothing! JIS has most of the vacancies, senior and junior, full- and part-time, and continues to include them in its newsletter until the deadline for application has passed. Some vacancies are also listed on the website British Archaeological Jobs Resource or BAJR (www.bajr.org.uk), though rarely do jobs appear here and not in the IfA JIS. Academic posts can be sought through the website http://www.jobs.ac.uk, though again most archaeology posts also appear in the IfA JIS. Of course, all larger employers (and some smaller ones) have a 'current vacancies' page on their website, and others have a page for potential volunteers.

In truth, JIS combined with a search using Google or similar search engines, with an appropriate combination of keywords ('archaeology' + 'jobs') will produce much if not all of what is currently available.

It is worth stating again that, as in all aspects of employment, vacancy rates will reflect current political and economic trends. Growth in the property market for example will generate development opportunities, and with so many archaeologists working in the commercial sector it is easy to see the impact this has on career opportunities. Equally there may be regional trends, such as housing growth areas, in which development will make further field archaeology a requirement. Of course one can only assess the vacancies currently available at the time one is actually looking, but it is worth taking note of the wider trends.

Most of the vacancies that arise are for jobs in the commercial and curatorial sector ('contractors' and 'curators'). In the commercial sector, early career vacancies are typically for excavation, site or project assistants, to work on particular field projects. As so many projects are now in advance of development, or assessing the archaeological implications of planning applications, many of the projects are small in scale and short in duration, so employees can expect to move swiftly between projects. Some landscape assessment projects are of longer duration however, and might involve excavation, field walking, trial pits and so on. Other projects may require employees to undertake desk-based study, at the local Historic Environment Record or a records office. Whether field- or desk-based, training will often be provided. Wessex Archaeology for example holds an annual training excavation for new recruits, something members of the public can also pay to attend. These posts with contracting units will suit people who enjoy digging, or outdoor and project-based work. They are also ideal for those wishing to progress within commercial archaeology. Many senior archaeologists took their first job after graduation at one of the units operating at that time.

Curatorial vacancies are different. Jobs may be in one of two main categories: working within the planning system, as a Historic Environment Record Assistant or Officer, or as an archaeologist working within development control, assessing planning applications for example; or commissioned by a national body to work on a national programme of study such as the National Mapping Programme or Historic Landscape Characterisation in England. In the first category, jobs can often be permanent and can suit archaeologists with a liking for more desk-based work, and half an eye on career progression within local government. Many of the present crop of county archaeologists and heads of sections started out as Sites and Monuments Records Officers and Assistants (as they were once called). These posts can also suit recent graduates with some relevant work experience and a good general grasp of British archaeology (more of this below).

The second category is more difficult, and could be seen as less attractive, as the posts are fixed term, usually of 2–4 years duration. However, they do provide valuable experience, working for a programme that often has a much longer shelf-life, with future vacancies in other regions as the programme continues to roll-out nationally. The organisational requirements of these commissioned projects also ensure that staffs are in regular contact with project managers at English Heritage for example, so it is a good opportunity to impress! Often, contracts are extended, and sometimes as local authorities expand, staff on these projects find themselves in an ideal position to take up a permanent post. More often than not, these are good positions that lead to better opportunities in the future.

Getting an Interview

With several hundred archaeology graduates every year, many of whom have ambitions to become professional archaeologists or work elsewhere within the heritage sector, and some of whom will have relevant higher degrees, it is inevitably a competitive field. We tend to believe though that, once selected for interview, things are more open. Anyone selected for interview has been selected on the basis that they could do the job; that – on paper at least – they have what it takes. So, arguably, getting to the interview is the hard part! Here we provide a few ideas of how this can be done, in a way that is fair to the employer and to the candidate.

The first stage, long before the curriculum vitae, involves building the experience and knowledge that will together constitute a strong application. There can be a presumption here that, even at university, perhaps even before attending university, you know precisely what you want to do and where you would like to work. This is rarely the case, but if you do, then great. Typically, this preliminary step on the career ladder might involve course selection at university and work experience. The first is dictated somewhat by the courses and modules on offer at the university you have an interest in attending. You may even select a university that offers more vocational courses. That is not to say the more theoretically driven courses should be avoided; far from it in fact as employers will want to see evidence for academic rigour, and the ability to question and analyse data in different ways. But a mix of the more theoretical and vocational elements might be good to achieve. If a heritage module is offered, then that may be particularly helpful. There may be other opportunities too. A dissertation can cover a topic where research is applied in some way or closely relevant to the career path you are considering, as can essays or other assignments. Much heritage information is now accessible online for example, notably Historic Environment Records and English Heritage's PastScape site (http://pastscape.english-heritage.org.uk/). The Archaeological Data Service has some of the Extensive Urban Survey reports produced by local authorities for many of England's small towns. These are all potential quarries for further analysis, interrogation and critique – and no one minds a good, reasoned and robust critique. So there is plenty of scope for studies and assignments that can enhance one's future prospects.

It may seem unfair and unprofessional sometimes to take employment without financial reward, but it can also have benefits. There are opportunities for unpaid work experience but you will have to ask; employers will not come looking for you. If you think a career in local government might be for you, write to your local county archaeological service and ask about work experience, perhaps just a week's work over the summer, entering data onto their GIS for example or cataloguing the results of new or recent projects. Some employers may also provide the opportunity to 'shadow' existing members of staff, attending meetings for example. You will not get paid, but you will learn a lot. You may decide that a particular area of work is not for you – but even that experience has had a positive outcome. Work experience is nearly always beneficial. But you need to be bold and ask. Of course, there may be people you know who have wider contacts and can make an initial introduction, but it will inevitably come back to you in the end.

Additional to this is the idea of a portfolio. Employers will rarely ask for one (except perhaps for some design and graphics posts), but they can have advantages. If, say, you took a heritage management module which involved preparing a management plan, or an essay directly relevant to the post you have applied for, or your dissertation had a direct bearing on what the post involves, then why not 'show and tell', especially if it is something that you were pleased with or which achieved high marks. Even if you did not get the high marks you hoped for, take it anyway and explain how you have learnt from the experience, how you know where you went wrong. You cannot insist on showing this to an interview panel, but you can mention that you have brought it. More often than not, they will offer you the opportunity to present your work. But do not take too much, just one or two items, and do not dwell on it for too long.

Two final things – being a member of the IfA will always help, whatever grade of membership you opt for, and a full driving licence will often be useful too. Some jobs will require it.

Let us move now to the point where an interesting job has been advertised, for which you appear to fit the person specification (often reduced to 'person spec'). Once you reach this point, the first thing involves you being bold and courageous. We are firm believers in contacting the organisation (and sometimes a specific named person) to talk about the post at an early stage, and before you begin your application. Surprisingly few people do this, but it is worthwhile. Making the call demonstrates to your prospective employer that you are keen and that you use your initiative. It is also likely to set you apart from most other prospective candidates, as most will not be as brave as you.

The application itself is the next step. Often there will be a specific application form, as opposed to the CV, but the same principles apply. Some people find self-promotion quite difficult, but this is one occasion where it is necessary. It is a job you want, and there will be others wanting it just as much. It is a competition and you have to be competitive if you want to win. Think hard about the CV or application – keep it simple, tight and to the point. Think hard about the job you are applying for, the skills and experiences they are after, and the personal specifications. Your CV (and the essential covering letter) must address these points. We will deal with the CV and the letter in turn.

Curriculum Vitae

The CV should have several key sections to it:

* Personal details
* Educational background

- Professional background
- Academic record (where relevant)
- Referees.

Preceding all of this, however, should be consideration of an informative and representative front page. Put yourself in the position of an employer, faced with 50–100 CVs and job applications, many from new or recent graduates, often with similar backgrounds. Show them who you are on the front page, and what you can provide that others might not. Personal details are essential here, but maybe something besides: some relevant modules in which you performed well, or interesting fieldwork, or a persuasive, well-written but of course brief personal statement. Set yourself apart. Promote yourself. Tell your potential employers why they should pick you for interview. What makes you an interesting prospect and potential colleague?

Let us think about these sections of the CV in a little more detail.

Personal Details

This is simple. This section is for all the vital information one has to include – name, contact address and details, whether one has a driving licence, and membership of professional bodies. If you are a member of the IfA, at any grade, put it here.

Educational Background

This section includes the schools and university you attended, the dates, grades and – at university – the modules, units or courses you took and the marks awarded (where known). Make sure the most relevant units are clear and obvious – do not hide these away! For example, if you are applying for an aerial photographic post, and got a very high mark in an aerial photograph interpretation module, then make sure this information is prominently displayed.

Professional Background

If you have a history of employment, include previous employers in this section with an outline of your main responsibilities (e.g. staff management, whether or not you were a budget holder, etc.) and tasks. Mention which excavations you worked on, for how long, and in what position. This is also the place for voluntary work and any unpaid work experience. You might also like to highlight some of your main achievements, or how you overcame particular difficulties or challenging situations (such as accommodating changes in working practices, or new and additional responsibilities like being a budget holder, or managing staff). But be brief and to the point.

Academic Record

If you have any publications, have given talks or lectures, been awarded grants or awards and prizes for academic work, then include it in this section. As your career progresses, this section can take over your CV, but initially it will be fairly modest.

Referees

Select these very carefully! You need to be sure your referees will take their role seriously, and of course acting as referee is a significant responsibility. You need to ensure that they have the job description and so-called 'person spec' to consult and use; that they have your CV and that they know why you want the job and what you feel you have to offer. The referee also needs to know you and your capabilities well-enough to present your case in as positive and honest a way as possible. Where possible, ask a referee who knows the area of work you are looking to move into – someone that once worked in local government, for a local authority job for example.

Above all, attention to detail matters. There is nothing worse that a strong candidate with relevant experience and a shoddy CV. The key is not to rush it. When applying for lots of jobs at once, you could be forgiven for printing off multiple copies of the CV and letter (see below) and just mailing them out to all and sundry. Employers will notice when this happens, when the application is a general one and not specifically tailored to the particular requirements of a specific post. Have the job title on the top of the CV for example and the date. Ensure some of your experiences are specifically matched to the Job Description. Demonstrate to your prospective employer that you have thought carefully about the job and about your application.

An accompanying letter is important too, and needs to be carefully crafted to address the needs of the post, and your suitability and enthusiasm for it. It needs to be well written and neatly presented, reflecting the ordered and well-organised person they wish to employ. No silly remarks. No photograph (unless one is requested – in which case be suspicious!). Just simple, coherent and to the point: why you want the job and why you are the best person for it. Be bold. It is a competition, remember. Briefly summarise the CV by stating what relevant experiences you have, including particular courses at university, relevant work experience and personal qualities. For many jobs (and where only one job is advertised), only 6–7 people may be interviewed for a post for which 60–70 will apply. You need to make sure that you are the one in ten that is selected. You need to set yourself apart, and the CV and letter is the only place to do that. So make sure everything relevant is in there that you have presented yourself as an interesting, efficient, dynamic person who would fit well into the team. Then sit and wait.

The Interview

If you do not get an interview – do not be too downhearted. Nobody has success every time, and there will be occasions when you feel knocked-back, especially if you felt the job was one you could easily have done.

But if you are selected, then you are in with a chance. One of the authors was once told that the best way to approach an interview was not necessarily to attempt to talk yourself into the job (running the risk of being brash and overconfident), but to make sure you do not talk yourself *out* of it. If you are not the most confident of people, this approach could serve you well. You will inevitably be nervous or apprehensive, and it is worth knowing that those on the panel may well be apprehensive too! We also suggest that it is best to just be yourself – and that if they like you as a person, then you are in a good position. Remember what you have already done before getting to this stage: you have supplied a CV containing a summary of your achievements to date, and from that they have clearly decided you could do the job. So now it may be more down to personalities and impressing them with your interest in the post and the work the organisation does, your enthusiasm and your ability to think on your feet. So, be friendly, warm, open and (of course) polite. Answer the questions you are asked clearly and coherently. Do not talk for too long and stick to the point.

Make sure that you have done your research, and throw one or two references to what you have learnt into the interview. Look at the organisation's Corporate or Strategic Plan for example, to find out what their future plans and ambitions might be, or new areas they might be looking to expand into. If you know who is on the panel (and some organisations will provide this information), find out something about them – things they have written for example, or interests. Again, it may be possible to tailor some of your answers to particular areas of interest or expertise to engage the panel in discussion or debate. And finally, always have at least one question to ask that is not about salary. 'When could I start?' for example.

It is hard to advise people on how to dress for an interview. One approach is simply to dress 'appropriately'. For a management job, a suit is probably best; for other office jobs a jacket (for men) and equivalent for women; for a field archaeologists' job, it is best not to wear a suit! A good rule of thumb is to wear a smart version of what you would expect to be wearing at work – then the panel can envisage you in the role.

If your interview was successful, great. But if not it is likely to have been a valuable experience, which you can draw on in the future. You can (and should) always seek feedback on your performance, which most employers will readily provide. Just write to them or email and ask, or call them. Even better, try to discuss it with the chair of the panel – you can then ask him/her directly about your strengths and weaknesses. You not only want to know 'what went wrong', but also what was good and what could you improve on for next time.

Various websites offer CV and interview advice. Rather than provide specific examples of these, readers are advised to use the search engines. The good websites should be fairly obvious.

Higher Education

Which University?

The Higher Education or HE sector provides a diversity of opportunities for those seeking a career in archaeology, heritage and the historic environment. In most of Britain, a high proportion of those leaving school at 18 years old will attend university or higher education institutions. The government plans are for that to increase, to 50% in due course. In 2005, 405,000 students attended their first year at university, a rise of 28,000 on the previous year. The number of overseas students also increased, by 4.3% on 2004. Of those university entrants every year, several hundred enrol on archaeology or heritage courses. And there are plenty to choose from: 29 at the last count, though this figure does fluctuate somewhat as some smaller departments close down. Crucially, it is important to look at the closer details of the courses and units on offer as they do vary considerably. As we have seen, some universities offer a more theoretical perspective than others; some are more vocational. Obviously, the place to look first is online: put 'archaeology' and 'university' into Google and any department worth its salt will appear in the first few pages. Look at the staff pages too – what are their research interests and current research projects? And not only the core staff, but also look up visiting lecturers and fellows, as it is sometimes these staff – people often working in the profession – who provide specialist courses, in heritage for example, or aspects of environmental archaeology.

You should also look at the department's RAE rating. RAE is the Research Assessment Exercise, last conducted in 2007 and being replaced by the Research Excellence Framework (REF). A panel of peer reviewers assess the publications and research quality of individuals from every department that is 'research-active'. It is a rigorous but important exercise that ultimately sees the departments graded, with 5* being the maximum that can be achieved. This is both a reflection of quality and productivity of a department's staff, and of its research culture; but it also partly determines future funding. A high-RAE rating means that the department can continue to develop its research. This matters to students partly because it means that lecturers are introducing significant new material and ideas to the curriculum and partly because there is a freshness about their delivery – it is not the same old stuff being regurgitated year after year. And perhaps most important of all, there is a good chance you will have the opportunity to work on some of these exciting projects, often in exotic places.

However, do not overlook another important measure: that of the Quality Assurance Agency for Higher Education (QAA). The QAA audits universities on a rolling programme and looks at teaching rather than research output. The quality of teaching is an important factor, especially for undergraduates.

The choice of university is definitely a personal choice, and cost may well be a determining factor. But the following considerations may help you to make that decision:

1. Course content
   Does it match with my own interests and expectations?
2. Lecturers
   Do they seem an interesting and dynamic bunch?
3. Research projects
   Are there some interesting projects that I may be able to work on? This includes the current crop of PhD students – is there a healthy number working on some exciting and innovative projects?
4. Success
   Is it a successful and popular department? Have a look at student comments and feedback, often available online
5. Location
   Is it a place I could happily spend 3 or 4 years?
6. University
   Does the university itself have good facilities, and a good social scene?
7. Further studies
   Are there opportunities to pursue my studies there if I chose to do so? What are the available MA programmes for example?

Getting into university is based on your previous academic achievement, basically your A level results or equivalent. You may be looking to progress directly from school or college, or enter HE as a mature student. If you are taking a gap year, there may be opportunities to undertake some archaeological work by way of preparation, and this you could do at home or abroad. You may be from Britain or overseas (and in either case there are of course lots of additional opportunities to study archaeology and heritage outside Britain – in the USA, Australasia and Europe for example). For Britain, there is a clear starting point, and your next step should be to contact UCAS – the Universities and Colleges Admission Service (www.ucas.com). Here you can find out what the various universities and colleges have to offer and the grade entry requirements (be realistic!) and you can apply online. In Britain, the academic year begins in September/October, so an application much earlier in the year is necessary. It is also much earlier in the year that most universities hold 'open days', and sometimes up to a year ahead of entry. So do take the opportunity to visit before deciding finally on your first choice. A clearing process then takes place in August once the year's A level and Higher results have been published.

In summary, the application process involves you making up to five choices, in order of preference. Some universities may have enough applicants to select only from those who place them as first choice. But our advice is to use the check list above to make the initial selection, then visit the universities concerned to decide your order.

Further Studies

Whether to continue to postgraduate studies will depend on a number of factors, not least your desire to do so, the additional costs involved, and whether your class of degree allows that possibility. But there is another question which you may wish to consider: will it be advantageous to do so? The answer to this will depend on your chosen career path. If you want to work in the commercial sector, you may find that there is no immediate advantage, though it might help with career progression in the future. For other paths, such as local authorities or heritage agencies, where competition is fierce and vacancies less common, anything that might give you the edge could be helpful. You need then to think which MA or MSc course is most relevant to the area you are hoping to move into. Or you may deliberately seek out degrees that meet skills gaps within the heritage sector. The IfA can advise on this, though GIS in heritage applications is an obvious one.

If you are undertaking a Masters degree already, or have recently completed one, the next stage might be to consider further doctoral research. Exactly the same points apply. You may wish to undertake a research programme for its own sake, and certainly it is unlikely that a PhD would do your prospects any harm! But if you are looking for a PhD to help with a particular career move, think hard about this and try to establish, by speaking with people that know, whether there really will be an advantage, or whether work experience may be a better use of your time.

If 'heritage' is the direction you wish to take, a number of MA/MSc programmes are available in Britain that deal directly with this. You will also find a significant heritage component (or can create one for yourself) in Masters programmes that focus on landscape archaeology, archaeology and computing and conservation. The key to all of this though is research, and all of the necessary information can be found online.

Training and Continuing Professional Development

Once you have completed your university education and hopefully found employment, your education really begins! Obviously you will learn a lot 'on the job', and grow in confidence and develop expertise over time. When you start you will be going to others for advice. It is surprising how quickly that is reversed, and people start coming to you, especially if you have joined the office with a particular skill not shared by others – GIS for example. But a significant development over recent years, not least since the IfA came on the scene, has been Continuing Professional Development or 'CPD'. There is a recognition within the profession, and crucially amongst many employers, that CPD matters, and is something worth the investment of staff time and resources. Larger organisations sometimes run their own training courses, while others are organised by universities. Oxford University's Department of Continuing Education organises an annual programme of 1-day courses for example, all of direct relevance to heritage professionals and university students (http://www.conted.ox.ac.uk/courses/).

Finally, there are conferences. Some are more academic in their scope and purpose – the annual Theoretical Archaeology Group conference for example (now matched by Nordic and US 'TAGs'), always held at a British university shortly before Christmas and frequented by early career researchers, many presenting their work in public for the first time; the annual IfA conference, held annually before Easter and targeted more at historic environment professionals; and the European Association of Archaeologists conference, held at a European location in September each year and representing a mixture of professional and university-based research.

The great thing about CPD is that the benefits of participating in all of these opportunities are recognised by employers and line managers. Provided you can make a case for attending, couched in terms of your professional (or indeed personal) development and provided there are sufficient funds to cover it, the presumption *should* be that you can go. That does not mean you can go to all the conferences and attend all training courses – you will have to be selective and make a reasoned case for each one!

Getting Research Funding

As this handbook provides guidance and advice for people wishing to work in Britain, many of the grants are likely to be in the home countries of applicants. For this you will need to search online as this is a huge subject that is necessarily beyond the scope of this book. But once in Britain the options for research funding are numerous and diverse (and highly competitive), as this short section will explain.

Research grants vary in size and scope, and the conditions attached to them vary also. If you are based in a university, then you may be encouraged to apply for one of the major research grants awarded by the Luverhulme Trust, the Arts and Humanities Research Council (AHRC), or the Economic and Social Research Council (ESRC). The AHRC supports research within a huge subject domain from traditional humanities subjects, such as history, modern languages and English literature, to the creative and performing arts. Many university-based archaeology research projects are funded by AHRC. It also funds postgraduate study, for taught Masters courses and research degrees. In addition, on behalf of the Higher Education Funding Council for England, it provides funding for museums, galleries and collections that are based in, or attached to, higher education institutions in England.

The AHRC was established on 1 April 2005 and replaced the Arts and Humanities Research Board. The decision to create the AHRC underlines the importance of high-quality research in the arts and humanities for the cultural, creative and economic life of the nation. As with the other research councils, the AHRC is an independent non-departmental public body, established by Royal Charter and accountable to Parliament through the Office of Science and Innovation.

The ESRC funds research and training into social and economic issues. It has an international reputation both for providing high-quality research on issues of importance to business, the public sector and government and for its commitment to training excellence, which produces world-class social scientists. ESRC is also an independent organisation, established by Royal Charter, and which again receives most of its funding through the Government's Office of Science and Innovation. A number of heritage and archaeology programmes are supported by the ESRC.

Other funding streams for major research projects are available through the British Academy and the Society of Antiquaries of London, the Heritage Lottery Fund and English Heritage. All can provide research grants to researchers within (and in some cases outwith) the HE sector. Grants vary considerably. With the British Academy for example, grants are awarded each year with four separate deadlines at 3-month intervals. English Heritage and to a much lesser extent the other national agencies provide grant selectively, and are dependent largely on the ability of the proposed project to deliver on particular and predetermined research priorities, usually set out in published research frameworks or strategies. The Heritage Lottery Fund target projects that seek to preserve or make accessible the nation's heritage. In addition are numerous smaller grants. The Council for British Archaeology for example has a Challenge Fund, with small amounts of money to set up projects that will attract further funding from elsewhere as they develop. A number of the national period societies, as well as local amenity and local history societies, have small amounts of grant to fund research projects.

For all grants and other funding, an application will be needed, explaining what is intended and when, what is the justification for the project, how the work will be undertaken and by whom, why you are qualified to do the work, how you propose to publicise it and curate the final archive, and who will benefit from it. Some funding applications involve completing an application form, as with the British Academy; others will involve producing a Project Outline or a Project Design. For English Heritage, this will be to MoRPHE guidelines (English Heritage 2006; http://www.english-heritage.org.uk/upload/pdf/MoRPHE-Project-Managers-Guide.pdf), though much the same information will also be required by others. Sometimes this will be in response to a Brief supplied by the client or the commissioning body. In these cases, the Brief should be studied very carefully and all of its points addressed. They may want details of insurance and indemnity for example; and clear evidence of your qualifications to undertake this particular commission.

If your research is for an area with which you are familiar, then much of the ground work will have been completed already. You will know the local curators and landowners; and you will be familiar with the lie of the land. But if it is an unfamiliar area, or an area where you haven't previously worked, then some preparatory groundwork will be necessary. You should stay in the area for a few days, giving yourself sufficient time to talk to the local curator, travel around to gain an impression of the landscape, of land ownership and where you can get essential supplies. Talk to members of the local community – in the pub, the local shop. And do your research on the history of the area, and any current issues that have a bearing on your proposed work. Write to the parish council. If it is a suburban area or village, talk to the local historical or amenity society. Often one good contact – someone that holds status locally – will be invaluable in ensuring good relations with the entire community.

Once work begins, consultation and networking should occur constantly. It can be difficult sometimes, but always find the time for visitors and interested bystanders: allocate this task to someone, on a rolling daily basis. And offer to talk to people about your work at the earliest opportunity: a short talk in the village hall for example, and an item for the local newspaper. This relationship should remain strong even after the project is complete. A copy of the final report should always be made available locally.

One Year Studying Archaeology in the UK: A Canadian Perspective

Adrian Myers (Stanford University)

Soon after my arrival in the UK from Canada, I realised that though the two countries' mores are different, they're not *that* different… we speak the same language, after all. Or so I thought. For more than once in the year that followed, the supposedly subtle differences between Canadian, and British English, would be cause for embarrassment!

After finishing a first degree in my own city, I was accepted to the University of Bristol's Department of Archaeology. I was excited for a year abroad – 'a change of scenery' – and at the prospect of completing an MA in 1 year, versus the standard two required by most North American universities. Another attraction to the UK was the diversity, and specificity, of the programmes offered: Bristol has a programme developed specifically around the sub-discipline of *Historical Archaeology*. I was excited, and apprehensive, to learn that there would be few constraints – geographic or temporal – on what topics I chose to work on.

After the first day, I knew it would be a great year. Everyone was genial and encouraging, building my confidence in face of initial anxieties. *And it was a great year*. The programme was packed with trips to museums and to historic sites and landscapes – we even took a memorable journey to Lundy, an island in the Bristol Channel…sea sickness tablets were free of charge.

The department was international – my tutor was American – and in my cohort of ten students, only two were bona fide Brits! We became friends and between projects we met at the pub to decompress. To our benefit, classes were often led by guest lecturers, specialists in different fields. This allowed for insight into specific areas of historic archaeology and for personal connections to be made. One evening a week, the department hosts a special guest lecturer – and quoting the weekly emails that announce these events: 'Wine will be served'!

My year of studying in the UK was a balance between rewarding hard work, and equally rewarding relaxation… with minor adventures throughout – I could tell you about driving an old Land Rover on the 'British' side of the road for the first time! Back in Canada, and planning a career in archaeology, not only do I have this year of learning and fun behind me, but I also have a post-graduate degree from a respected institution abroad which demonstrates experience and self initiative on any CV.

Conditions of Employment

Most archaeology jobs in the UK are waged. That means there is a salary which should be sufficient to cover living expenses including rent. Some projects may even provide accommodation, while most employers will cover expenses while away from home, on project work for example. Employment conditions vary hugely though, as we saw earlier. Although most posts included in the IfA's 'Profiling the Profession' survey were permanent, a significant number were of shorter duration. This is much more likely with early career posts, which by definition will be less well paid.

But other than that, employment conditions will be the standard conditions that exist in any professional employment, with provision for national insurance and pension contributions. There will also be the option of union membership.

Union Membership

Prospect is one of the main unions for archaeologists, with hundreds of members in almost 20 archaeology units across the country. Intended to be a voice for those in technical professions, the union has been vocal in trying to establish a proper career structure for archaeologists since it was founded in 2001, and in 2003 launched a seven-point manifesto for archaeology, which sought to raise the status of the profession and improve its terms and conditions.

Prospect advises, defends and supports members, if they have a problem at work. They also negotiate pay and conditions; campaign for jobs and standards; offer valuable benefits and services; and influence employers and government.

Joining the union usually incurs a monthly membership fee, and it is for you to decide whether this is worthwhile. At the start of a career, or in a new job, everything can seem rosy, and the chances are it will remain so. But occasionally things can go wrong, and when they do the union can be a useful ally. The union is well placed to advise on all sorts of work-place issues and to provide expert advice and guidance if the going ever gets tough.

Public-sector workers (especially those in local authorities) may prefer to join *Unison*, which is a union for public-sector workers of all professions.

Keeping Safe and Within the Law

Any archaeological work will require permission, even if it is only from the owner of the land. But first you should contact the local authority archaeologist to discuss what you have in mind. This is partly a courtesy, but also sensible given that the local authority curator is best placed to know what archaeological work has been done in the past, and any other proposed projects in the near future. They may also be able to help with ownership information, and any legal constraints. Failing that ownership is often easy to establish. Start with the nearest farm or property. If they do not own the area you are interested in and do not know who does, then try the next nearest and so on. One can also now obtain ownership information online through the Land Registry for a small fee (www.landregistry.gov.uk).

Legal constraints can also be easily established. The simplest way is online via www.magic.gov.uk, a site that lists, maps or provides links to all heritage designations from Sites of Special Scientific Interest to Scheduled Monuments. If there is a legal constraint, then an application to the statutory body will be required. This may take some time to be processed (perhaps even months) and could ultimately be rejected. There will certainly have to be a very clearly thought-out and robustly argued project design if Scheduled Monument Consent (SMC) is to be granted. This applies to excavation, but also any form of geophysical and metal detecting work. It remains illegal to use a metal detector on a scheduled monument without prior consent from the Secretary of State.

Other than that, nothing needs to be done. If the owner gives consent, the local authority archaeologist is aware and supportive, and there are no legal constraints then you can proceed. In Britain, there is currently no requirement for a licence to excavate archaeological sites.

Health and Safety

Health and safety is important, whether a lone-worker surveying or field-walking in remote areas, or a manager of an excavation. Either way, it is your responsibility to ensure you are operating in as safe an environment as possible. The best way to achieve this is to anticipate problems and ensure measures are put in place that mini-mise the risk. This procedure is standard practice now in British archaeology and is known as Risk Assessment. Risk Assessment documents should be thought about, carefully prepared and shared in advance with everyone involved in the project. It is then a matter of ensuring working practices take these potential risks into account at every turn, whether it be: providing details of where you will be if working alone; monitoring the height and profile of spoil heaps; being vigilant with wearing safety boots, high visibility jackets and hard-hats; giving regular health and safety briefings to visitors etc. It is rare to hear of accidents on archaeological sites. Careful prior consideration of risk will ensure we keep it that way.

We have very few living pests in Britain, which makes archaeological work less challenging than in other parts of the world. There are tics of course, which can cause illness and – in rare cases – paralysis. For people working in areas of low brush and bracken in warmer months, keeping legs covered is a good idea. Mosquitoes and midges are also a nuisance in summer, but are not known to cause anything other than itchy bites. Standard over-the-counter sprays can provide adequate protec-tion. Other stinging insects are wasps, bees (rarely), and hornets – the old adage seems to work though; do not annoy them and they will not annoy you. The best advice is to have sting relief close to hand.

Finally snakes: there are not many of these and nearly all are harmless. Only the adder can bite – this would be unpleasant but is not usually life-threatening. Adders live in open heath or moorland habitats, many of which have been lost under forestry plantations, farmland, development or encroaching scrub. Females are nearly always a red-brown earthy colour with the males being slightly smaller and a much lighter colour, most often a striking slate grey. Both sexes have defined black zig-zags down their backs. The pattern resembles a shadow cast by a fern, which is why a lot of people, and predators, do not see them.

Although every project should have a First-Aid Kit and an appointed first-aider (make sure you know who it is, and where the kit is when you first arrive on site), you should have your own too, and keep it close to hand. And this applies not only to site work, but any time. Keep it in your day pack. If you drive a car you should have one there as well, with additional bandages that may be helpful in the event of a minor accident. For your smaller personal kit, you should have plasters, sting relief, burn ointment, some pain killers and – if you wish – antiseptic cream. This should cover most minor burns, stings and scrapes. But this is a specialised area, so we will let the specialists say more about it. The following text boxes provide much more detail.

First-Aid Tips for Lone Workers

Paul Jeffery (English Heritage)

Some jobs require archaeologists to work alone, out-of-doors and sometimes in remote areas. In these situations, particular first-aid skills, knowledge and equipment are particularly important. A broken ankle might only be a minor injury if working with others but, if isolated, could lead to hypothermia and death! Do not panic though. This advice, added to a recognised course, should give you confidence and it could just save your life.

When dealing with injury or illness remember:

- Your safety
- Where you are! OS six figure NGR or postcode
- Stay calm
- Never move unless in danger of further injury or death
- Call for help as soon as possible (999 or 112)

Heart Attack

It is impossible to give yourself CPR. When alone, you need to spot the signs and act before you stop breathing! Respond to:

- A crushing pain in the chest which often wraps around the body. This may spread, or just affect arms, throat, neck, jaw, back or stomach. Pain does not go away with rest
- Breathlessness, pale and sweaty skin
- Feeling sick, weak or dizzy
- A rapid and weak pulse.

You must:

- Get help immediately – especially if pain has lasted more than 15 min
- Sit in a comfortable position
- Phone an ambulance
- Chew an aspirin tablet if you have one, unless you have an aspirin allergy.

Bleeding

Bleeding can be caused by many accidents. It must be stopped as soon as possible to prevent your condition from deteriorating. In the event of a wound:

- DO NOT remove an embedded object
- DO NOT apply direct pressure over it if there is a foreign object in it, but pad around
- DO NOT use a tourniquet.

You should:

- Expose the wound
- Apply direct pressure over the area using a sterile dressing if possible. Raise and support the limb above the level of your heart
- Lie down
- Apply a sterile dressing
- Consider calling an ambulance.

Clinical Shock

Shock is a major killer. Look for:

- Cold, clammy, sweaty skin
- Rapid, weak pulse
- Thirst
- Yawning
- Nausea
- Weakness and dizziness.

You should:

- Keep warm
- Stay calm
- Get comfortable
- Lie down, raise legs
- Loosen tight clothing
- Call an ambulance.

Broken Bones

Falls, trips or falling objects can break bones. You should:

- Remain calm and avoid unnecessary movement
- Support the injured limb above and below the break
- Call an ambulance if unable to walk to help
- Keep warm.

First-Aid Equipment

Paul Jeffery (English Heritage)

The table below shows the minimum required for kits if you are working in Britain. In addition, risk assessment or personal needs may require other items. The suggestions below the table for personal use are exactly that, suggestions for things you might want to have and to use in an emergency but which you cannot administer to others under current UK HSE regulations (Table 8.3).

Table 8.3 Standard equipment for first-aid kits, based on guidance from the HSE approved code of practice

Content description	Vehicle/individual kit	First-aid boxes (excavation)
Guidance leaflet IND(G)4	1	1
Individually wrapped sterile adhesive dressings (assorted sizes S, M and L)	6	20
Sterile eye pads with attachments	–	2
Triangular bandages (individually wrapped)	2	4
Safety pins	2	6
Dressings sterile unmedicated:		
Medium 12 cm×12 cm	–	6
Large 18 cm×18 cm	1	2
Individually wrapped moist cleansing wipes (alcohol-free sterile)	5	10
Pairs of disposable gloves (not laytex)	1	2

Notes:
1. Cleansing wipes – non-alcoholic, non-antiseptic, should only be kept where soap and water are not available.
2. Scissors, adhesive tape and disposable aprons may also be kept in the container if there is room.
3. Where tap water is not available and eye wash facilities are needed, sterile water or saline in disposable containers (at least 1 L) should be provided (the marked expiry dates should be checked regularly).

Travelling or trek type First-Aid kits can be supplemented with the following items of personal equipment.

- One pair tuff cut scissors
- One foil survival blanket
- One small make-up type mirror (to check cuts to face and out of sight places!)
- One military style battlefield dressing (best kept in coat pocket)
- One penlight torch
- Light stick or flare.

Personal Medicines and Hygiene

The following suggestions are for sole use of the individual and it is up to individuals to choose a product suitable for them:

- Paracetamol and aspirin, and any prescribed medication you may require (Note: Aspirin is for use if you suspect you are having a heart attack. Other painkillers will have no effect in this instance and are for normal headaches etc.)
- Water-free anti-bacterial gel (for personal hygiene)
- Sting treatment (stingoze or similar), Antiseptic cream or spray.

Individuals who have allergy problems may wish to carry antihistamine tablets (such as Piriton) or cream. If in doubt, seek advice from your GP.

'Keep the Car Running'

Cassie Newland (University of Bristol)

Most archaeologists use cars or vans either for getting to and from work, or as part of their job. I even 'excavated' one once! But here I just want to give some basic tips on how to stay safe and avoid unnecessary risk.

First, buy a manual. Manuals have useful pictures that show you where everything is. If you cannot afford a manual, your local library will have them to lend. Check oil and water levels weekly and before long journeys. Add more fluid as necessary. This not only prevents damage through overheating but can also be linked to bigger problems so keep an eye on how frequently a top up is required. A visual check of hydraulic and other fluids can be undertaken at the same time. Always use the correct grade of oil for your engine. You can find out the grade recommended by asking at any car parts shop. When topping up the radiator remember to use the correct proportion of antifreeze in the water. This will not only keep your car running in winter, it will also keep it nice and cool in summer.

Check your tyres regularly, especially before long journeys. A combined tread and pressure gauge can be bought very cheaply. Check for a good depth of tread and uneven wear patterns (wear only on the inside/outside/stripe down the middle) as these can give you advance warning of developing problems. Always keep tyres inflated to the correct pressure. This can normally be found on a sticker inside one of the doors.

Follow your vehicle's maintenance regime religiously, especially if you have a diesel engine. Oil and filters should be changed when your manufacturer recommends. You can find this out from your newly bought manual, a car parts shop or the manufacturer themselves. Many vehicles also have a 'summer' and 'winter' setting on their air intake, often marked with a 'snowflake' or 'sun' image. It is usually a very simple job to switch from one to the other, sometimes just the flick of a switch. Using the appropriate setting will ensure that your car starts on a cold day and runs in a fuel efficient manner in warmer weather.

Do not wait until the petrol gauge is knocking on empty to fill up. Older fuel tanks can harbour sediments that can harm your fuel filter and injectors. If your diesel has done a few miles, try to keep it at least a quarter full at all times. If you get a scratch or scrape, apply wax to protect the exposed metal until you can get it fixed properly. Get any stone chips in your windscreen drilled and glued immediately. Not only will it save you money but also it might save your life!

The Countryside Code

- Be Safe – plan ahead and follow signs
- Leave gates and property as you find them
- Protect plants and animals and take your litter home
- Keep dogs under close control
- Consider other people.

For further details go to: www.countrysideaccess.gov.uk

I Just Don't Know What to Wear…

Martin Short (Ministry of Defence, and one-time archaeologist)

Throughout a working life as both an archaeologist and soldier, I have spent long periods of time wishing I was (a) warmer, (b) drier, (c) less uncomfortable and (d) working in an office. Whilst making sensible choices about clothing is only part of the picture in managing the risks associated with working outdoors: it can literally make a life or death difference. This short section looks at some of the issues (Fig. 8.1).

Our bodies, when exposed to the cold, will limit the amount of blood pumped to extremities to preserve heat within the vital organs. That is why our hands and feet are the first things to get cold – they are being sacrificed, in a sense, for our more important core body parts.

Fig. 8.1 I just don't know what to wear… the 'look' of a British archaeologist. (Drawing: Martin Short)

Hands and feet have a low volume but a big surface area which means that they lose heat quickly and if one has wet gloves or socks then heat loss is accelerated. In all weathers, a pair of woollen socks and a thin pair of wicking socks should be used together. This helps the feet breathe and prevents blisters by allowing the socks to slide against each other. In winter use thicker woollen socks but keep the inner wicking pair. Most people find a pair of breathable water-proof gloves is a good investment to keep hands warm and comfortable.

Our heads have a large exposed surface area and a dense blood supply that is not diminished when exposed to cold, so an uncovered head will lose heat rapidly. For the same reason, an exposed head should be protected in summer as over-heating is possible. A wide brimmed hat is useful for this.

Just as our bodies try hard to protect our core area we too should treat this area as a priority because relatively minor fluctuations in core temperature can allow conditions such as hypothermia and heat exhaustion to take hold. The impact of these conditions can make a serious situation considerably worse, if they progress to a stage where our ability to navigate or make rational decisions are affected.

Even on a very cold day it is possible to be comfortable in light clothing, if we are physically active. When walking fast, mattocking or shifting spoil heaps our bodies need a lot of energy and heat is a by-product of such muscular activity. It is only when our level of activity drops that we start to feel cold. The secret to effective outdoor clothing is the discipline of 'layering'. Clothing needs to be worn in multiple layers rather than as a few thick garments. As we warm up we can strip off layers, as we cool down then add layers. It makes sense, therefore, to buy clothes that are easy to put on and take off.

In general, the layering approach needs to stop wind and rain getting in and allow water vapour or sweat to get out. Layers are divided into three types:

- Wicking layer: This is the inner layer, sometimes called a base layer, and should feel comfortable against the skin. It needs to dry quickly and pull sweat away from the skin towards the next layer of clothing, where it can evaporate. Cotton is bad at this but some synthetic fibres or silk are excellent.
- Insulation layer: This layer or layers should keep you warm and dry as the weather gets colder or your level of activity declines. It should also provide ventilation so that moisture wicked away from your skin by the inner layer keeps moving. The best insulator is air (trapped in an open weave or knit fabric such as fleece). Try to find garments that are machine washable, and anti-pill.
- Shell layer: This waterproof layer (jacket and over-trousers) should allow perspiration vapour to vent, while blocking wind and rain and reducing heat loss. If your level of physical activity is high, however, then even manmade membranes such as Gore-Tex will not prevent you getting wetter from your own sweat than from the elements. Many people use a wicking

and shell layer during hard work in poor weather conditions, whilst keeping the insulation layer safe and dry in a waterproof bag for use later.

Legs are not part of the body core and choosing trousers often ends up being more a personal choice. Jeans should, however, be avoided as they soak up water like a sponge and will certainly teach you the meaning of wind chill very quickly. I try to avoid trousers with seams in the groin region as these chafe mercilessly when they get wet – my personal favourites are army surplus trousers as these are well made, designed for the outdoors and generally dry out quite quickly.

Last but not least is footwear – which for outdoors means good quality boots with ankle support, but not trainers. You should always try on new boots in the afternoon as your feet swell during the day. Use the two layers of socks you would normally wear and make sure the boots are comfortable in the middle range of tension on the laces. You may wish to consider getting boots fitted with shock-absorbing insoles such as Sorbothane which are also very good insulators, if you are prone to cold feet. As a general rule, the more stitching on the uppers of the boots the more likely it is that water will get in so look for a 'one piece' leather upper to be on the safe side. Good quality soles are essential. I always go for a good grip pattern and avoid soles with cut-away angles at the back of the heel as this prevents the boot being firmly dug into slopes when going downhill.

Outdoor safety is mostly about common sense, planning and self-discipline. While I cannot do anything about environmental hazards such as poor weather and difficult terrain, I can make sure that I choose appropriate clothing and use the layering approach. I can take spare clothes and make sure that I keep them dry. I can get training to improve first-aid and navigation skills, I can make sure that I do not push beyond my physical abilities and I can try and plan for the unexpected. Most importantly, if I am unable to prevent, reduce or plan around risks, I can postpone the work to such a time as it is safe.

Summary

This chapter could have been the first in the book – it certainly contains some of the most important information and tips that could perhaps contribute to getting a job, finding the right course or avoiding a sticky end, having followed some health and safety tips. But whether it comes first or last, the essence of this book is most clearly evident in this chapter. Our reason for writing this book was to produce something for budding archaeologists, whether already based here in the UK, but most especially for those currently living overseas and with plans to come and work in archaeology or the heritage sector in Britain. Although much information is provided, the situation is fluid, and while some of the basic guidance here will remain relevant, some specific points – about employment prospects, for example – will change. For that reason, readers should make use of what we include here, but supplement that with a good search of online resources. These will be easy to find with an appropriate combination of keywords.

It is often said that making a career in archaeology or heritage is made difficult through a comparative lack of opportunities and poor pay and career structure. To our mind that is a rather bleak outlook. Our view is rather more optimistic. Our large glass of real ale is half full, not half empty. Despite the recent downturn there are still jobs, and there is a career structure. And pay is much better than it was. Archaeology is a great career, and surely one of the most rewarding for those with a passion for the past. So why not give it a go?

References and Further Reading

Aitchison, K. 1999. *Profiling the Profession: a survey of archaeological jobs in the UK*. Institute of Field Archaeologists/Council for British Archaeology/English Heritage.

Aitchison, K. and Edwards, R. 2003. *Archaeology Labour Market Intelligence: Profiling the Profession 2002/3*. Bradford: Cultural Heritage National Training Organisation.

Aitchison, K. and Edwards, R. 2008. *Archaeology Labour Market Intelligence: Profiling the Profession 2007/8*. Reading: Institute of Field Archaeologists.

English Heritage 2006. *Management of Research Projects in the Historic Environment: The MoRPHE Project Managers Guide (MoRPHE)*. London: English Heritage. http://www.english-heritage.org.uk/upload/pdf/MoRPHE-Project-Managers-Guide.pdf

Appendix
Useful Web Resources

Entering the Country

UK government Border Agency Web site: http://www.ukba.homeoffice.gov.uk/
http://www.ukvisas.gov.uk
http://www.workingintheuk.gov.uk
http://www.gov.im/dti/employmentrights/workpermits.xml

National Agencies

http://www.english-heritage.org.uk
http://www.cadw.wales.gov.uk
http://www.historic-scotland.gov.uk
http://www.gov.im/mnh/
http://www.jerseyheritagetrust.org
http://www.guernseyheritage.com
http://www.culture.gov.uk
http://new.wales.gov.uk/about/departments/heritage/?lang=en
http://www.nationaltrust.org.uk
http://www.nts.org.uk
http://www.hlf.org.uk
http://www.snh.org.uk
http://www.naturalengland.org.uk
http://www.britarch.ac.uk
http://www.mla.gov.uk
http://www.museums.co.uk

J. Schofield et al., *Archaeological Practice in Great Britain: A Heritage Handbook*,
World Archaeological Congress Cultural Heritage Manual Series,
DOI 10.1007/978-0-387-09453-3, © Springer Science+Business Media, LLC 2011

Careers Advice

http://www.learndirect-advice.co.uk/helpwithyourcareer/jobprofiles/profiles/profile404/
British Archaeological Jobs Resource (BAJR or 'Badger'): http://www.bajr.org/

Link for Online HERs and Much More: Heritage Gateway

http://www.heritagegateway.org.uk/gateway

Planning Systems and Research Frameworks

England and Wales (including details of planning reform):
http://www.planningportal.gov.uk/england/genpub/en/1102425564249.html
West Midlands Regional Archaeological Research Framework:
http://www.iaa.bham.ac.uk/research/projects/wmrrfa/index.shtml
East Midlands Regional Archaeological Research Framework
http://www.le.ac.uk/ar/research/projects/eastmidsfw/
North West Regional Archaeological Research Framework
http://www.liverpoolmuseums.org.uk/mol/archaeology/arf/
http://www.english-heritage.org.uk/characterisation
English Heritage *Change and Creation* document: http://www.changeandcreation.org
Welsh national research framework: http://www.archaeoleg.org.uk/
Mining research framework: http://www.vmine.net/namho/research.asp
Scotland: http://www.scotland.gov.uk/Topics/built-environment/planning
Scottish national research framework (ScARF): http://www.socantscot.org/scarf.asp
Historical Metallurgy Society Metals and Metalworking' framework: http://hist-met.org/metalsframeworkall.pdf

Underwater Archaeology

Seascapes project: http://www.english-heritage.org.uk/server/show/nav.8684
English Heritage's Maritime Archaeology Team and projects:
http://www.english-heritage.org.uk/server/show/nav.1276
The Nautical Archaeology Society: http://www.nasportsmouth.org.uk/

Archaeological Organisations

IfA: http://www.archaeologists.net
ALGAO: http://www.algao.org.uk/default.htm
FAME: http://www.famearchaeology.co.uk/

Council for British Archaeology (CBA): http://www.britarch.ac.uk/
RESCUE: the British Archaeological Trust: http://www.rescue-archaeology.org.uk/

Education

Universities with archaeology departments:
British universities offering archaeology and related subjects, go to UCAS at www.
ucas.com and search on 'archaeology', 'heritage' and similar.

National Curriculum: http://curriculum.qca.org.uk/key-stages-3-and-4/subjects/
history/History_and_the_national_curriculum_aims.aspx

Research funding sources:
http://www.ahrc.ac.uk/
http://www.esrc.ac.uk/ESRCInfoCentre/index.aspx
http://www.hlf.org.uk
http://www.britac.ac.uk
http://www.leverhulme.ac.uk
http://www.sal.org.uk

Unions

http://www.prospect.org.uk

Advice on Archaeological Practice

Archaeological thesaurus: http://thesaurus.english-heritage.org.uk
Guide to field survey: http://www.helm.org.uk/
Harris matrix: http://www.harrismatrix.com
HELM online library of EH and local guidance: http://www.helm.org.uk/server/show/
nav.19701

Archives

'Access to Archives' (a2a) portal at: http://www.a2a.org.uk
The Archaeology Data Service (ADS): http://archaeologydataservice.ac.uk/

Aerial Photographs

National Monuments Record collections of aerial photographs: http://www.english-
heritage.org.uk/server/show/nav.20088

The Cambridge University Collection of Air Photographs: http://venus.uflm.cam.
ac.uk/

Excavation and Standards

MoLAS excavation manual:
http://www.museumoflondon.org.uk/laarc/guidelines/ASM_3edn_1994.pdf
IfA Standards and Guidance:
http://www.archaeologists.net/codes/ifa
HELM online library of EH and local guidance:
http://www.helm.org.uk/server/show/nav.19701

Handling Metals

English Heritage Archaeometallurgy guidelines: http://www.helm.org.uk/upload/
pdf/Archaeometallury.Centre%20for%20Archaeology%20Guidelines_2001.
pdf?1236850388
Historical Metallurgy Society Data Sheets http://hist-met.org/datasheets.html

On Site Safety and Health

First aid information and courses
British Red Cross: http://www.redcross.org.uk/firstaid.
St John Ambulance: http://www.sja.org.uk
http://www.amtrainingservices.co.uk

Health & Safety information and courses
UK Health & Safety Executive: http://www.hse.org.uk
http://www.amtrainingservices.co.uk
Oxford University Continuing Education: http://www.conted.ox.ac.uk

Index

Printed by Printforce, the Netherlands